LEGENDARY LOCALS

OF

PINE CITY

MINNESOTA

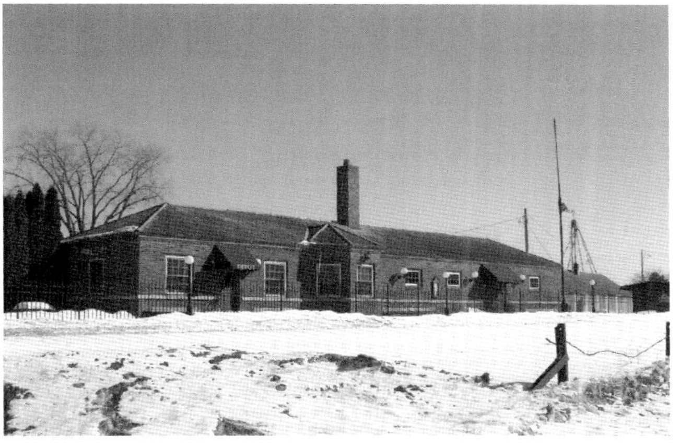

I0806219

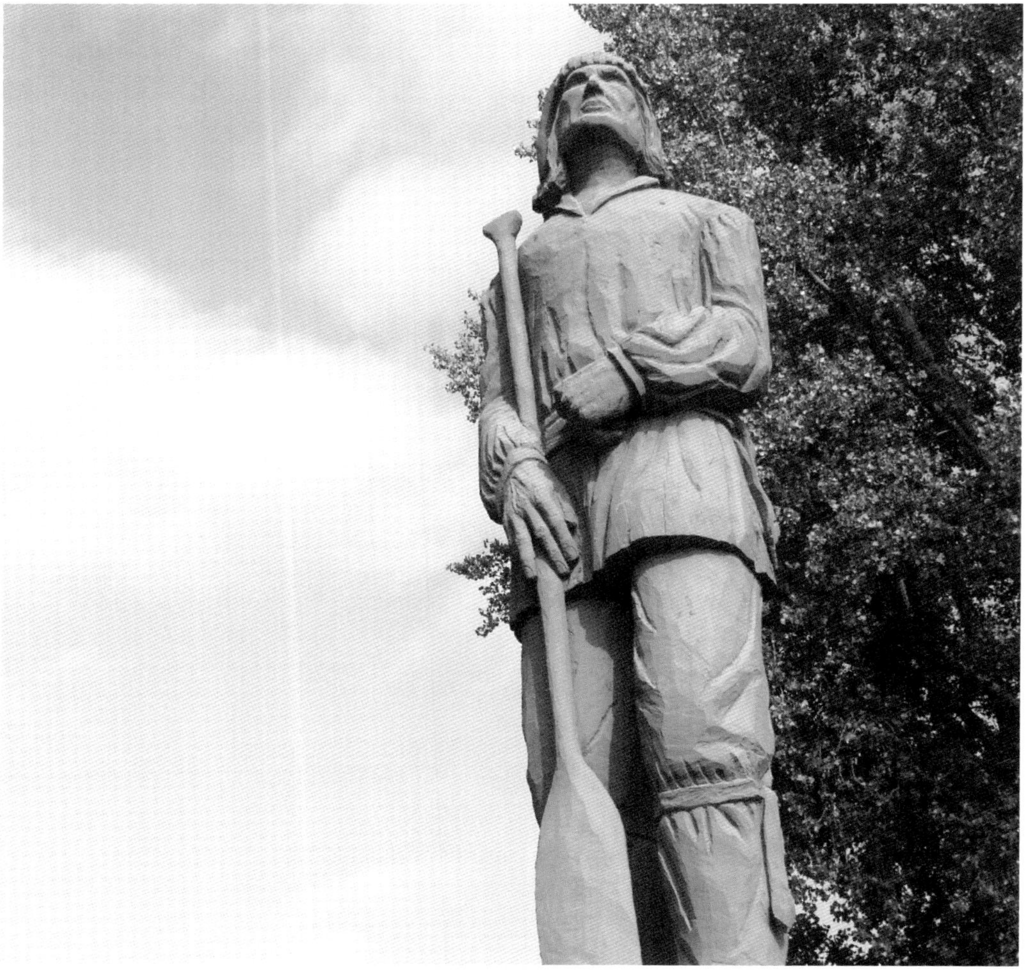

François, the Voyageur
The carver of this once 42-foot-long redwood log, Dennis Roahair, passed away at the age of 60 on April 20, 2013. The famous roadside statue sits overlooking downtown Pine City on the north shore of the Snake River. François, as locals call him, is legendary in his own right. (Author's collection.)

The Depot at Pine City
Pictured is the Pine City Depot after it was restored by Bob Haedt. (Author's collection.)

LEGENDARY LOCALS

OF

PINE CITY

MINNESOTA

NATHAN JOHNSON

LEGENDARY LOCALS

ISBN 978-1-4671-0119-6
Legendary Locals is an imprint of Arcadia Publishing
Charleston, South Carolina

Printed in the United States of America

Library of Congress Control Number: 2013944575

For all general information, please contact Arcadia Publishing:
Telephone 843-853-2070
Fax 843-853-0044
E-mail sales@arcadiapublishing.com
For customer service and orders:
Toll-Free 1-888-313-2665

Visit us on the Internet at www.arcadiapublishing.com

This book is dedicated to the people of Pine City, whom I love very much, and without whose stories the history in this book would not have been possible.

On the Front Cover: Clockwise from top left:
Jean Lindig Kessler, Princess Kay of the Milky Way (Courtesy of Richard Lindig; see page 77), Andy Greder, writer (Photograph by Noah Sikkink; see page 79), Karla Nelsen, bodybuilder (Courtesy of Karla Nelsen; see page 47), Roy Carl Carlson, legislator (Courtesy of the Minnesota Legislative Reference Library; see page 24), Martin Rike, rescuee (Photograph by Noah Sikkink; see page 111), Kristen Seuntjens, arts advocate (Photograph by Noah Sikkink; see page 111), Amy Olson, actress (Courtesy of Amy Olson; see page 76); Anna Dickey Olesen, politician (Courtesy of Library of Congress; see page 34), Bob Mould (Courtesy of Gaelen Hadlett; see page 87).

On the Back Cover: From left to right:
Shane Bauer, detainee, and mother Cindy Hickey (Photograph by Noah Sikkink; see page 44), Rhiannon Sauter, softball record holder (Photograph by Noah Sikkink; see page 52).

CONTENTS

ACKNOWLEDGMENTS

I greatly acknowledge the work of all prior Pine City historians, whose efforts serve as a foundation for this volume. For sharing their personal photographs for this project, I thank each and every individual, family, business, and institution who parted with a photograph, even if only temporarily.

Most importantly, I wish to thank God for giving me vision to begin this project at a very young age and for the strength to see this project through. I also thank my family, friends, and loved ones for their support along the way.

Finally, my immeasurable gratitude goes to photographer Noah Sikkink of Hinckley, Minnesota, for taking so many outstanding photographs that appear throughout this book, capturing the essence of some of the legendary people of Pine City.

INTRODUCTION

Too many people don't tell their stories because they feel they don't have a good ending. But it is not so much about what the ending of the story is, it's not so much about the climax, or some sort of Hollywood-type ending; what's important is the narrative, the emotion, the character and the context and the details that tell people's stories. People should be more willing to do that.

—Andy Greder, Pine City, May 25, 2013

Pine City. The name sounds like a soap-opera locale. But it is a real place, nestled among pines, no less. The town has been the setting for books and theater productions and has been referenced in film. Playwright Craig Wright, best known as the writer of HBO's *Six Feet Under*, set a series of plays in Pine City: *The Pavilion*, *Orange Flower Water*, *Molly's Delicious*, *Melissa Arctic*, and *Grace*. The latter takes place in Florida, but is about people who come from Pine City. These plays have been performed across the United States.

Author Dean Hovey wrote three mystery novels set in Pine City: *Where Evil Hides*, *Hooker*, and *Unforgettable: A Pine County Mystery*. The Larry Millett book *Sherlock Holmes and the Red Demon* is set against the backdrop of the devastating Hinckley fire and in the Pine City area. And author Richie Ryan's adult fiction, *What We Are: Richie's Story* and *What We Are II: Summer Heat*, are set in Pine City. In the motion picture *Drop Dead Gorgeous*, starring Kirsten Dunst, the fictitious "Miss Pine City" character was portrayed by an actual Pine Citian, Amy Olson.

Perhaps what makes people want to write about Pine City and use it as the setting for their stories is that it is the quintessential American small town, with a Main Street, town square, and downtown café serving up gossip for breakfast and meatloaf for lunch. People still roll up their sleeves to put on a plethora of events throughout the summer and rally behind the football team on fall Friday nights under the lights. "Places like Pine City are replacing suburbs as the next wave in community development," said Jack Schultz, author of the book *Boomtown USA*. He said Pine City was among a group of small towns nationwide poised to boom and outperform metropolitan areas.

Pine City is different from other towns its size. For starters, there is so much history here. It started out small enough to not be counted as a city but rather a village; it was uprooted and moved to a location near the railroad; and it has endured hardships and been resilient enough to see success. By and large, the people made Pine City then, and it is the people who are making it now. Every life is important, and everyone who lives leaves an impression on the world—but the notoriety each attains can vary greatly. Some people come and go with barely a mention; volumes are written about others. When examining a town whose history dates to 1881, the variety of people is staggering. Yet, in that entire multitude, some people stood out.

This book isn't about dignitaries who have visited Pine City, or notable people who made history while visiting here. It is about people who claim Pine City a part of their story—and about stories that are made because of certain Pine City people. It is also not about those in town everyone knew, like "Bicycle Betty" Lou Larsen, who passed away at age 82 after moving to Duluth, though she was legendary in her own regard. In 2011, a Guinness World Record was set at the Frisbee golf course in Voyageur Park for most holes of disc golf played in a 24-hour period. The feat didn't warrant the inclusion of the record setter, Dan Schnabel, in this book. That is not to say that beating the previous record by over 100 holes and finishing with 1,305 holes played (including three aces) was not notable. It was very notable. It is just that Schnabel was not from Pine City, nor did he live here.

This is also not meant to be a comprehensive compilation of the notable people of Pine City; nor is it meant to capture everyone who did anything of significance. Everyone measures success differently, and most people achieve something of significance in their lives. Mostly, this book is meant to help those who moved city-ward and those who remained in, or moved back to, their hometown gain understanding and connection with some of their old associations. The moral of this story could be, "You can be from anywhere—even Pine City, Minnesota—and be somebody." Included here is an amazing assortment of characters. It has been that way since the beginning. Selecting a few of the tens of thousands of people who have lived in Pine City over the years was a difficult task. But some did stand out for a variety of reasons. The following profiles shed light on these individuals.

CHAPTER ONE

Military Personnel

Pine City has always had a high regard for America's veterans, regardless of their branch, rank, or duty. Many men and women throughout the years have served their country to ensure its way of life. In appreciation, the City of Pine City donated land, and monuments have been erected with participation from local veterans' organizations, dedicated to those individuals who went to war and never came back. On Memorial Day each year, a town parade, followed by a ceremony at Birchwood Cemetery, remembers those who lost their lives in service to their country. A Veterans Day recognition dinner is held each year at the American Legion Heath-Perkins Post No. 51 to remember all veterans, past and present.

In 1992, memorials were dedicated at the Pine Government Center—for veterans of World War I, the Civil War, Korea, Vietnam, and World War II—and at the B.F. Davis Post Grand Army of the Republic. At the Birchwood Cemetery circle is a memorial for all veterans who have served. At Woodpecker Ridge Park, a memorial marker recognizes those who served in Operation Desert Storm. At the Pine City Public Library, a memorial is dedicated to the memory of the members of the 3rd Division Minnesota Naval Militia. At the Veterans of Foreign Wars, a flag is flown in memory of all departed veterans and a memorial is displayed to recognize all military personnel who served in the Vietnam conflict.

These are some of the ways the community has shown its reverence for those who have served. Under the leadership of Jessica Paulson and by nomination of Cindy Foster, in 2011, Pine City was officially proclaimed a Yellow Ribbon City by Gov. Mark Dayton for its work in recognizing and supporting its veterans. Pine City's citizens are proud of all of those who served.

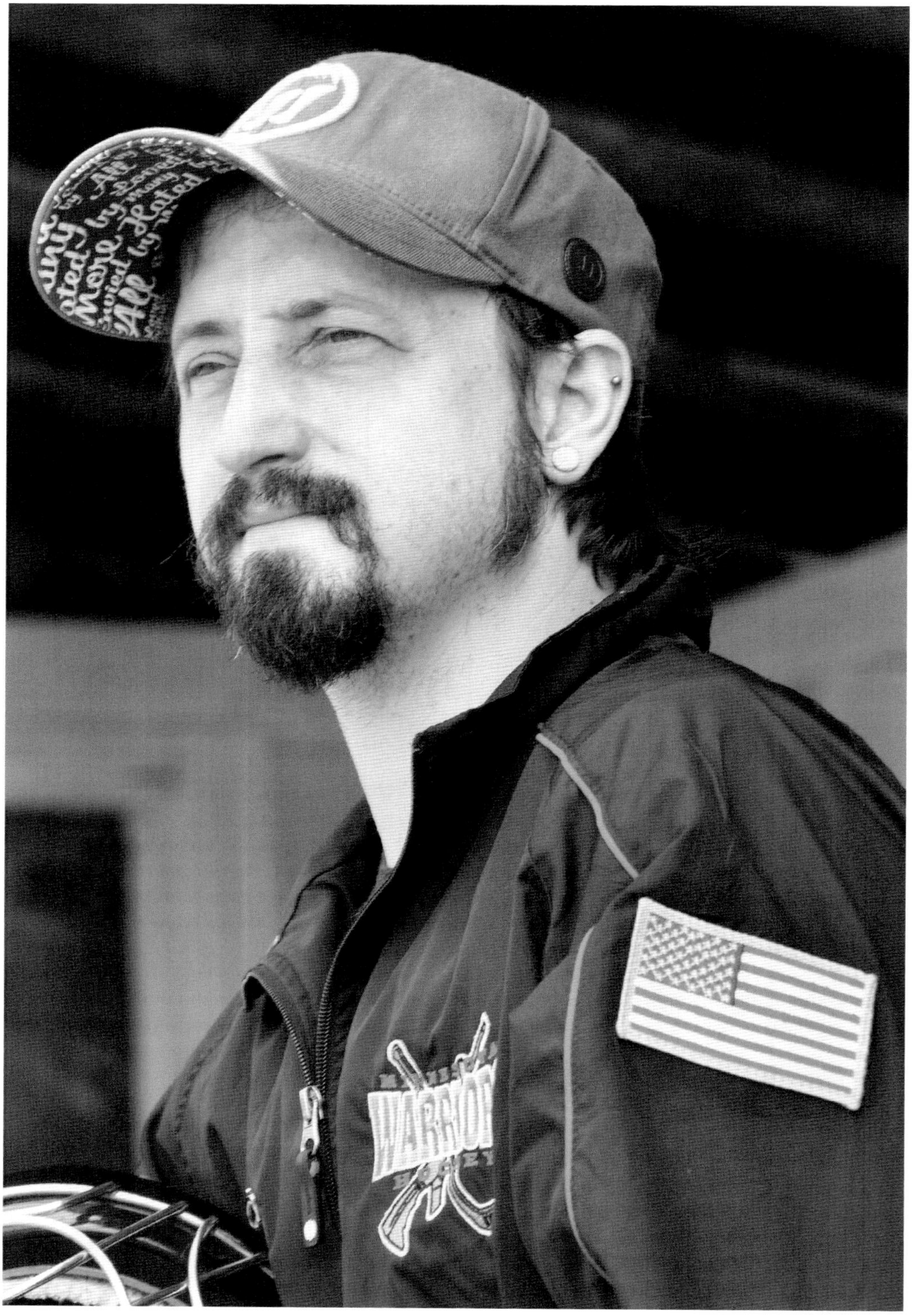

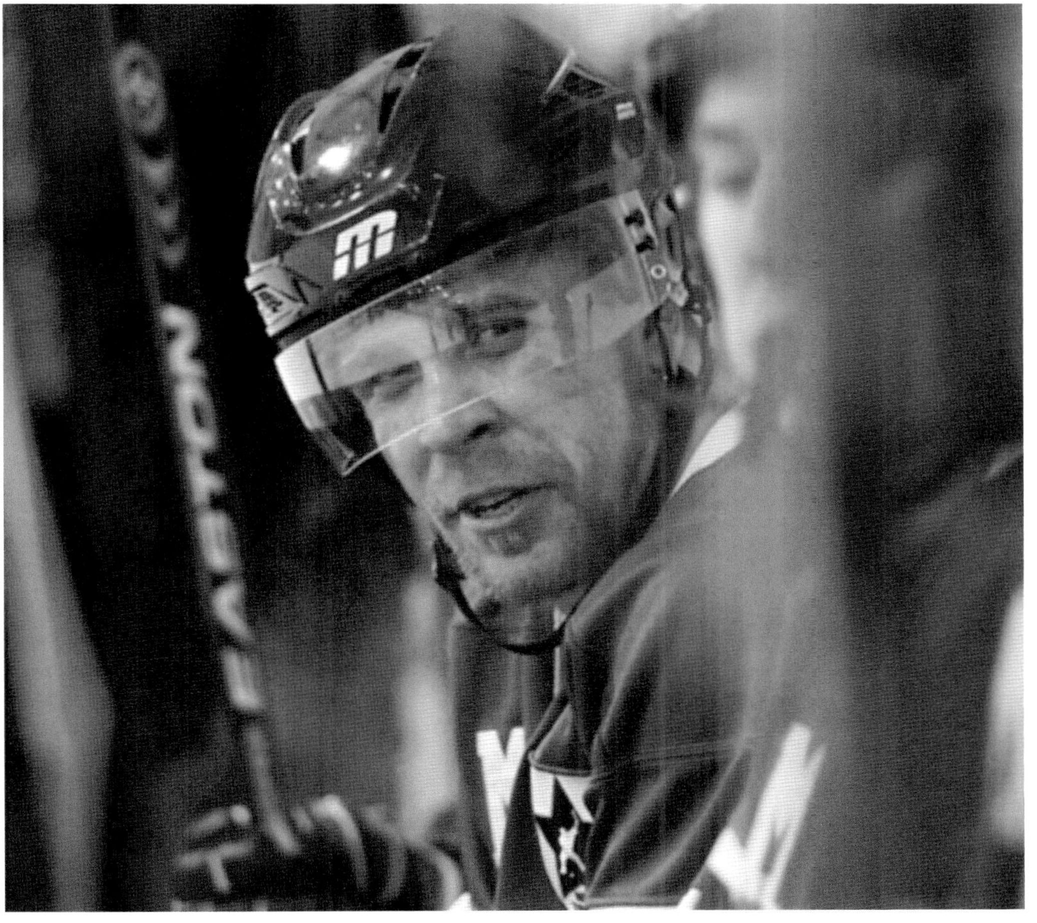

Mark Stanford and Jeremiah Lord (ABOVE AND OPPOSITE PAGE)
Fans watching Minnesota Wild games in the 2012–2013 season saw television commercials for the Minnesota Warriors Ice Hockey Program, organized for US military personnel who have been wounded, injured, or otherwise disabled. The program assists veterans with reintegration into civilian life. In the commercial, a standalone shot showed Pine City's Mark Stanford, who proudly wore his green Warrior jersey.

Stanford (opposite page) was born April 22, 1978, in Arizona. Like all of the men in his family, he joined the military. It was the year 2000, and his first assignment was with air defense. He later went to Korea and was injured. He suffered from depression, anxiety, and post-traumatic stress disorder (PTSD). He also had back injuries, knee and vision problems, and ringing in his ears. He began to avoid big crowds and sometimes could not shake the feeling that he was being followed. Stanford ended up moving to Pine City, because his family was close by in Mora, Minnesota. He bought a house in Woodpecker Ridge. Al Lindgren, of the Warriors, was asked to find another goalie, and he called upon Randy Lee of Pine City, who connected Stanford with the program.

Jeremy Lord (above), another Pine Citian on the Warriors team, also suffered from PTSD. Before he joined the team, he was going through a rough time, feeling that his life was on the line. His aunt referred him to the Warriors. Both Stanford and Lord made the 60-mile drive from their Pine City homes to Vadnais Heights to play hockey. They did not join the Warriors for therapy or support, but they found those things nonetheless in the brotherhood they received. (Opposite, photograph by Noah Sikkink; above, courtesy of Jeremiah Lord.)

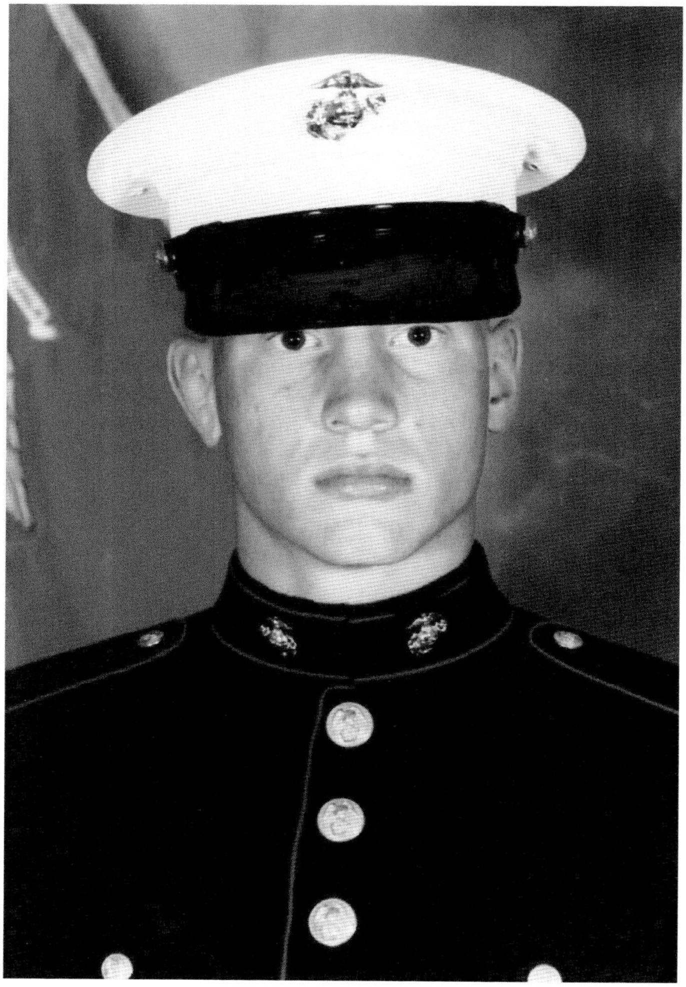

Daniel Fedder

M.Sgt. Daniel L. Fedder died at the age of 34 on August 27, 2010, while supporting combat operations in Helmand Province, Afghanistan, during Operation Enduring Freedom. He was born on July 31, 1976, in Mora, Minnesota. He attended Grasston Christian Academy from first through sixth grades. He later attended Pine City High School, graduating in 1994. His accomplishments included wrestling, football, speech, and participation with the Heritage Players. A 16-year veteran of the Marine Corps, Fedder became a highly decorated soldier and went on to receive a plethora of awards and decorations. He was serving his fourth tour overseas, and his first in Afghanistan, when he was mortally wounded by an improvised explosive device (IED). During his tour in Afghanistan, he demonstrated incredible courage in disposing of more than 25 IEDs. His actions saved the lives of countless fellow service members and Afghan civilians. Fedder had dedicated nearly half of his life to military service.

On September 6, 2010, a funeral service for Master Sergeant Fedder was held at the Pine City National Guard Armory. Many dignitaries, including Minnesota governor Tim Pawlenty, were in attendance. City streets were lined with community supporters for the funeral procession from the armory to Birchwood Cemetery. On June 5, 2012, House Resolution 3220 was unanimously passed. The bill designated the US Postal Service facility at 170 Evergreen Square Southwest in Pine City as the Master Sergeant Daniel L. Fedder Post Office. (Courtesy of Jackie McKellar.)

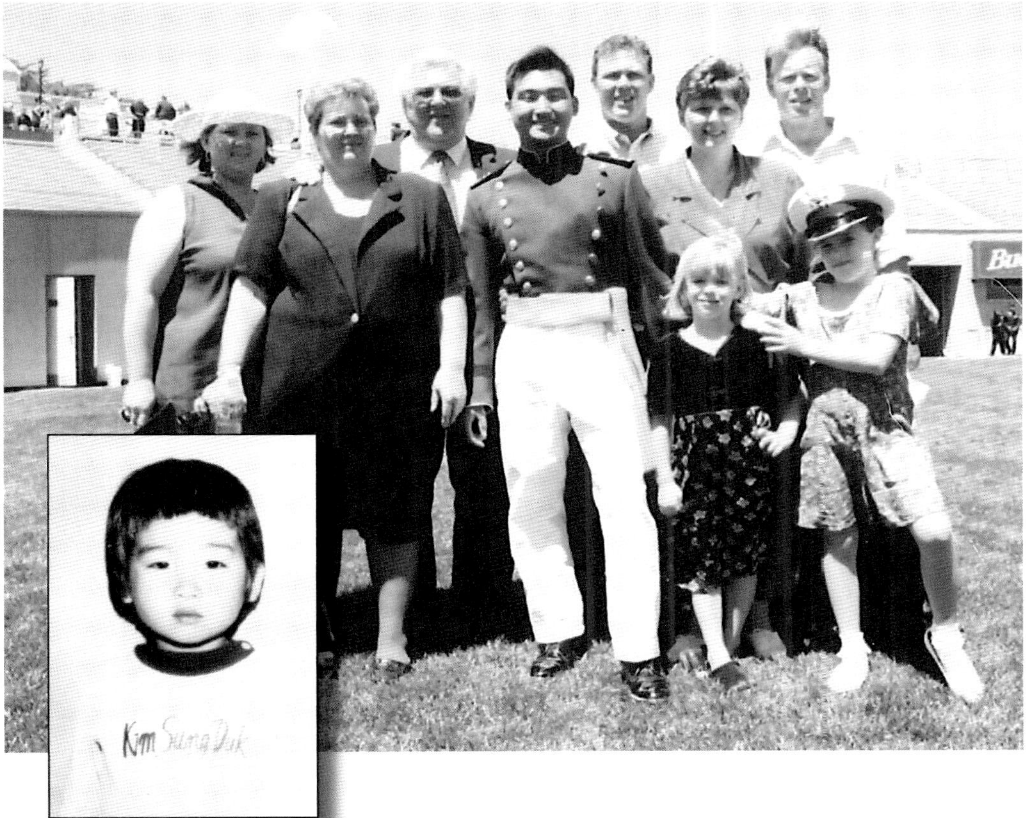

Brian Bauman

Brian Bauman, born Kim Sung-duk in South Korea, was adopted in 1977 at the age of three by Steve and Elaine Bauman of Pine City. During high school, Brian earned straight As, was student council president, and made varsity in three sports. After graduating high school in Pine City in 1992, Bauman had a bright future ahead of him, but he had a major obstacle to overcome. It started with a stomachache that wouldn't go away, exhaustion, and a loss of appetite. At the age of 21, the senior in the US Air Force Academy was diagnosed with leukemia and was told he had five years to live without a successful bone marrow transplant. The chances of finding such a match: one in 20,000.

After failing to find his biological mother or a matching donor in the United States, Bauman's parents looked for a Korean candidate. After searching through 7,000 registered potential donors, the person was found in Army sergeant Suh Hankuk, age 23, who was flown by the Red Cross to the United States to provide what he hoped at the time would be life-saving assistance. "Considering the relatively small number of people registered with our bone-marrow bank, we are very happy that we have found a match for Bauman so soon," the Red Cross told the Associated Press. Several Pine Citians registered to be bone marrow donors at a local drive in 1996, when the search was taking place. The Bauman family was sincerely appreciative of everyone's support throughout the whole ordeal. (Both, courtesy of Steve Bauman.)

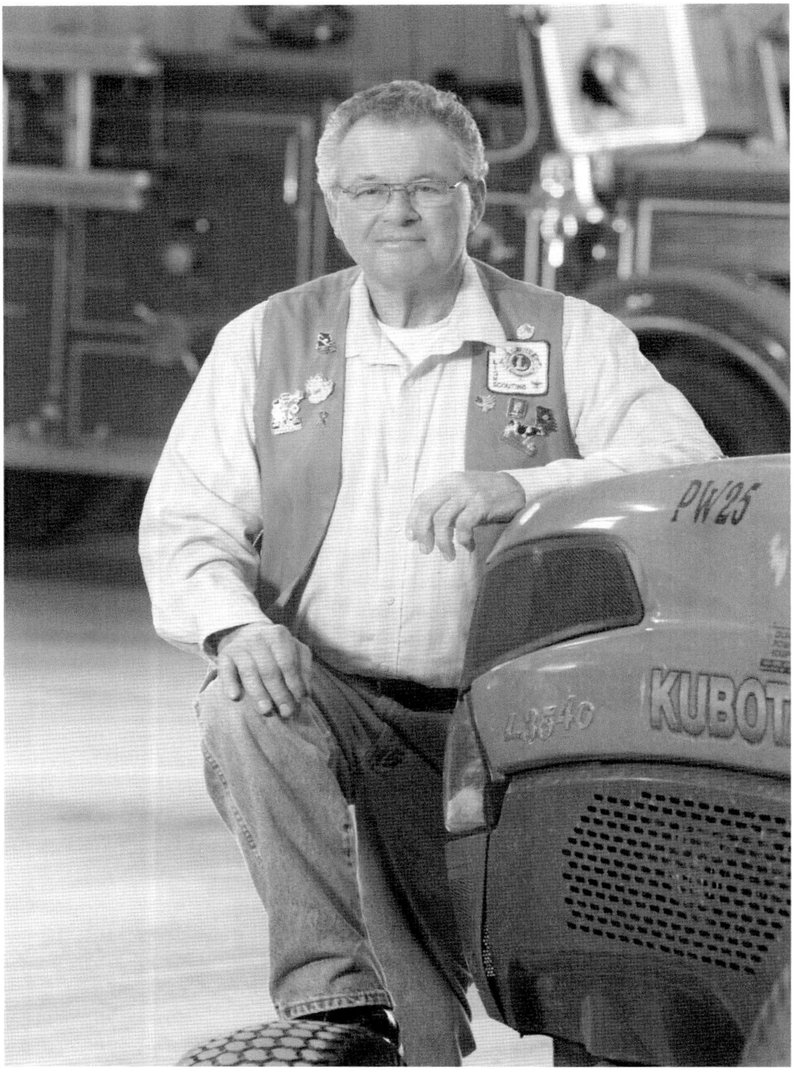

Jim Zaun

James "Jim" Alan Zaun, a Vietnam veteran, served in the Navy from 1962 to 1965. He patrolled off the North Vietnam coast in 1964 aboard the destroyer USS *Wedderburn* (DD-684). Major American involvement in Indochina began after the Gulf of Tonkin incident in November 1964. The North Vietnamese supposedly attacked the USS *Turner Joy*, and the resulting Congressional resolution vastly increased the number of American military personnel in the region.

Even though he served almost 40 years before, Zaun did not join the VFW until after the attacks of September 11, 2001. He served as president of the Pine City Lions and currently is a member of the board of directors as the immediate past president. Zaun has served as commander of both VFW Post No. 4258 and the Pine City American Legion. In addition, he was a president of the Lions Club, member of the Salvation Army, Boy Scouts, and Cub Scouts. In 2006, he was named Pine City's Citizen of the Year. In 2011, Zaun received the Melvin Jones Award, the highest honor given by the Lions Club International Foundation. Zaun is an employee of the Pine City Public Works Department and has volunteered his time as a Red Cross blood-drive coordinator. (Courtesy of Gross Productions.)

Harold Kick

Harold Kick was born on May 6, 1924, in Pine City, where he lived his entire life. He graduated from Pine City High School in 1942, in the early months of World War II, and enlisted in the Air Force. He met his wife, a local, in 1951, and the couple had two children, Brian and Becky. For most of his working years, he was employed at the post office. He also did some carpentry and farming.

Pine City's Veterans of Foreign Wars Post No. 4258 was organized in July 1945. Harold Kick is one of the last surviving charter members. He was a first lieutenant in the US Army Air Corps and served as fighter pilot. After arriving home from Italy, he was invited to join the VFW, despite not knowing what it was. He paid his $5 dues and has been a member ever since.

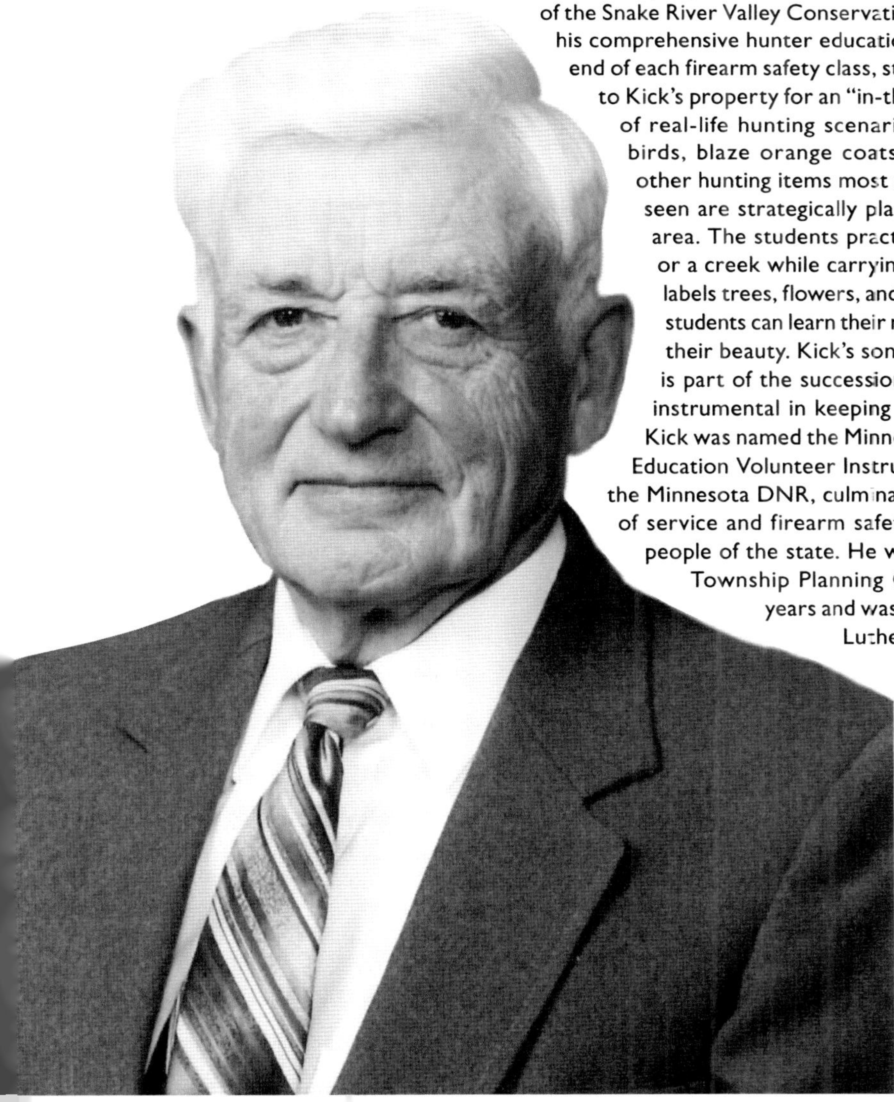

For over 50 years, Kick has taught nearly 3,600 students the importance of firearm safety as a Minnesota Department of Natural Resources (DNR) hunter education instructor. His classes were so effective that they were videotaped and used by state agencies as an example of how to organize and conduct a successful firearm safety program. Since 1946, Kick has been a member of the Snake River Valley Conservation Club, praised for his comprehensive hunter education field trips. At the end of each firearm safety class, students were invited to Kick's property for an "in-the-field experience" of real-life hunting scenarios. Mounted deer, birds, blaze orange coats, deer stands, and other hunting items most students have never seen are strategically placed throughout the area. The students practice crossing a fence or a creek while carrying a firearm. He also labels trees, flowers, and other vegetation so students can learn their names and appreciate their beauty. Kick's son-in-law Steve Hallan is part of the succession plan and has been instrumental in keeping the program going. Kick was named the Minnesota Firearm Safety Education Volunteer Instructor of the Year by the Minnesota DNR, culminating nearly 50 years of service and firearm safety education to the people of the state. He was on the Pine City Township Planning Commission for 10 years and was involved in the Zion Lutheran Church, where he served on the council for about 20 years. He was named Citizen of the Year in 1993. (Courtesy of Harold Kick.)

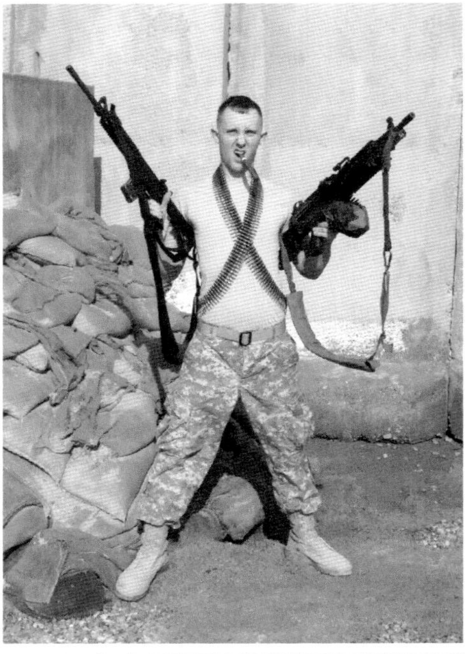

Ashley Ackley

Specialist John Ackley, now Ashley Ackley, of the 34th Red Bull Infantry Division of the Minnesota National Guard, is paving the way to be the first person to reenlist in the military as another gender. Among the 131 Pine City troops returning from Kuwait in 2012 was Ackley, a transgender veteran who changed her name and her birth certificate and is in the process of undergoing hormone treatments in advance of a complete sex-change operation. Ackley said of the feat to become the first veteran to reenlist as a different gender, "Even the Veterans Administration hospital is handling the hormone treatments." In an interview on CNN on June 6, 2012, Ackley spoke about why she is fighting Army Regulation 40-501, which sees transgendered people as "administratively unfit." The policy applies to anyone who has undergone or attempted to change his or her gender. The Minnesota National Guard will not have a say in Ackley's fate; instead, it is the jurisdiction of the Army. Ackley, a contradiction of stereotypes, has become a source of pride in the LGBT community. She loves to work on her Chevy Corvair, about which WCCO-TV reported, "Not every woman can repair a classic car, but not every man will go for a pink interior." (Both, courtesy of Ashley Ackley.)

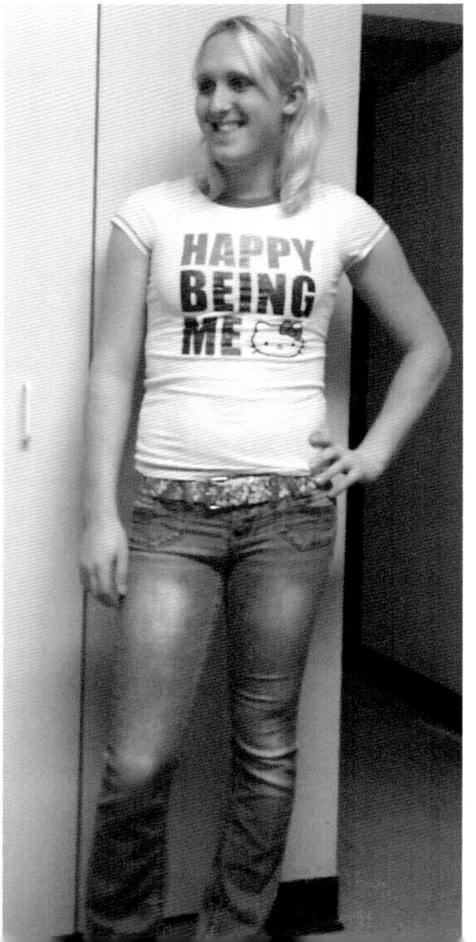

CHAPTER TWO

Pine City's Past Legislators

The legislators who came from Pine City and worked in St. Paul made their respective marks. There were not many over the years—11 in all—but this chapter gives a look into the lives of these men who were the voice of Pine City at the state capitol.

It was not known which political party Adolph Munch belonged to, but he was the first Pine City resident to serve in the Minnesota House of Representatives, in 1872, representing District 28, which at that time encompassed Aitkin, Chisago, Kanabec, and Pine Counties. Munch, born in 1829 in Prussia, came to Minnesota in 1852 and then moved to Pine City, where he was a merchant. He served a one-year term, from January 2, 1872, to January 6, 1873.

Randall K. Burrows, also known as R.K., served in the Minnesota Senate in 1874, representing District 28. He was the first senator to come from Pine City. Burrows was born in 1929 in Connecticut and lived the single life. According to *History of the Saint Croix Valley* by Augustus B. Easton, Burrows came to Pine City in 1869 and, with Adolph Munch, built a large stave mill on the shores of Cross Lake. This proved an unfortunate investment, resulting in litigation, during which time the mill was destroyed by fire in 1878. A manufacturer by trade, Burrows served in the 16th legislative session. His seat was contested by John Hallburg of Center City. The senate referred the question to the people, and in the election that followed, Burrows was defeated. He moved to the Dakotas in 1879 and died three years later.

Dr. M.A. Brawley served in the Minnesota House in 1876, the second Pine Citian to ever do so. He was born in 1850 in Ohio. Brawley came to Pine City in 1873 and became the Pine County coroner. For a time, he served as the county auditor. He was a physician by trade and served in the 18th legislative session after residing in the area for just three years. There are no photographs available for Munch, Burrows, or Brawley.

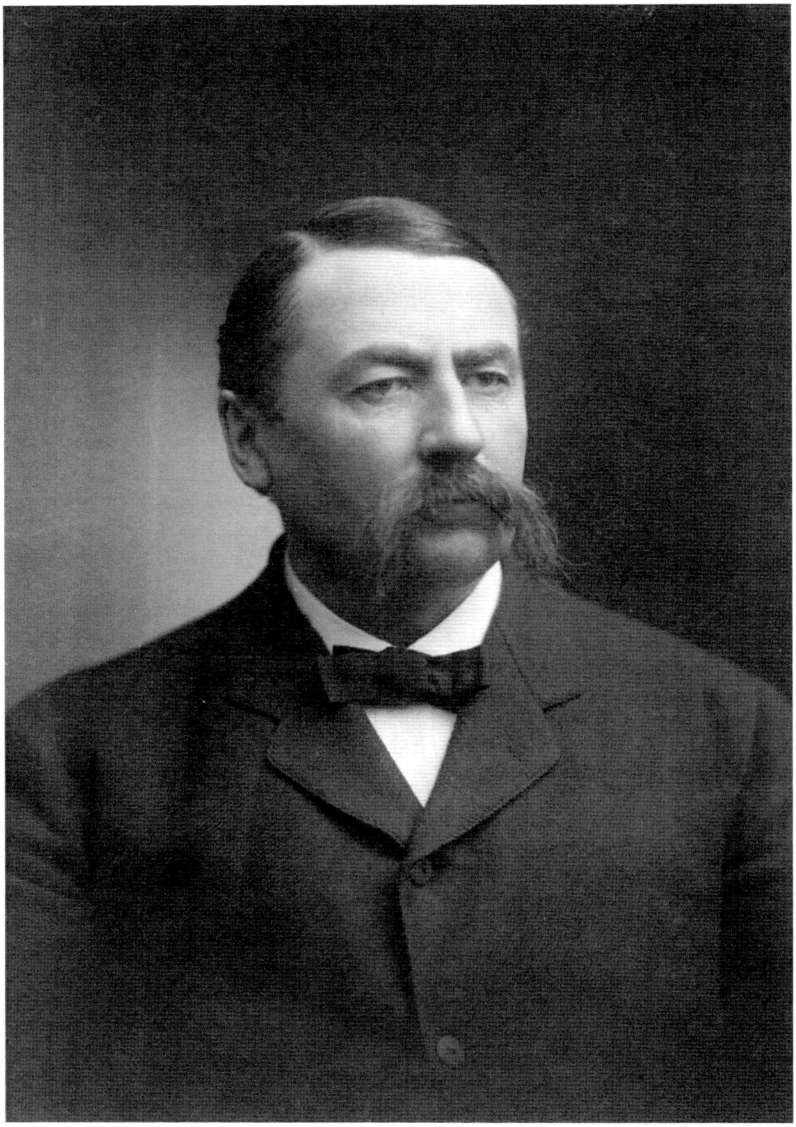

Levi McKusick

Levi H. McKusick, also known as L.H., served in the Minnesota House from 1883 to 1886 and from 1889 to 1890. A Republican, he was also elected to the Minnesota Senate, where he served from 1899 to 1902. McKusick, of Scottish and English ancestry, was born in the mid-1850s in Maine. He attended Maine Common Schools, St. Stephen Academy, New Brunswick, and three terms at Maine State Normal School. He attended college for one course, but studied law and was admitted to the bar in the spring of 1878. McKusick moved to Pine City in the late 1870s and was the Pine County attorney 16 years beginning in 1878.

A Methodist, he was married and had five children, Clinton, Fred, Alice, William, and Marion. His father, Levi E., served in the Maine Legislature. In addition, two other family members served in the Minnesota Legislature, John McKusick and William McKusick. Levi died in 1913. (Courtesy of the Minnesota Legislative Reference Library.)

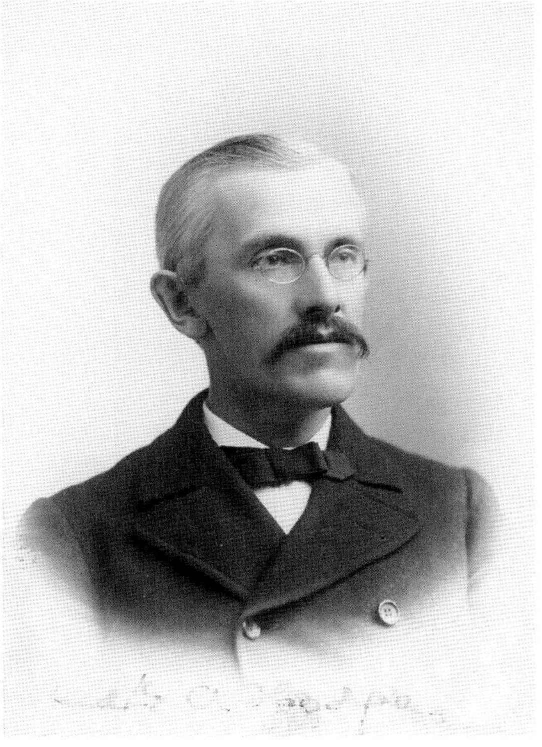

Fred Hodge

Frederick Augustus Hodge was the third person from Pine City to be elected senator, serving in that capacity from 1895 to 1898 as a Republican. The Senate district covered Chisago, Kanabec, and Pine Counties. Hodge was born in 1853 in New Hampshire. He came to Minnesota in 1870 and, while living in Pine City, was in the real estate and loan business. From 1876 to 1894, he was the Pine County auditor. Hodge served in the 29th legislative session (1895–1896) and in the 30th session (1897 to 1898), which was the second half of his Senate term. He died in 1922. (Courtesy of the Minnesota Legislative Reference Library.)

L.C. Pedersen

Pedersen was born in Denmark in 1862 and immigrated to the United States in 1879. He settled in Alden in Freeborn County, where he engaged in farming until 1894, when he moved to Lincoln County. There, he organized and conducted a creamery and livestock business. Later, Pedersen became engaged in the retail hardware and mercantile business and in the development of cutover land in Pine County. He served as president of the First State Bank of Askov and was a major factor in the exceptional development of Pine County into a dairy region by Danish emigrants. It was here that he decided to run for the Minnesota House, winning a nonpartisan election. Pedersen served two sessions, from 1919 to 1922. He then moved to Pine City to run for his second term in office, which he won.

He always took a prominent part in movements that he considered beneficial to the community in which he resided, and his dominant personality carried weight and influence for any activity in which he was engaged. L.C. Pedersen died in Askov, Minnesota, on February 16, 1929. A resolution was read by his successor, Rep. Joe Therrien. It said, in part, "The passing of Hon. L.C. Pedersen created another vacancy in the rapidly diminishing ranks of those sturdy, typical pioneers who not only 'made Minnesota' but 'made America,' men whom no obstacles could long delay, no difficulties deter, and no dangers daunt." (Courtesy of the Minnesota Legislative Reference Library.)

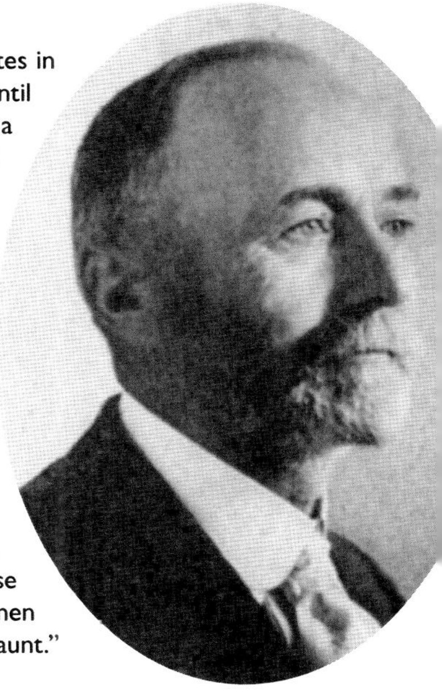

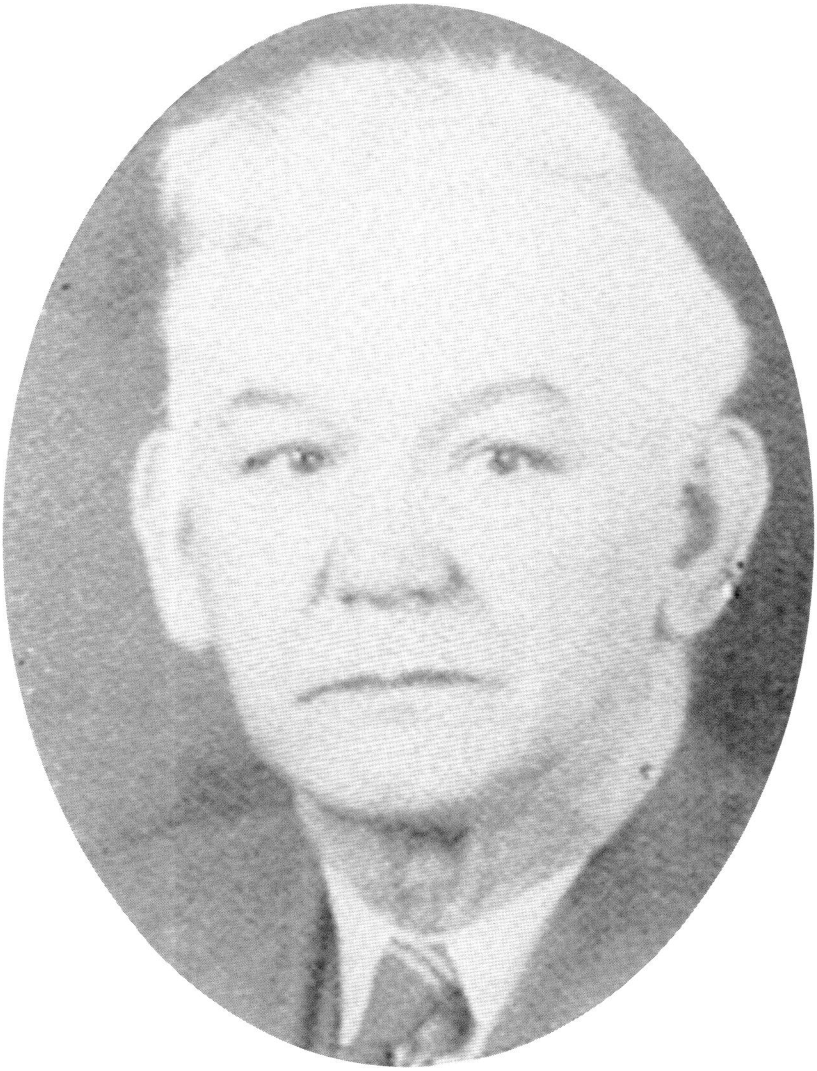

Joe Therrien

Joseph Edward Therrien was the longest-serving Pine Citian in the Minnesota Legislature (1923–1930 and 1943–1946). Born in Canada on March 17, 1879, he came to Two Harbors, Minnesota, with his parents in 1882. He attended school in Two Harbors and then studied law with the Lake County attorney and Sen. Charles A. Towne's office. He was deputy and clerk in practically every office in the Lake County Courthouse.

Therrien married Jennie MacDermaid in 1900, and the couple had seven children. After moving to Pine City in 1908, he was the auditor for Pine County for eight years. From 1917 to 1920, he was a judge of probate for the county. Therrien was the operator of the Pine County Abstract Co. when his political career began. He was elected on November 7, 1922, and served in the following legislative sessions: 43rd (1923–1925); 44th (1925–1926); 45th (1927–1928); 46th (1929–1930); 53rd (1943–1944); and 54th (1945–1946). All were nonpartisan elections, but Therrien did participate in the Conservative caucus in his final run. He died on October 7, 1953, in Pine County. (Courtesy of the Minnesota Legislative Reference Library.)

George Clem

George I. Clem served in the Minnesota House of Representatives from 1947 to 1948. Although the election was nonpartisan, he was a member of the Conservative caucus. Clem was born in 1910 in Fairmont, Minnesota. A former teacher and school principal, he was an insurance agency member when he was elected to office. He was married with two children, a son and a daughter. According to the May 21, 1953, edition of the *Askov American*, Clem had a rock collection, and he traveled around, displaying and explaining it. Clem was Pine City's Citizen of the Year in 1977. He died in 1988 at the age of 78. (Courtesy of the Minnesota Legislative Reference Library.)

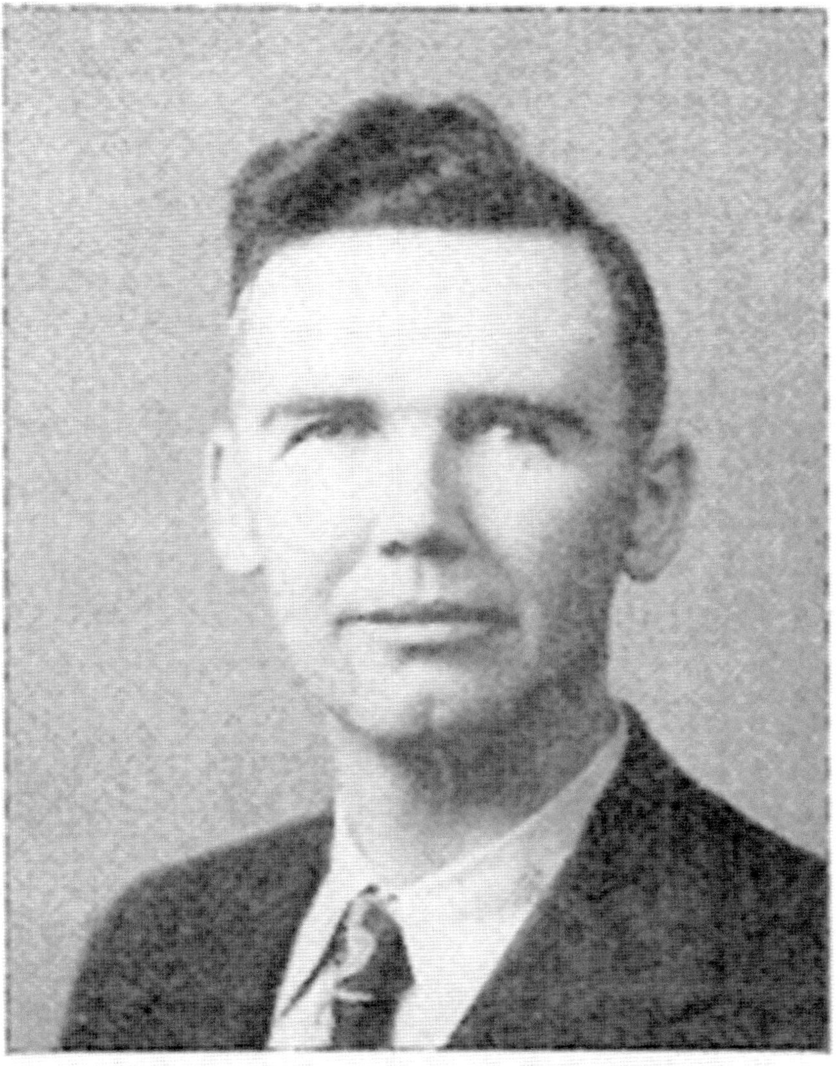

GEORGE I. CLEM
Fifty-sixth District

Joe Karas

Karas was a state representative who served in the Minnesota House from 1949 to 1956. He was born in Rice County on January 22, 1891. In the October 28, 1948, edition of the *Askov American*, during his first legislative campaign, an advertisement (shown here) paid for by Karas described him as "A Home Product and A Man of Experience." It was a nonpartisan election, but Karas was a part of the Liberal caucus at that time, running against George Clem.

Karas was a farmer and a manager of Farm Mutual Fire Insurance Company. The husband and father of two children, a son and a daughter, served on a local town board for 22 years. He was a member of the following legislative sessions: 56th (1949–1950); 57th (1951–1952); 58th (1953–1954); and 59th (1955–1956). In his later two terms, he was a part of the Conservative caucus. Joe Karas died in May 1981 at the age of 90. (Author's collection.)

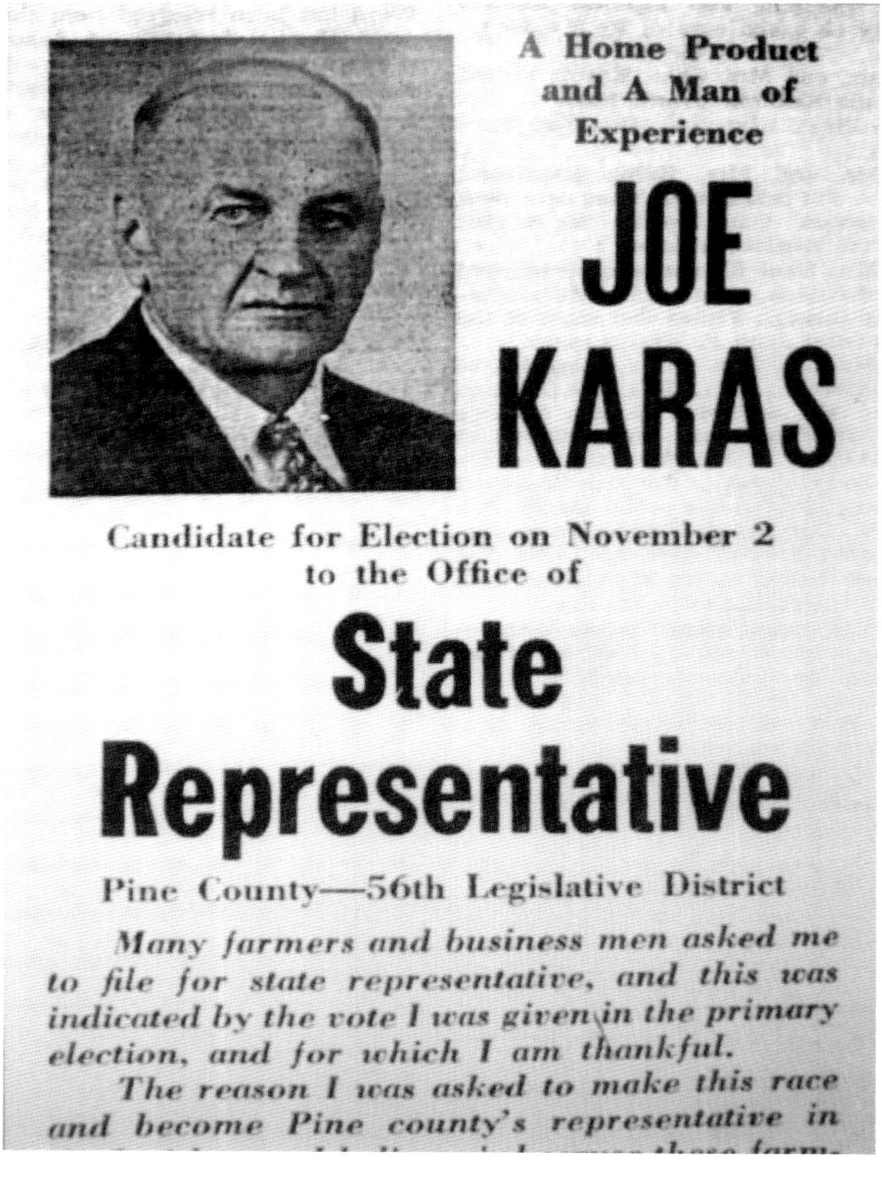

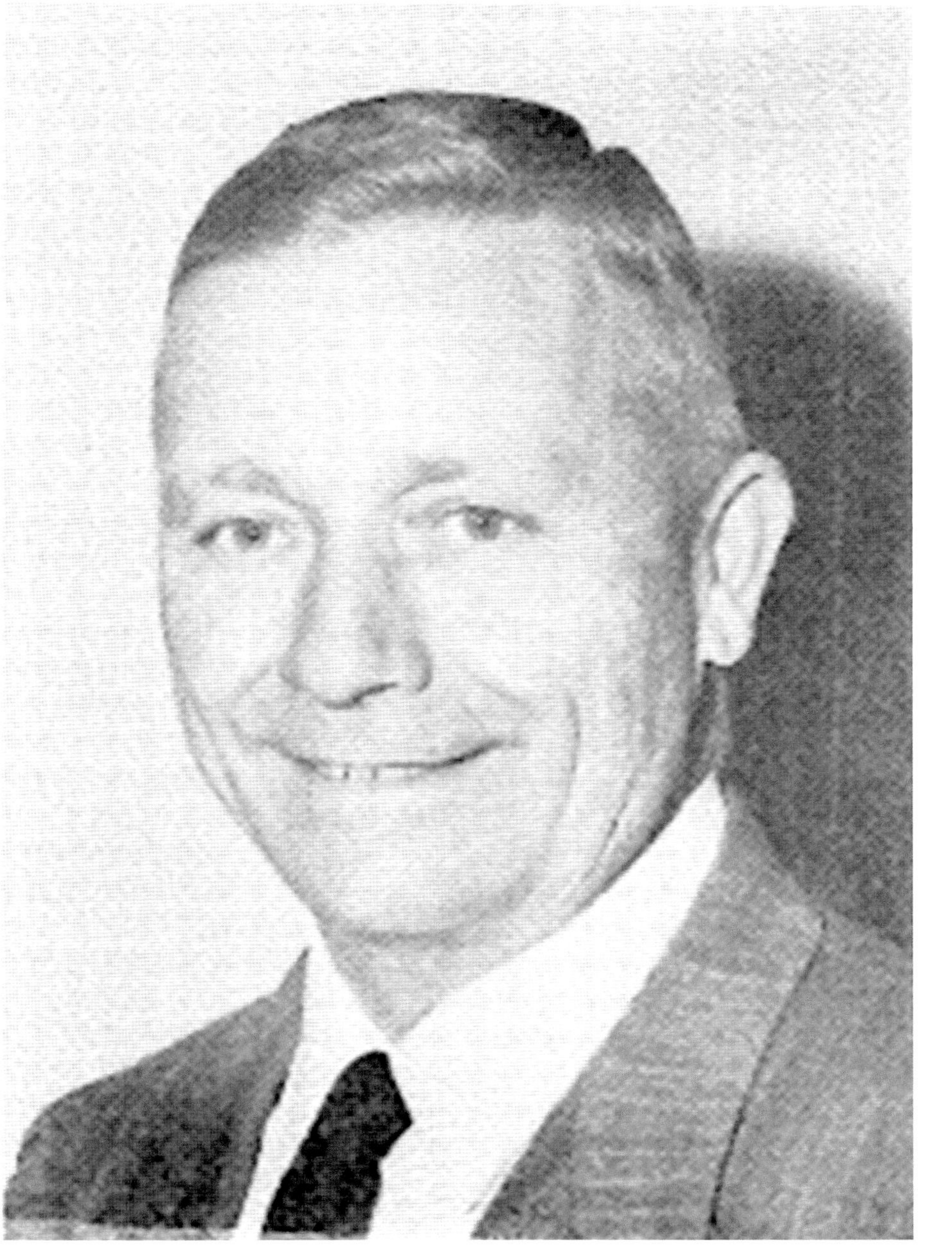

Glenn Truesdell
Born on June 1, 1909, in North Dakota, Truesdell was a man of many trades. He ran a gas business, was an assessor and auctioneer, and was a farmer. He married Bessie Zeman, and they had two daughters, Darlene and Shirley. The family was Presbyterian. Truesdell served in the Minnesota House from 1959 to 1960. A member of the Liberal caucus, he won a close election his first time running. It was 3,231 votes cast for Glenn, 3,010 votes for Joe Gimpl. The district encompassed all of Pine County at that time. He served in the 61st legislative session (1959–1960). Truesdell died in December 1992. (Courtesy of the Minnesota Legislative Reference Library.)

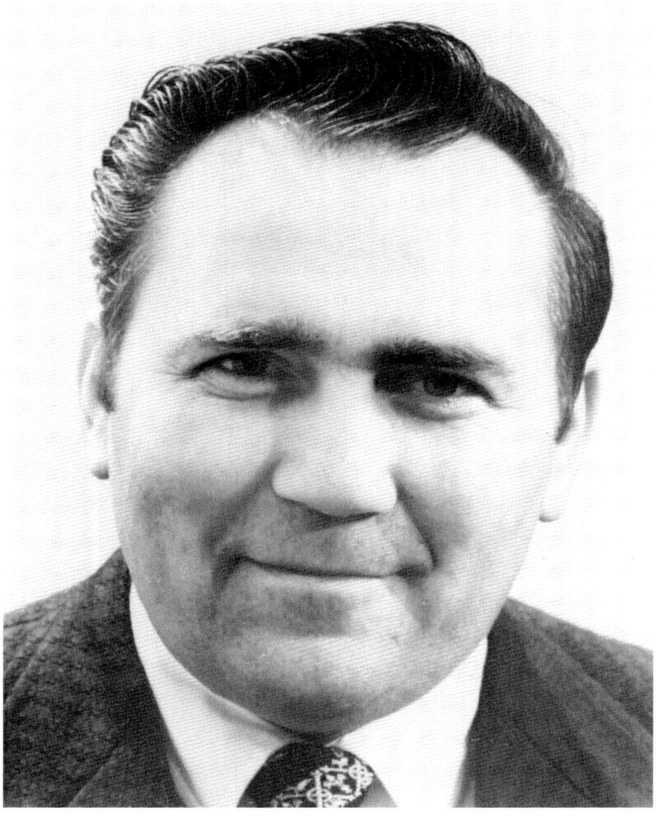

Roy Carlson

Roy Carl Carlson, the most recent Pine Citian to serve in the Minnesota Legislature, was born on May 4, 1937, in Minneapolis. He graduated from Robbinsdale High School in 1955 and went on to serve in the US Army in Germany. In 1962, he met Sharon Wee, and they were married in June 1964. The couple had five children, Connie, Sherri, Cary, Terri, and Mary. In 1965, Carlson earned a degree in industrial education, and in 1968, a master's degree in vocational education, both from the University of Wisconsin–Stout. Due to his love for carpentry, he taught industrial education and worked in construction in the Minneapolis area until 1973. After moving to Pine City in 1974, he ran for the Minnesota House of Representatives and won. After one term, he ran unsuccessfully for the Democratic-Farmer-Labor (DFL) party endorsement for Minnesota Senate in the 1976 primary election, losing to Florian Chmielewski. In 1978, he ran against Doug Carlson and contested unfair campaign practices related to the latter's distribution of helium-filled balloons reading "Re-elect Rep. Doug Carlson." A grand jury ruled that this didn't violate the law, so Doug Carlson retained the seat.

Carlson owned and operated Ma & Pa's Energy Econo Nook in Pine City. After moving to Isanti County, he worked on remodeling projects and returned to teaching. He owned the Ann River Swedish Motel in Mora, Minnesota, from 1990 to 2002. Carlson then attended Bethel Seminary in Roseville, Minnesota, to become a chaplain. He then became involved in Senior Citizens Ministries. He conducted Sunday services at a New Brighton nursing home with his second wife, Marjorie Fletcher, whom he married in February 2005. Throughout his life, Carlson remained extremely active in the DFL Party, campaigning and promoting various local, state, and national candidates. Carlson was also active in the following organizations: Boy Scouts, 4-H, MN-WI Livestock Show, Pine City Cabin Fever Days, Korbel Ice Arena, MCCL, Moraklocka Days, The Gideon's International, and Minnesota Family Nice. Roy Carlson died at the age of 73 on April 11, 2011. (Courtesy of the Minnesota Legislative Reference Library.)

CHAPTER THREE

Notable Mayors

There have been several significant mayors throughout the years. One example is Dr. Robert L. Wiseman, who served from 1910 to 1912. He was a physician and, in 1905, when the Pokegama Sanatorium opened its doors for the treatment of incipient tuberculosis, he attended to the medical work of the institution, along with Dr. Longstreet Taylor of St. Paul. Wiseman Square was named after him.

And then there was Julius Dosey, elected mayor at four different periods during Pine City's early development. He was born in Prussia on June 9, 1851, the son of Otto and Margaret Dosey. His father was a stock and grain buyer who died in 1888. Julius's mother died in 1894. Dosey received his education in his native country and came to America in 1866, starting work at once as water boy for a crew of railroad constructors on the New Jersey Central line. The following year, he drove mules on the Morris Canal and, in 1869, worked on the Belvidere & Delaware Railroad. After short stays in Omaha, St. Paul, and Rush City, Minnesota, Dosey came to Pine City, working in the woods during the season of 1870–1871. In 1871–1872, he worked at the Pine City Lumber Company as a packer and explorer; and in 1872–1873, he worked on the Knife River.

In 1874, Dosey engaged in logging for himself for about four years, then took up work for the St. Paul & Duluth Railroad land department, estimating timber near the Carlton and St. Louis Rivers. From 1879 to 1881, he helped estimate large tracts of timber on Cloquet River in St. Louis County. In 1881–1882, he helped to estimate similar tracts on Sand Creek, Crooked Creek, and the Lower Tamarack in the eastern part of Pine County. In the summer of 1882, Dosey made the estimate of the Mille Lacs Lake Indian Reservation in Mille Lacs County. In 1883, he went to Rainy Lake and, with Mahlon Black, worked for the Winnipeg Lumber Company, estimating timber. He continued to cruise in northern Minnesota for iron and pine timber, and in 1885, he started working for Philip Harris and David Tozer, estimating pine timber on Snake River.

In 1886, he was employed by the David Tozer Company, estimating timber in Minnesota, Wisconsin, and Washington. Dosey was married on November 21, 1875, in Pine City to Elizabeth Drews of Chicago, daughter of H.H. and Elizabeth Drews, who relocated to Rush City. The couple had eight children: Ida, who went on to become deputy county auditor; William, who worked in the telephone business; Ernest, cashier of the Pine City State Bank; Anna, a school teacher; Daniel, a lumberjack; Elizabeth, a music teacher; and Julia and Esther (occupations unknown). The family belonged to the Presbyterian Church. Elizabeth Drews Dosey died on July 7, 1907, at her home in Pine City. Julius Dosey, a Democrat, was a member of the village council for over 20 years. In 1875, he served one year as town assessor and the following year was elected county commissioner, holding the position for four years. Dosey was elected mayor of Pine City and served several terms (1899–1901; 1906–1909; 1912–1919; and 1926–1928). His fraternal associations included membership in the Modern Woodmen of American and the Ancient Order of United Workmen.

This chapter profiles five other mayors who contributed to Pine City's history.

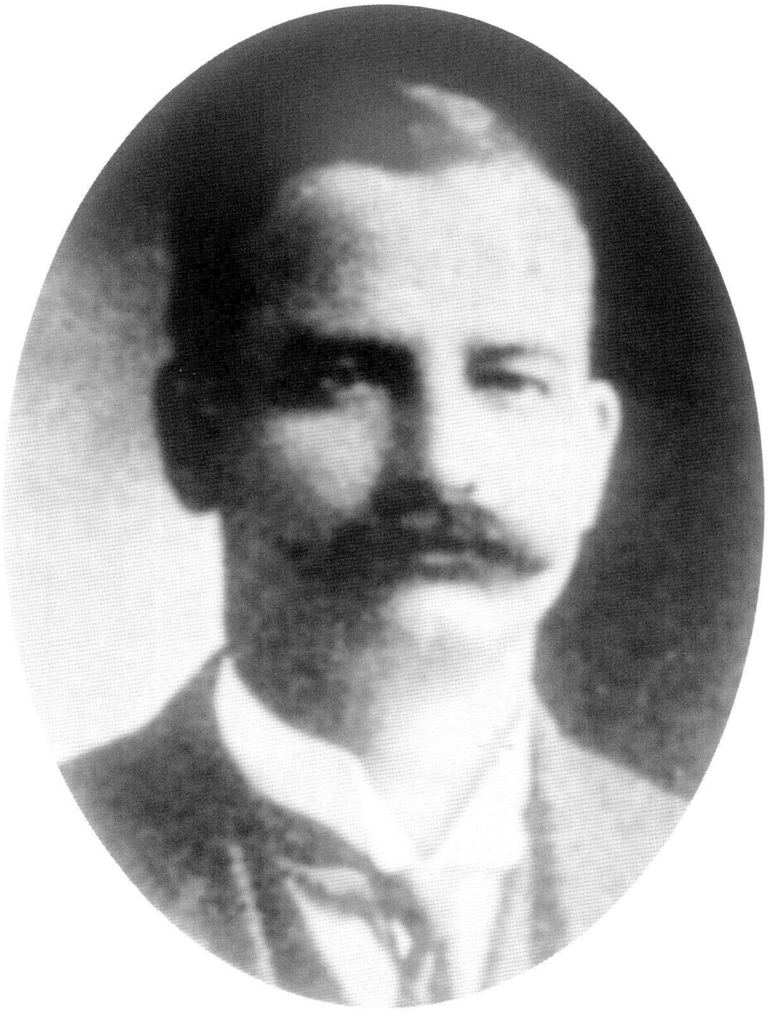

John Breckenridge
John Younglove Breckenridge, the fourth mayor of Pine City, was three times elected to the office, serving from 1897 to 1899. He was born on May 7, 1864, in Vermont. At an early age, he began working at a lumber company in Connecticut as a collector. In 1883, Breckenridge became employed by railway contractors in St. Paul.

In 1886, he married Lizze E. Stone, a pharmacist with a drugstore in Pine City, opened three years prior. He gained his apprenticeship under her guidance. Since 1887, this drugstore was named Breckenridge's Pharmacy and was widely known as being the finest pharmacy between the Twin Cities and the Twin Ports. John Breckenridge became assistant pharmacist of the store after taking a course to learn the job in 1897. In 1900, he became a full-fledged pharmacist by examination, and he stayed in the pharmacy business for 30 years. Breckenridge also was Pine City postmaster, appointed in 1889 and holding the office for four years. He was reappointed in 1898 and held the office for 18 years. A Republican, he was chair of the congressional committee of Pine County for over 20 years. He also served as president of the Commercial Club and as president of the Pine County Agricultural Association. Breckenridge, one of the most public-spirited people of the community, belonged to the Masons, Knights of Pythias, Ancient Order of United Workmen, and Sons of the American Revolution. (Author's collection.)

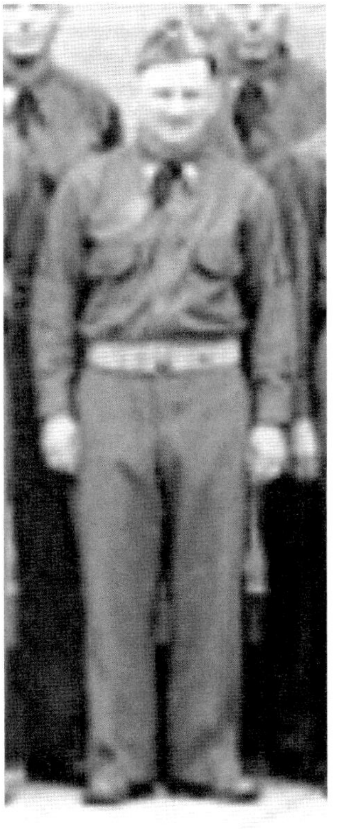

Leonard Machart
Machart was born in Kansas on September 30, 1898, to Frantisek Machart and Mary Mraz. In 1915, Howard Folsom of Pine City established the *Brook Park Banner* newspaper, replacing the *Brook Park Enterprise* (the town's first paper), according to the Pine County History Blog. Leonard "Scoop" Machart, 16, purchased the *Banner* the following year. For the next year and a half, he printed the paper himself with a hand-rolled press. He was attending high school at the time. Machart married Grace Elphick, and the couple had one child. He was mayor of Pine City from 1947 to 1951. The Romanesque Revival courthouse building, erected in 1886, was struck by lightning, the following year after Machart left office, causing it to burn down. A new one replaced it two years after the fire. Machart also served as president of First National Bank. He passed away on February 20, 1980, at the age of 81. (Author's collection.)

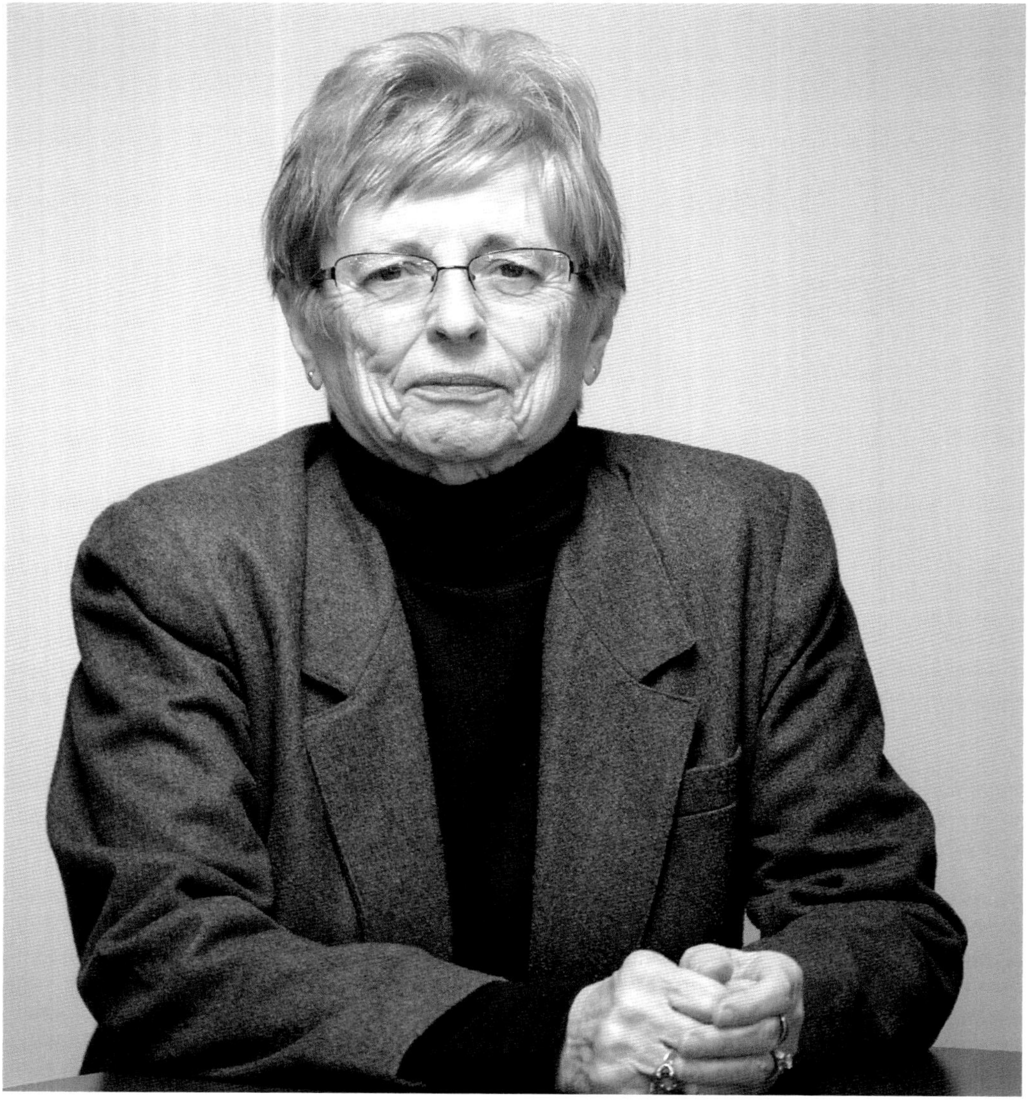

Jane Robbins (ABOVE AND OPPOSITE PAGE)
Jane Robbins was the first female mayor of Pine City. She was elected in 1992 as the city's 32nd mayor and was reelected every two years until 2011, when she did not file for reelection. She was the longest-serving mayor in the city's history. Pine City had a female mayor before Minneapolis did; Sharon Sayles-Belton was elected in 1994.

In 2008, Robbins received the C.C. Ludwig Award, the League of Minnesota Cities' highest honor for an elected official. It was presented to her for going the extra mile, for her contributions to improved municipal government, for the admiration and respect of the general public toward her, and for her selfless conduct focused on the greater good of the community. In 2010, Robbins won the Women in City Government Leadership Award. She received this honor for her individual achievements in Pine City and for her leadership and mentoring roles both inside and outside of the community. Robbins was known for bringing her locally famous "sticky buns" to meetings, funerals, and community gatherings. (Above, photograph by Noah Sikkink; opposite, both author's collection.)

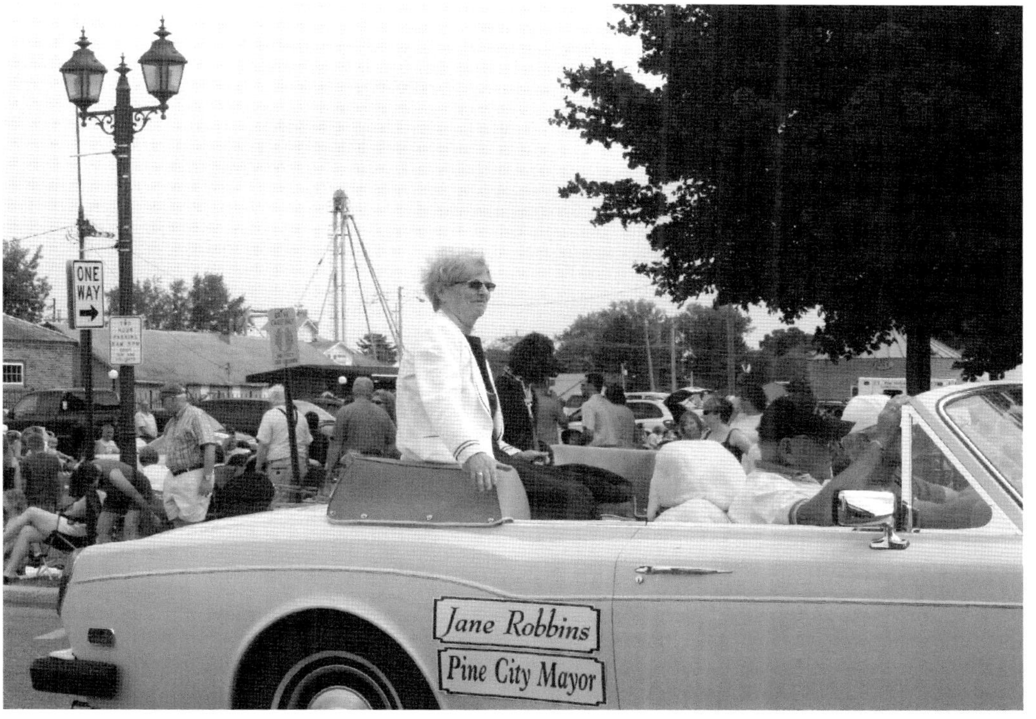
ONE WAY
Jane Robbins
Pine City Mayor

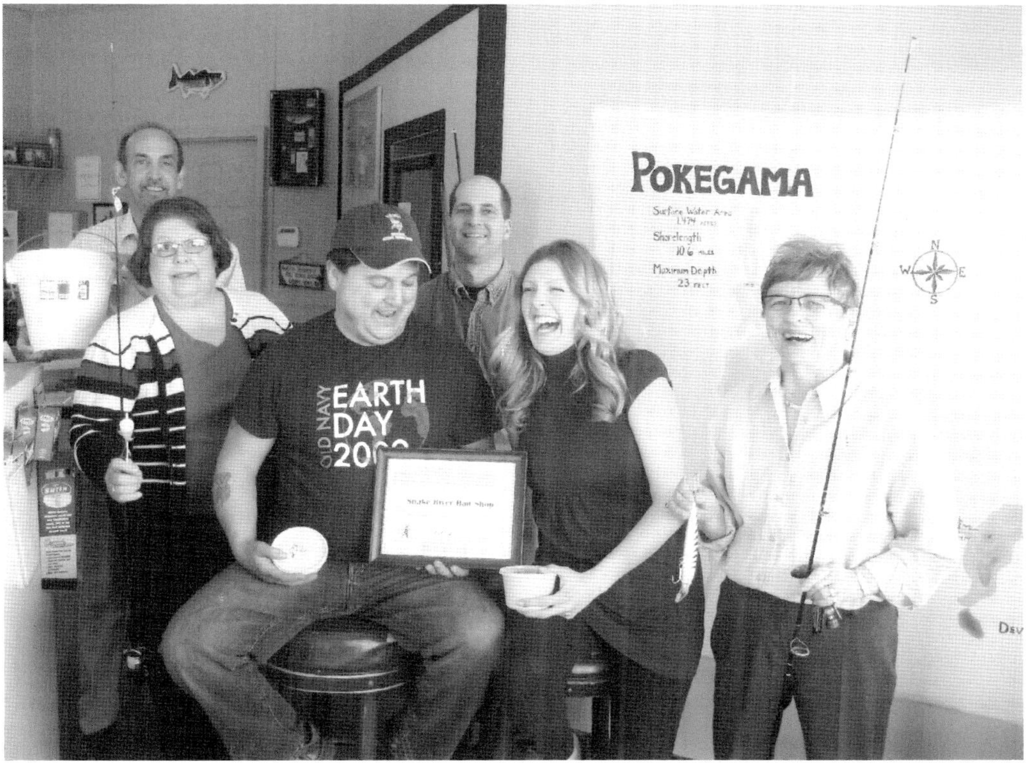
POKEGAMA
OLD NAVY
EARTH DAY

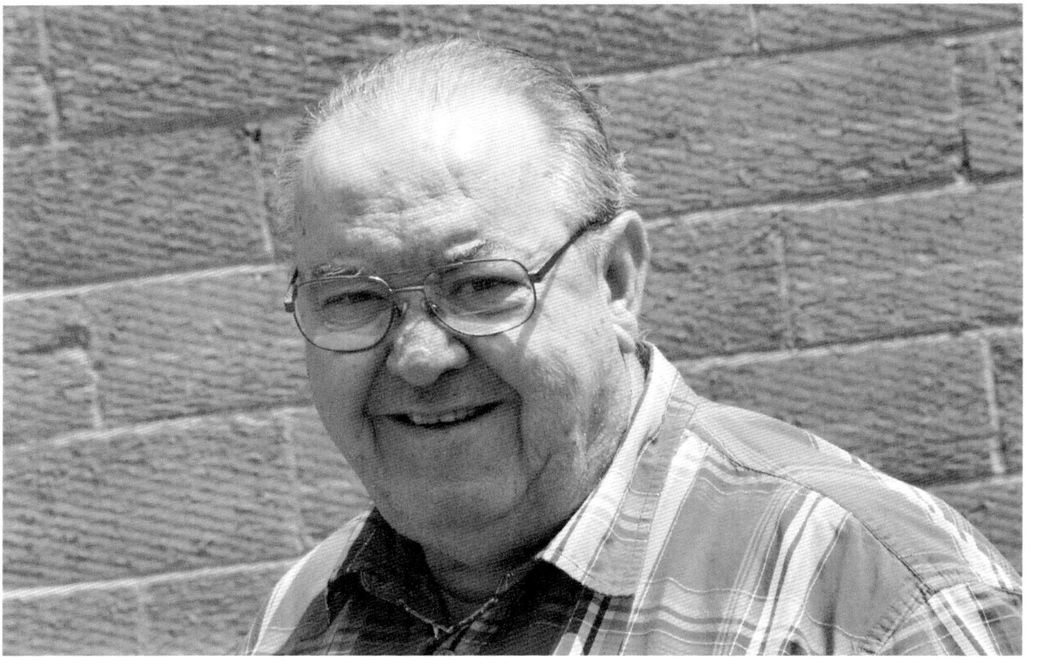

Paul Janssen

Perhaps it was in part because Paul Janssen saved downtown decades earlier that he was elected mayor in 2011. Janssen was born in Pine City on March 8, 1939. In his working years, he was a truck driver and, later, a welder. Every day, he waited for his truck at the downtown Mobil station, then went on to work. One morning in 1971, Mike Miller, the bulk truck driver and manager of Gehl Oil Company, was dumping gas at the downtown Mobil station, managed by John Armstrong. Janssen happened to look out the window of the station and saw gas spewing out of the pump. Soon, the station exploded into flames. Janssen ran out the front door, and Miller, engulfed in flames, went out another door. Janssen threw his jacket over Miller's head to try to extinguish the flames, to no avail. He took a fire extinguisher from his truck and applied it to Miller's feet and head, but the flames kept reigniting, and then finally went out.

Pine County sheriff John Kosicek responded, and an ambulance took Miller away. Meanwhile, gas was still being dispensed into the building. The sheriff ordered that the delivery truck be driven away, out of downtown Pine City. No one present would dare climb aboard the truck, so Janssen jumped into the 1,500-gallon fuel tanker and drove off, northbound on Old Highway 61, down the center of the street. Trailing behind him was about 50 feet of hose. A passerby, Donny Sauter, used an axe to chop the hose off and stop the flame. At the boat landing, Janssen was able to shut off the dispenser. No one died, though Miller had major surgery. One building was lost, but, by-and-large, downtown remained undamaged. (Photograph by Noah Sikkink.)

CHAPTER FOUR

Activists and Other Government Service People

There have been so many citizens of Pine City who have given their time to service or a cause. This chapter recognizes some of these people, from philanthropists to those who, despite being affected by circumstances out of their control, knew they had to dive in and help others. Though the county is among the largest in the state and encompasses the cities of Sandstone and Hinckley as well as Pine City, two of the longest-serving sheriffs in Pine County's history lived in Pine City: Hannes Rypkema (1931–1958) and John Kosicek (1971–1991). Rypkema, a World War I veteran, was synonymous with justice for 28 years in Pine County. He also received the Distinguished Service Cross, the second-highest military declaration awarded by the US Army. Kosicek, a lifelong resident of Pine City, knew the citizens and loved his community. He worked on local farms from a very young age and later drove heavy equipment before joining the Army in 1943. A World War II veteran, Kosicek continued to serve the community after his retirement as sheriff. He passed away on May 26, 2010. He did not see himself as a hero, but rather always said, "The only heroes in a war are the ones who died fighting for their country."

This chapter profiles Pine City residents who have reached out to others, including the following: philanthropist Bert Enger; the first woman to run for US Senate, Anna Dickey Olesen; the young conservative firebrand, Rudy Takala; Pine County's first woman commissioner, Eileen Anderson; same-sex marriage campaigner, Richard Carlbom; first female Minneapolis police chief, Linda Bergstrom; Congressman J. Adam Bede; longtime city clerk, Christine Bloomquist; Cindy Hickey; and Shane Bauer.

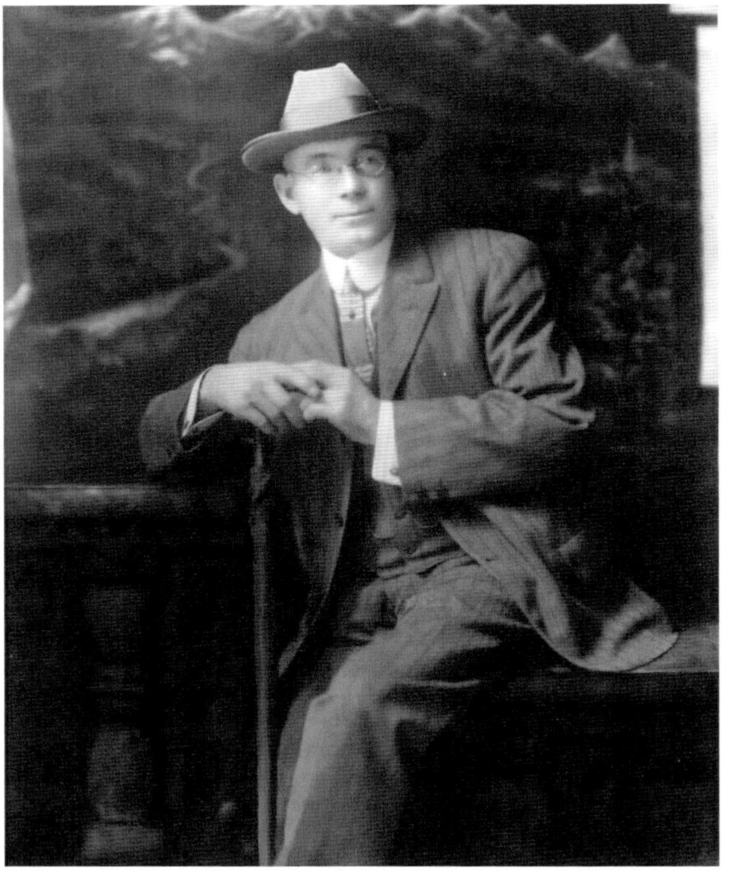

Bert Enger

An activist for city parks, Bert J. Enger was memorialized by the handcrafted, bluestone, 75-foot-tall Enger Tower in Duluth. The park the tower sits in also bears his name. The tower has provided panoramic views of the bay, Lake Superior, and the St. Louis River for Duluthians and visitors since it was erected in 1939. In Enger's lifetime, he spent leisure hours in admiration of the panorama of Duluth and its environs. From common laborer to merchant prince, Enger demonstrated that America is a land of opportunity for the immigrant, who in turn enriches the nation.

Enger, born in Norway in 1864, immigrated to the United States in 1877, at the age of 13. He lived on a farm in rural Pine City and then, after failing at business, he, along with his business partner, Emil Olson, relocated to Duluth and started a furniture business in 1903. In 1920, Enger anonymously donated $50,000 to Duluth toward its longtime goal of condemning and purchasing the land that would make up what was then called Zenith Park and an adjacent golf course. But Mayor C.R. Magney refused to take the donation without the benefactor coming forward. So Enger fessed up. When the golf course opened in 1927, it was named for him.

Enger died in 1931 of a stroke while vacationing in Honolulu. He bequeathed two-thirds of his estate to the people of Duluth and the Duluth park system. In 1934, Zenith Park was rededicated as Enger Park. In 1939, the tower went up at a cost of $30,000. The expenses were covered by Enger's earlier contributions. On June 15, 1939, the tower was dedicated in a royal affair: Crown Prince Olaf and Princess Martha of Enger's native Norway visited Duluth to celebrate Enger and the tower's completion. More than 5,000 spectators showed up for the event, and the tower's green beacon was added in honor of the royal visitors. (Author's collection.)

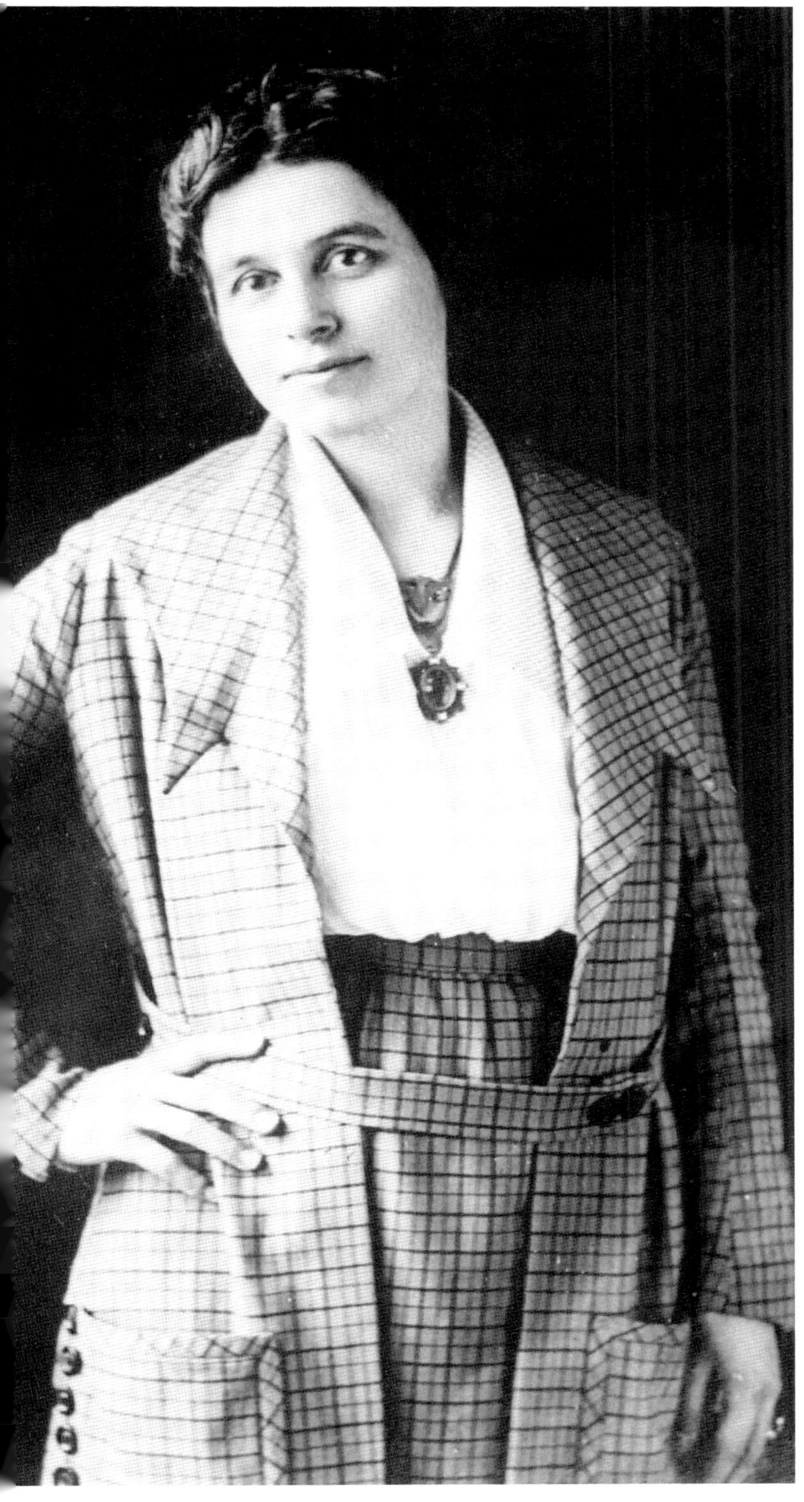

Anna Dickie Olesen
It was not until 2007 that Minnesota elected its first woman to the US Senate, Amy Klobuchar. But Anna Dickie Olesen of Pine City was the first woman, not only in Minnesota but in all of America, to run for Senate. She was born on July 3, 1885, in Cordova Township, in Le Sueur County. A member of the Democratic Party, she was the first woman to serve on the Democratic National Committee (1917–1924). In 1929, at the Democratic National Convention, she was mentioned as a possible candidate for vice president.

She was first married to Peter Olesen, superintendent of schools in Pine City (and later Cloquet, Minnesota), prior to her advancement in politics. She later married C.M. Burge. In the late 1930s, Anna served on the Minnesota State Planning Board and the Minnesota Resources Committee, and she was active with the General Federation of Women's Clubs and the League of Women Voters, among other organizations. Cited by the *New York Times* as being for the "common people," she campaigned across Minnesota in a Ford sedan. Anna died on May 21, 1971, in Northfield, Minnesota. (Courtesy of Library of Congress.)

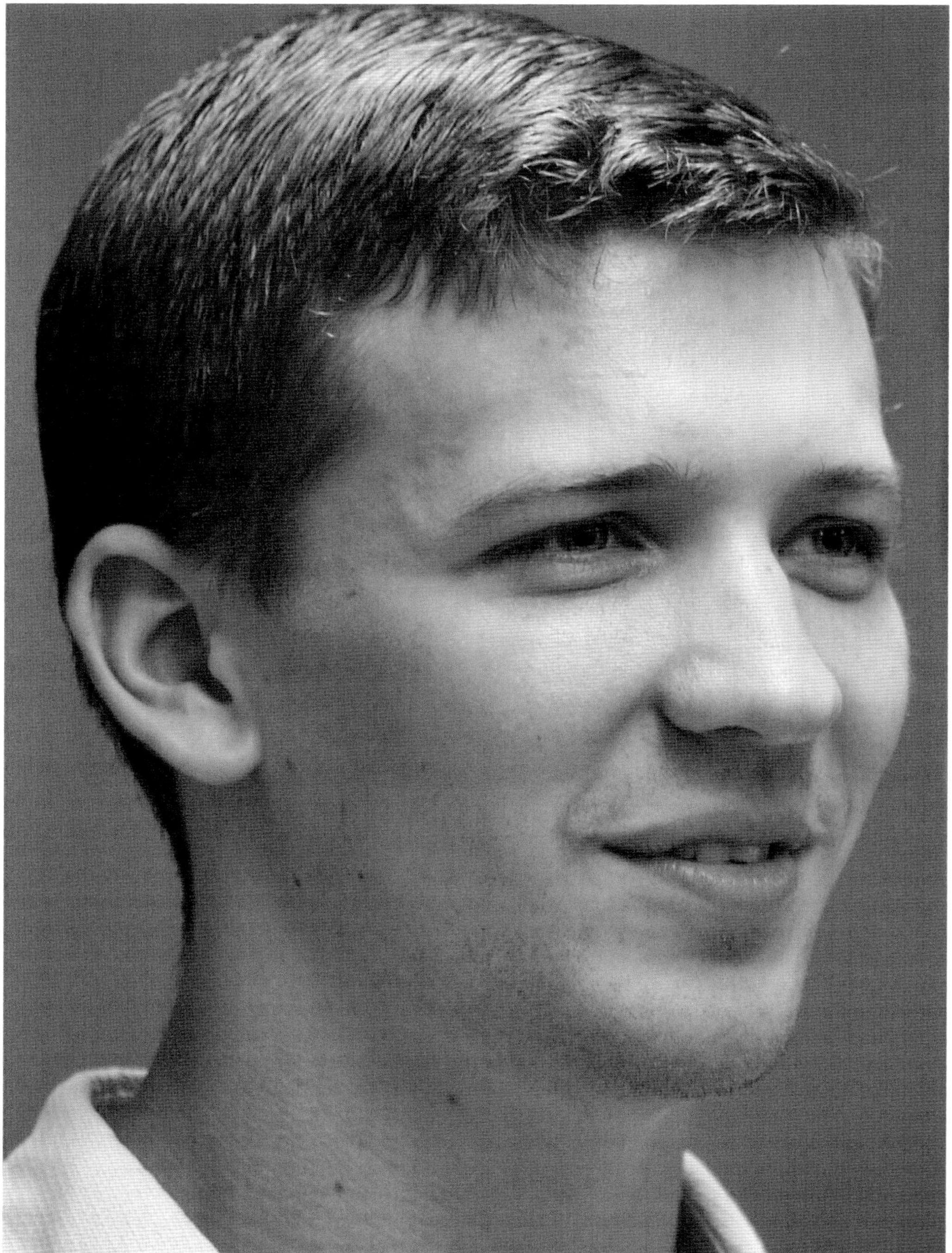

Rudy Takala

Born on November 30, 1988, Rudy Takala was raised on a dairy farm near Pine City and was homeschooled from first through ninth grade. He started at Pine Technical College at the age of 16 and graduated at the age of 20 with a degree in legal studies and economics from Hamline University. In 2006, at the age of 16, he was campaign manager for a Minnesota Senate candidate, Bill Saumer. Takala said he learned a lot about group dynamics in this role: "I thought that the [Republican Party] organization could do a lot more to respect people, include people and make people interested." He was appointed secretary of the Pine County Republicans and, at age 18, was elected chair, the youngest person to hold that position in any political party in Pine County. From there, he started a movement called "Simply Right" with the slogan "People over politics" in an effort to engage more people. The organization coincided with the Tea Party movement and was thus tied to it by several media publications, including *Politics in Minnesota*. In 2009, he announced his own candidacy for the Minnesota House of Representatives. He lost in the primary to Roger Crawford on August 10, 2010, despite carrying Pine County by a margin of 696 to 486 votes.

Takala has left an independent, yet conservative trail over the Internet. While considered a rising star in the Republican Party, he views himself as a voice that is critical of both major parties. Takala says he has an eye on party leadership. "[I] would like a political process that is more representative of average communities and less representative of lobbyists and people who are career politicians or political animals," he stated. Takala said he represents younger people in the Republican and Libertarian Parties. "The Republican Party doesn't represent ideas anymore. The Democratic Party represents ideas. The Republican Party is much more electorally driven, much more pragmatic; they don't really have a clear purpose as the Democratic Party does. That kind of drives young people away from it." But not Takala. (Photograph by Noah Sikkink.)

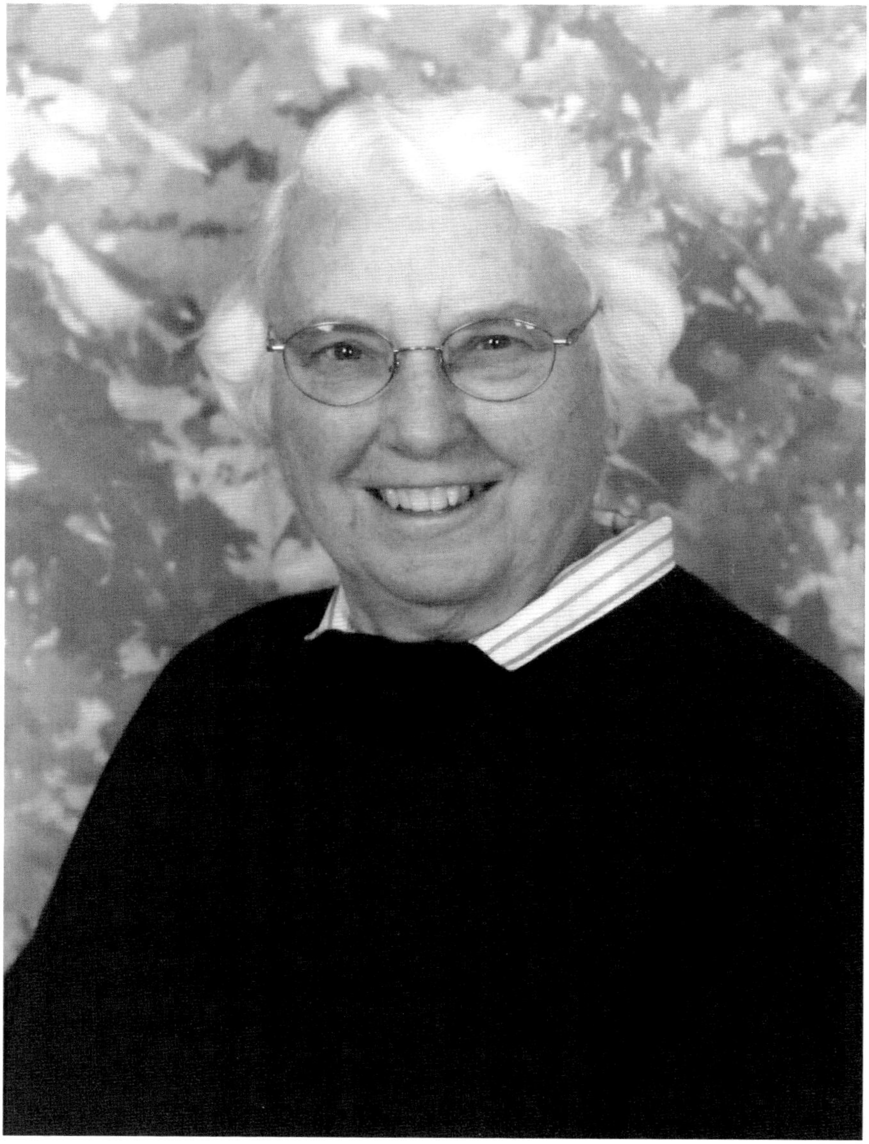

Eileen Anderson

The first female county commissioner in Pine County was Eileen Anderson, who took office in 1986 and held it until 2006. Prior to serving on the board, she was an accounting officer and fiscal supervisor for the human services department at the Pine County Courthouse. She worked for 40 years for the county. Then, she served for 20 more years, representing Pine County District One, before Steve Hallan defeated her. She was a voice for the Rush Line Corridor commuter rail, fighting for a park-and-ride to be constructed in southern Pine County. Anderson helped the county maintain continuity through some difficult issues, such as whether or not to split the county in two and the building of a new courthouse facility. (Courtesy of Eileen Anderson.)

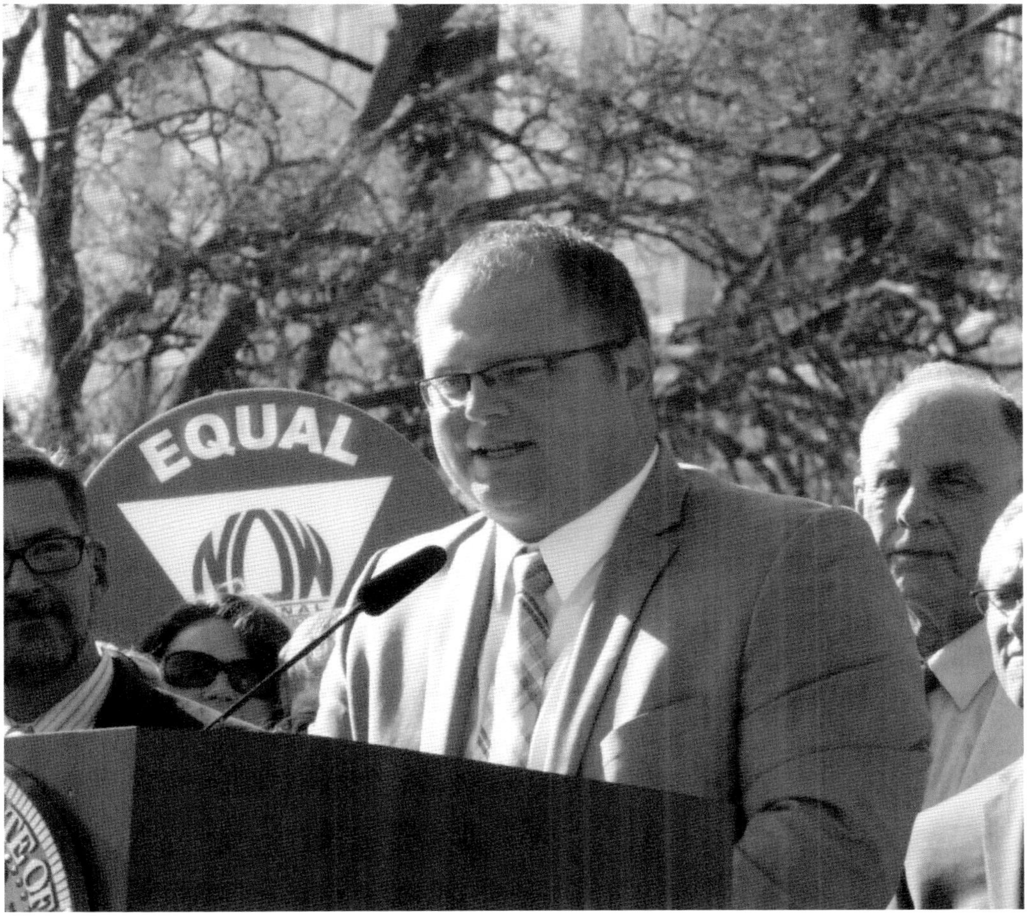

Richard Carlbom

While no single person is the public face of the successful drive for gay marriage in Minnesota, the man who gets the most credit from his allies for making it happen is Richard Carlbom. He grew up and attended elementary school in Pine City, citing those as his formative years. His parents owned the Chalet Motel in nearby Rock Creek. He attended St. John's University, graduating with a degree in political science. Soon after, he was elected mayor of St. Joseph, Minnesota, as an openly gay man. He also worked for the mayor of St. Paul and ran Democratic US Rep. Tim Walz's reelection campaign. But his career-defining job came at the age of 30, in 2011, when Minnesotans United for All Families hired him as its campaign manager. The issue of marriage equality came into focus when a GOP-led legislature put a same-sex marriage ban on the ballot. Carlbom led a successful campaign to defeat that amendment. "Every war—even a war of love—needs a general, and our general is quiet, and self-effacing and brilliant," said state senator Dick Cohen of Carlbom.

After the amendment was defeated, Carlbom and the rest of the Minnesotans United campaign quickly shifted to successfully lobbying a Democratic-controlled legislature to legalize same-sex marriage, which became law on August 1, 2013. In a stunning reversal from the tone of the previous legislature, Minnesota became the first state to defeat a gay-marriage ban after more than 30 were successfully installed around the country. Carlbom married his longtime partner, Justin Schramm, on December 20, 2013. (Courtesy of Richard Carlbom.)

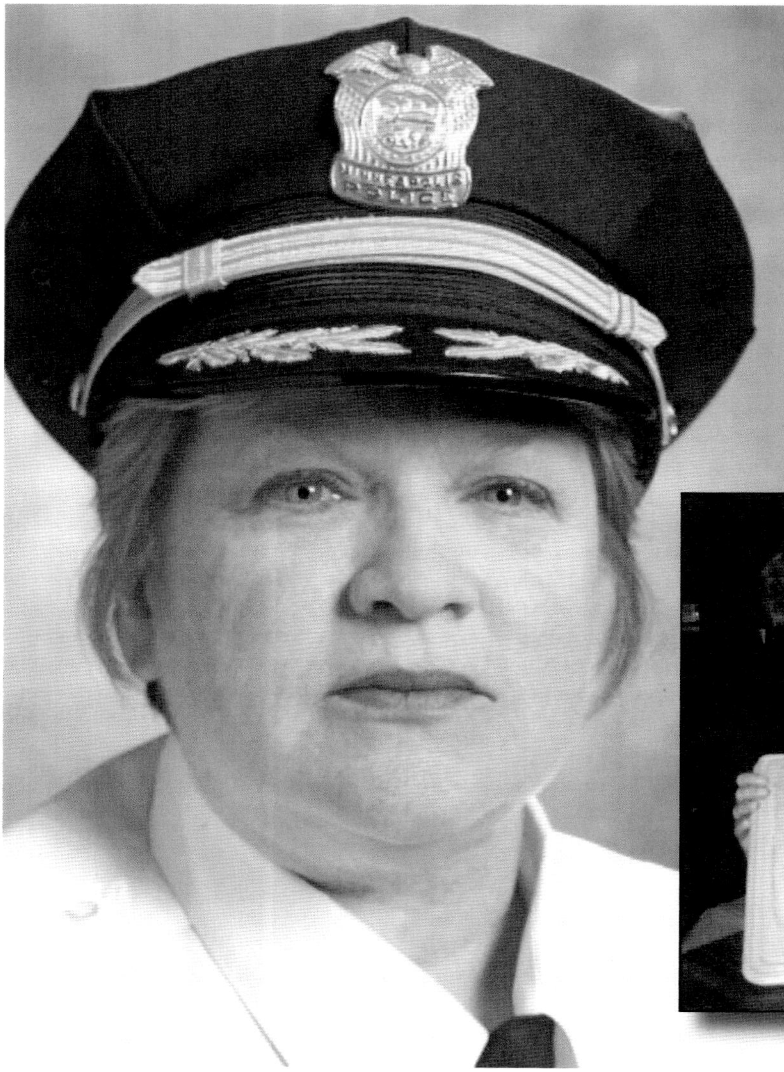

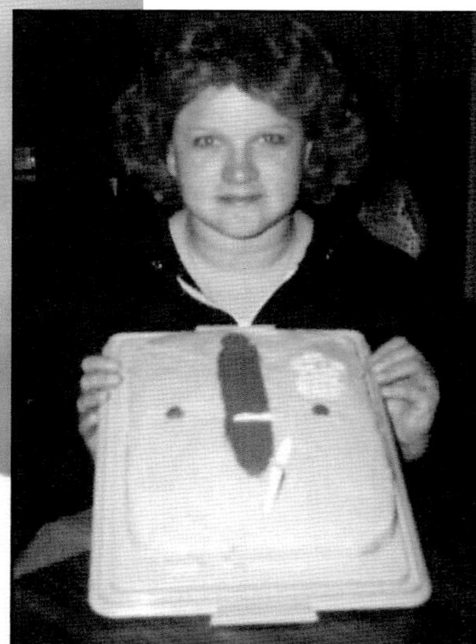

Linda Bergstrom

Linda K. Bergstrom loved her career and her colleagues, and she had a soft spot for stray dogs and cats. Born to August and Fidelia Milleren Bergstrom (the Milleren from Novak-Milleren VFW Post No. 4258), Bergstrom joined the Minneapolis Park Police Department as an agent in 1979. She had a career with the department for 34 years before dying suddenly at the age of 58 from respiratory failure. During her time with the Minneapolis Park Police, she rose through the ranks, becoming chief of police in July 2010. She was the first woman to hold all of those positions. Her obituary read, "She always considered the men and women she worked with as her extended family. Bergstrom always treated everyone with respect and always strived for fairness to everyone." Bergstrom went above and beyond the call of duty, rescuing stray pets from city parks, even meth labs. Some of the rescued animals became her own pets. She loved all animals, especially her three cats, Gussie, Lexie, and Tigger. She was recognized by her peers and the commanders at the Minneapolis Police Department, receiving a Medal of Commendation and two Awards of Merit. With honor, she wore badge No. 711, the same number her brother-in-law Larry Drellack wore until he retired from the force. (Left, courtesy of Barb Dupre; right, courtesy of Wendy Johnson.)

James Adam Bede

Bede was born on a farm in Ohio on January 13, 1856. He attended Oberlin College and Tabor College in Tabor, Iowa, and read law while learning the printing trade. He taught school in Iowa, Ohio, and Arkansas; was editor and publisher of several newspapers and periodicals; served as a representative for several western newspapers in Washington, DC, from 1888 to 1891; engaged in newspaper work in Pine City; served as US marshal for the district of Minnesota in 1894 during the great railway strike; and spoke at the first annual dinner of the Associated Press in New York. Bede was elected as a Republican and served from March 4, 1903, to March 3, 1909. He was the only US congressman to have come from Pine City. He was a great humorist with a rapid-fire delivery. When running for reelection, he had audiences in stitches during his speeches.

In his book *The Homesteaders*, which recounts life in early-20th-century rural Pine County, Minnesota, O. Bernard Johnson describes Bede's speaking style as follows: "If he said anything seriously about the issues of the day no one can recall, but I am sure that his humor got him many votes." But, he was an unsuccessful candidate for renomination in 1908 to the 61st Congress, and he returned to Pine City. At this juncture, he engaged as a publisher and lecturer. He moved to Duluth in 1927 and engaged in his former pursuits. He was also interested in the St. Lawrence inland waterway project. In an April 28, 1912, article, "How Humor Enlivens the Solemn Work of Congress," the *New York Times* reported: "Adam Bede was one of the most popular stump speakers and spellbinders of the present generation. His speeches were full of dry humor and his droll manner of illustrating his arguments by stories of the day never failed to win the applause of his audiences." Bede died in Duluth on April 11, 1942, and was interred in Birchwood Cemetery in Pine City. (Author's collection.)

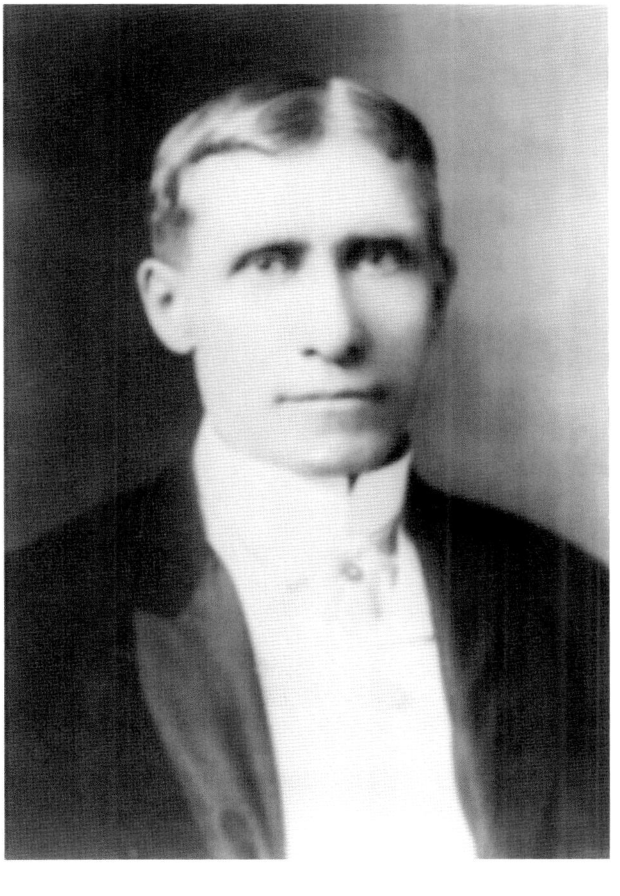

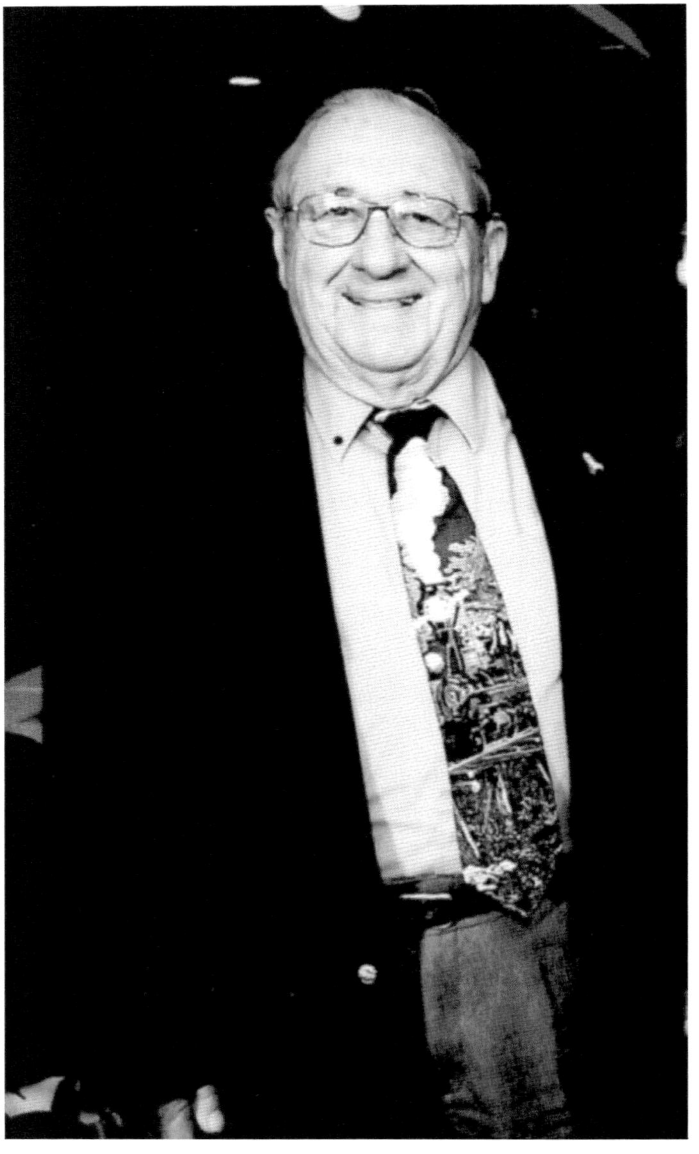

John Skluzacek

John Harold Skluzacek was born in 1933. He graduated from Pine City high school and went off to service. After his return, he went to work for the city and was a longtime city crew supervisor. He made national news on June 21, 1976, when he was fire chief. Sadly, he had to report that there were three children who died in a fire that destroyed a home six miles west of Pine City. Mr. and Mrs. Dale Bell, Dale's sister Mary, and four children escaped from the home before it was engulfed by flames. The victims and one other child, Victoria Bell, were sleeping on the top floor of the two-story home, and the others were sleeping downstairs when the fire broke out. Mary was awakened by Victoria's screams from the top of the stairway. In 1987, John and another longtime member of the National Guard, John Langenbrunner, retired from duty and were honored in a special ceremony at the armory in Pine City. Skluzacek became Citizen of the Year in 1999. (Courtesy of John Skluzacek.)

Henry Sommer

Sommer was born in Pine City on June 4, 1913, the fifth of eight children to Adolph and Sophia Eiles Sommer. He graduated from Pine City High School in 1930. His father died the same year. Sommer attended the University of Minnesota for one year, but returned home to help on the family farm. When the Pine City Cooperative was established in 1937, Sommer was hired as its first manager. Early on, he was station attendant, bookkeeper, and purchasing agent. He then was manager for 42 years until he retired in 1979. He served on the board of directors for Midland Cooperatives of Minneapolis for over 30 years and represented Midland on the National Cooperative Board for over 20 years.

Sommer married Evelyn Anderson on May 27, 1938, and they had five children: Gary "Butch," Judy, Sue, Mick, and Deb. Henry served on the Pine City Village Council during the 1940s and 1950s. In 1981, he was named Pine City's Citizen of the Year. He was also a member of the Snake River Valley Conservation Club (SRVCC). The fishing pier at the public access in Pine City was named Sommer Dock in his honor at a ceremony on June 6, 1986, attended by city council and SRVCC members and DNR personnel. He was a longtime member of the First Presbyterian Church, attending regularly well into his 90s. He also served on the church council. Henry Sommer was an enthusiastic sportsman. He took many fishing trips to Canada and to nearby rivers and lakes. He went deer hunting for 66 consecutive years at the hunting shack east of Hinckley and rarely came home without a deer. After one of his many elk-hunting trips to Colorado, he donated his bull elk mount to the SRVCC. He was an avid follower of the Twins and Vikings and enjoyed playing cribbage and 500. For many years, he played in the Pine Area Lions 500 Marathon and at the American Legion. He loved the outdoors and the family home on Cross Lake. A lifetime gardener, he was especially proud of his blueberry patch. Sommer loved being with his family, grandchildren, and great-grandchildren. He passed away at the age of 97 on September 18, 2010. (Courtesy of Judy Adams.)

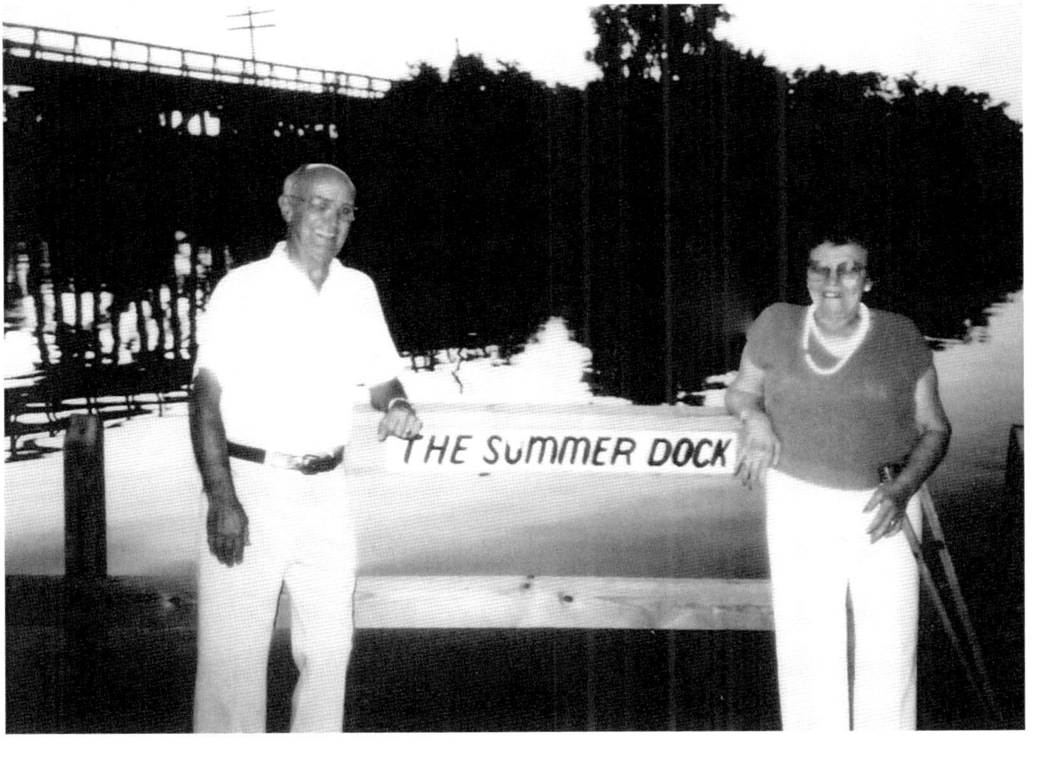

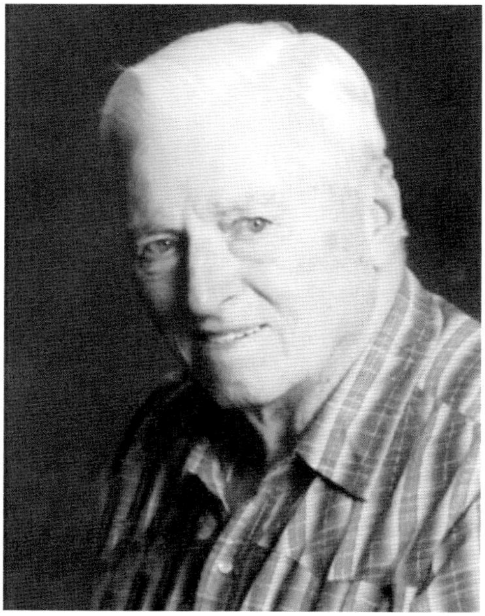

Ben Sauter

Sauter was a longtime Pine City business owner, council member, and a mayor of Pine City. He was born on January 29, 1921, in North Dakota. When he was two, his family moved to a farm west of Morris, Minnesota. He attended country school and lived on the farm with his parents, two brothers, and nine sisters. He married Irene Lesmeister of Morris on January 16, 1945. They made their home in Alberta, Minnesota. Sauter worked at Greens Milling Company and Chandler-Wilbert Vault Company during the winter months. In 1961, they moved to Pine City, and Sauter joined the United Farm Agency, a national real estate firm, and sold real estate for 28 years.

Sauter was elected to the city council of Pine City and served in that capacity for 16 years. He also served as acting mayor under Robert "Bob" E. Anderson. He was the civil defense director for a number of years, served on the Pine County Agricultural Society for 16 years, and was chair for 12 years. With Albrecht Erhart, he was instrumental in starting the Demo Derby for the Pine County Fair. He served on the Conservation Club for 16 years and was chair for 12 years. After retiring, Ben and Irene spent their winters in Arizona for many years and enjoyed camping with their family in the summer. Sauter died at the age of 90 in his Pine City home. (Above, courtesy of Susan Smetana.; below, author's collection.)

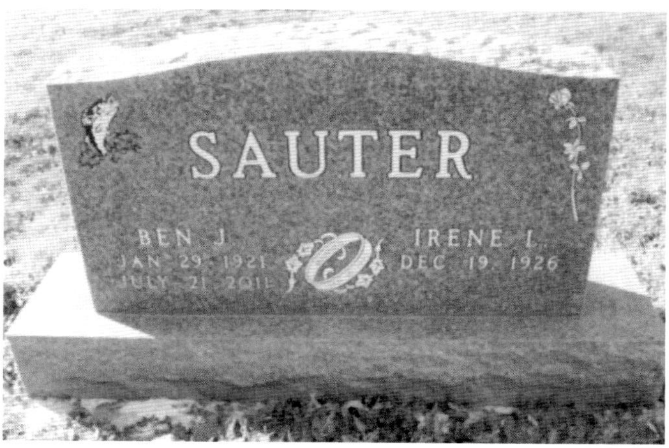

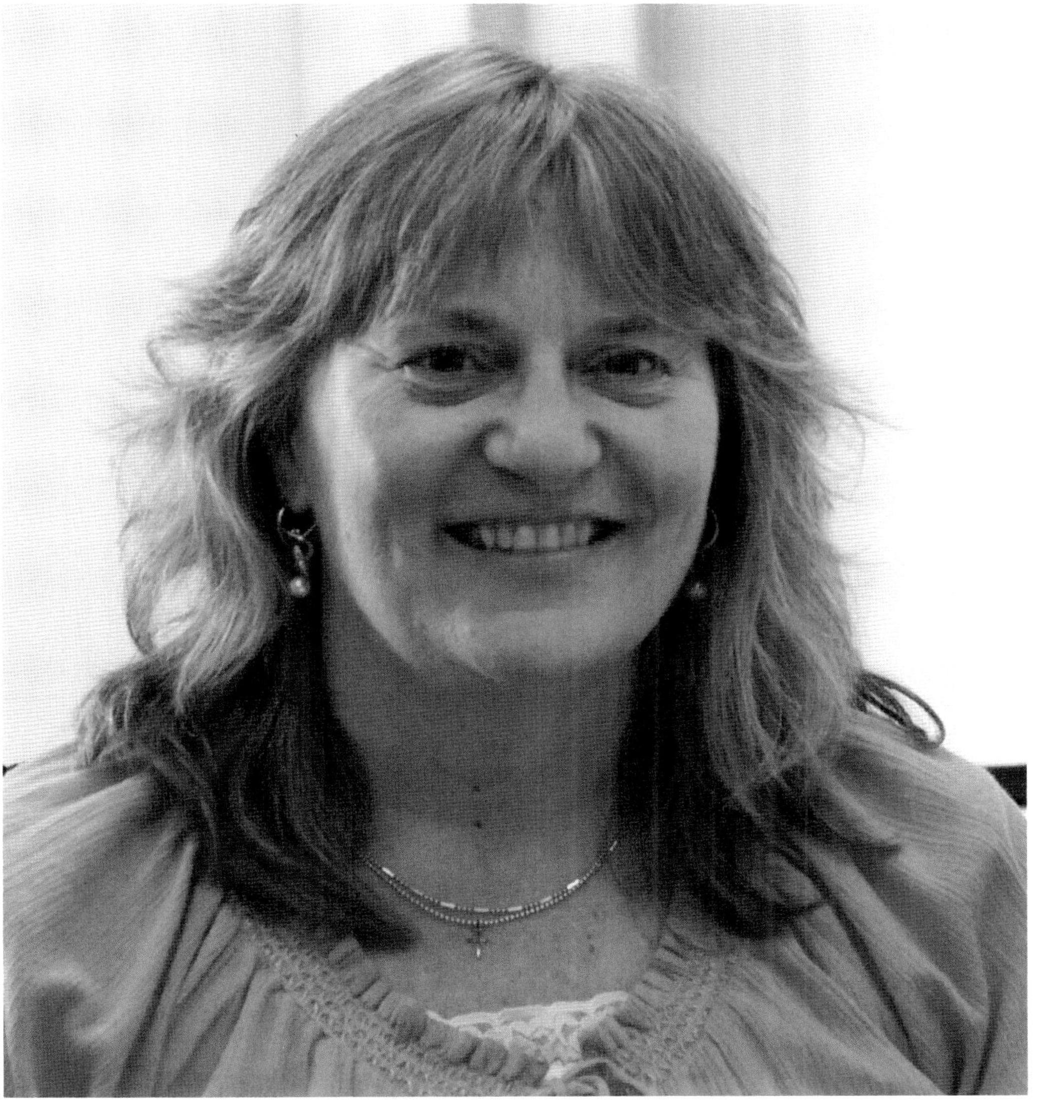

Christine Bloomquist

Chris Bloomquist worked as a clerk for the City of Pine City for more than 30 years. Over the years, her job underwent many changes, much to do with technological advances. There was only one computer in all of city hall when she started on October 19, 1983. A lot of personnel have changed during her time working for the city, including three mayors, four public works directors, and 12 city administrators. She was hired on as a deputy city clerk, became clerk, and then became assistant city administrator in her later years. Her starting wage was $5 an hour.

Chris and her husband, Hadley, came to love the area after making frequent visits to see her brother-in-law. They fell in love with a farm and moved to Pine City, with Hadley commuting to the Twin Cities for construction work. The two were inventors of a product for livestock, intended to create an audible sound to aid in the controlled movement of animals, suited for farmers, ranchers, auctioneers, and anyone who loads or moves livestock. "I've always had a passion to do the right thing for the City of Pine City, and to do a good job at everything I touched," Bloomquist said. (Photograph by Noah Sikkink.)

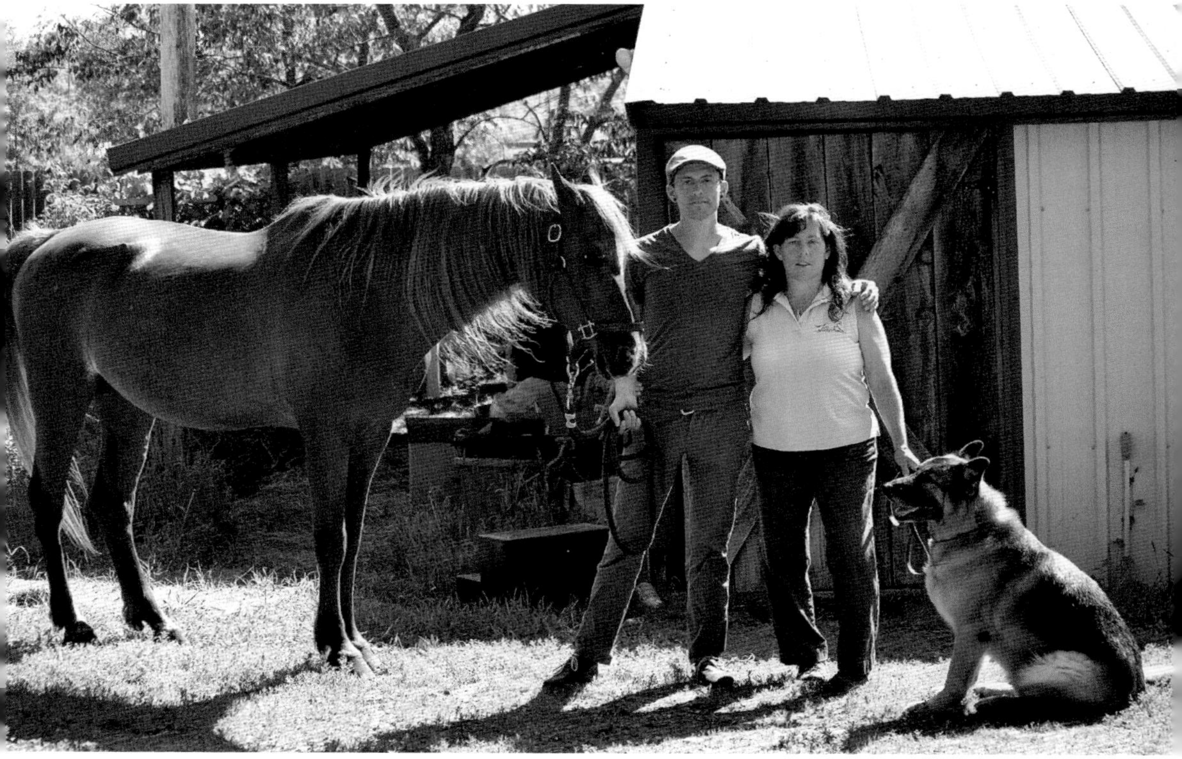

Shane Bauer and Cindy Hickey

On July 31, 2009, three Americans—Sarah Shourd, Shane Bauer (pictured), and Joshua Fattal—were taken into custody by Iranian border guards for allegedly crossing into Iran while hiking near the border in Iraqi Kurdistan. Iran claimed the three were spies but offered no evidence. The three Americans maintained they were on Iraqi territory at the time of the arrest and denied that they were involved in espionage or doing anything other than having a recreational hike. A wide range of voices, including UN secretary general Ban Ki-moon and the human rights group Amnesty International, called for the hikers' release. Desmond Tutu, Muhammad Ali, Alyssa Milano, Ashton Kutcher, Pres. Barack Obama, along with many other celebrities and governments, called for their release on grounds of inhumane treatment and lack of evidence.

Bauer, who grew up in Minnesota and California, is a freelance photojournalist and journalist who has written for *Mother Jones*, the *Christian Science Monitor*, the *San Francisco Chronicle*, the *Los Angeles Times*, and other media outlets, using his fluency in Arabic. Bauer and Fattal were friends from their days at the University of California–Berkeley.

The mothers of the three detainees, including Bauer's mother, Cindy Hickey (pictured), from rural Pine City, applied for visas in January 2010 to visit their children. The captives were united with their mothers for two days in May 2010. Shourd was released 14 months into captivity on humanitarian grounds, but Bauer and Fattal were convicted of illegal entry and espionage and were not released until September 21, 2011, after payment of five billion rial (approximately $465,000) bail. Bauer and Shourd, who were already in a relationship when they were detained, became engaged in prison and were married on May 12, 2012. On November 19, 2011, there was a welcome home celebration for Bauer at the North West Company Fur Post. According to the November 23, 2011, *Pine City Pioneer*, Hickey was quoted as saying, "I'm very grateful for the holidays this year. . . . All of my children will be home." Hickey's property, in a valley southeast of Pine City, is where she keeps horses, dogs, and other animals. She and Bauer used to ride horses together, and they hope they can do more of that in the days to come. (Courtesy of Noah Sikkink.)

CHAPTER FIVE

Athletes and Sports

Who was the best athlete to ever come out of Pine City High School? Some say Jerry Hoeffler (class of 1961, football and baseball), others claim Tom Nelson (class of 1980, basketball), and some say Rhiannon Sauter (class of 2007, softball). While that question is up for debate, what is beyond dispute is that there have been several athletic successes over the years in Pine City.

Wally Connaker worked for Pine City schools from 1970 to 2002, and then again from 2004 to 2009, his later years serving as athletic director. He saw a number of those successes.

According to Connaker, one of the biggest achievements of Pine City athletics took place during the 1961–1962 school year. The 1961 football team went undefeated, slaughtering rival Mora 41-0 and even clobbering the much larger Lakeville team 28-6. There was no state tournament then; if so, the team may have been Minnesota state champions. The 1962 baseball team, comprised of several of the same athletes, was undefeated going into the state tournament (a single-class tournament). From that team, Dick Kuzel and Jim Foster were named all-state.

The 1980 basketball team, the first to head to the Minnesota state tournament, consisted of Tommy Nelson, Joe Kessler, Tim Werner, Tom Seversen, and Pat Butler (son of the coach, Don Butler), to name a few. Of the team's 20 games, it lost just two, back-to-back, to Braham and Mora. The team had won three district titles in a row, from 1978 to 1980, and one in 1976, when Butler came on as coach. Three state championships were achieved by the Pine City Dragons: Tommy Nelson in the high jump (6 feet, 8.25 inches) in 1980; Tim Odegard in Class A golf (76-78, 154) in 1981; and Adam Olson, Mike Hansmann, Nick Cummings, and Jordan Pangerl in the 4-by-100-meter relay (43.70) in 2011.

This chapter covers not only Pine City High School athletics, but also athletes with Pine City ties that have had major successes. Pine City was home to the world's largest female bodybuilder and to professional wrestlers, baseball players, football players, and two National Hockey League draft picks. Moreover, the town has been home to a Paralympian, a professional snowcross racer, and at least one professional mixed martial arts (MMA) fighter.

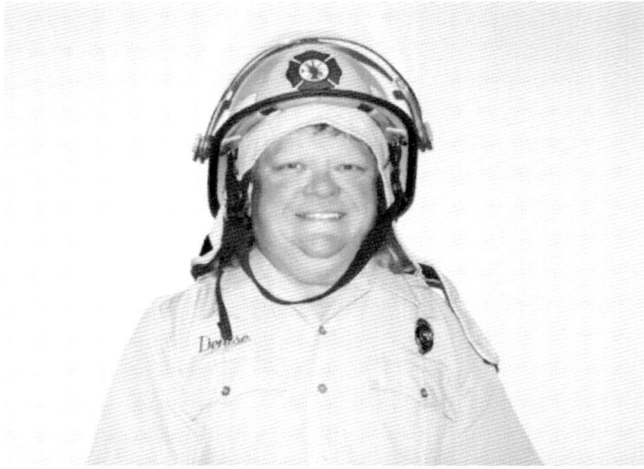

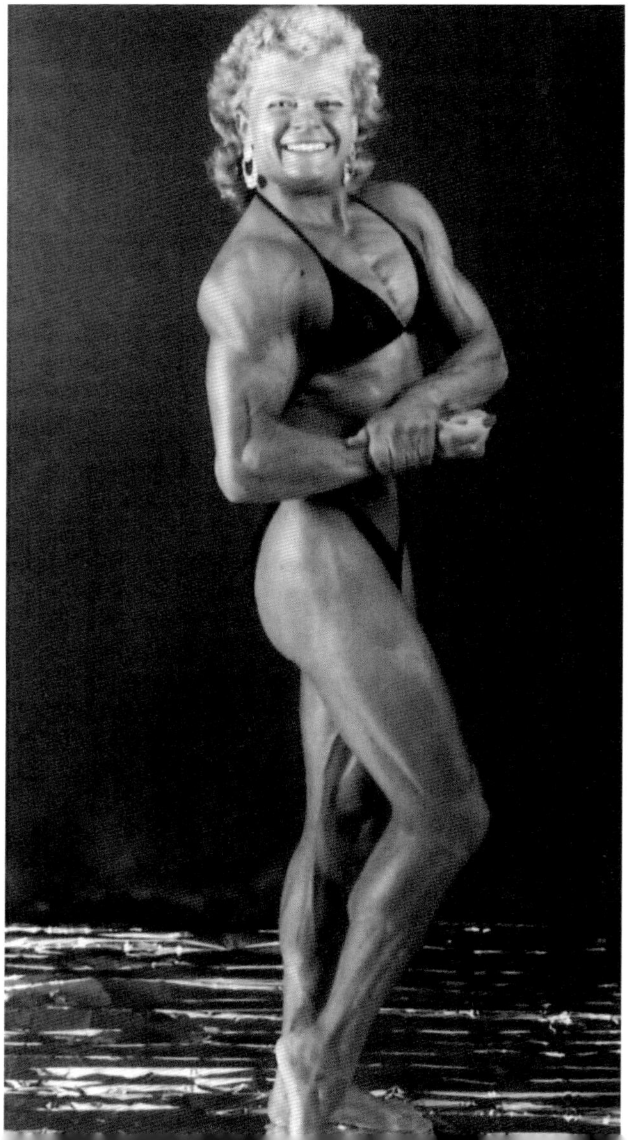

Denise Nelsen

Denise Nelsen, sister of Karla Nelsen, was the first female firefighter in Pine City. She was born on April 18, 1961. Always muscular, and at times self-conscious about it, Nelsen decided to make the most of her situation. Through a bodybuilding friend in the early 1990s, she heard that the St. Paul Fire Department had a callout for women firefighters, and she applied. She trained hard, running around her family's large tract of land west of Pine City on a mowed, 1.5-mile loop that was otherwise used by the family's mini-bikes. Firefighting seemed like a good fit to Nelsen, who was following in her sister's footsteps, as she developed her bodybuilding skills and went on to become 1990 Ms. Natural Minnesota, an award given by the National American Bodybuilding Association.

During trial testing, she checked into the Pine City Fire Department and later joined the department with the encouragement of fellow school faculty worker George Johnson. Despite growing up in a fairly conservative family, Nelsen broke the glass ceiling, becoming Pine City's first female firefighter. The PCFD was not only a place for her to be "one of the guys," it was to be a stepping-stone of sorts to get accepted to the St. Paul Fire Department. Nelsen, however, ended up staying in her hometown. She was later outed as a lesbian in her father's obituary, which mentioned her partner at the time, Anita Chavez. She said she was well accepted in the field, though some of the guys were a little leery about how they should act around her. A true athlete, Nelsen still holds school field-day records. (Both, courtesy Denise Nelsen.)

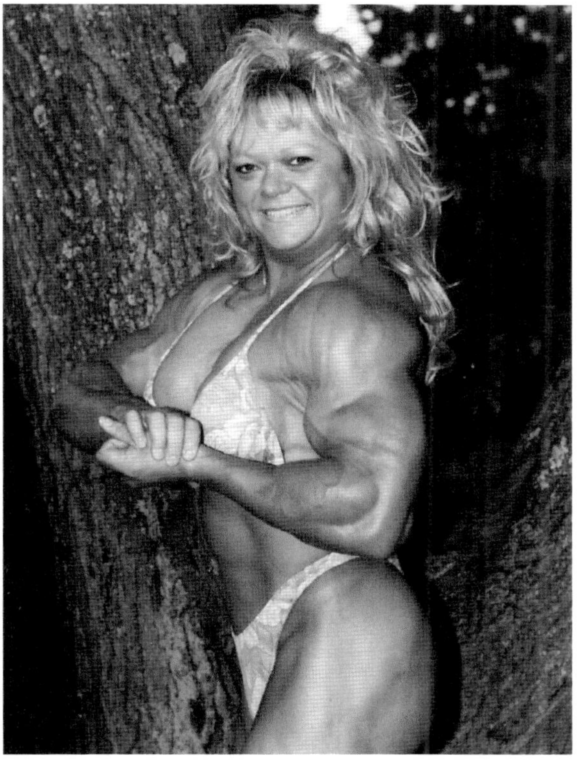

Karla Nelsen Blake

Karla Nelsen Blake, born December 9, 1965, is a former amateur female bodybuilder. She grew up in Pine City where she became involved in the fledgling sport. She graduated from Pine City High School in 1983. In her senior year, she was the first high school female athlete to qualify and compete in the state track meet. She was also the first female athlete to be inducted into the school's Athletic Hall of Fame. Her most competitive years as a bodybuilder were 1987 to 1996. She was 1989 NPC Ms. Minnesota; 1992 World's Strongest Woman (contest held in Japan); AAU 1993 Ms. America; and the National Amateur Bodybuilders Association's Ms. USA in 1994. That same year, she was fourth runner-up for the NABBA Ms. Universe title, losing because the judges felt she was "too big." Karla was featured in *Muscle & Fitness* magazine and in *Flex* magazine. She tried out for the television show *American Gladiators*, but was considered "too muscular" and "too masculine" for the show. In Japan, she appeared in that nation's version of the show.

In her younger days, she was self-conscious, but she grew to realize she had great genetics. At first, she would cover up as much as possible, but she began showing off and being proud of her physique. In competition, her heaviest was 210 pounds. She competed in the "strong" category, at three-to-four-percent body fat. She was widely regarded as the largest female bodybuilder in the world. With that notoriety, she began doing the talk-show circuit, appearing on such shows as KSTP's *Good Company*, hosted by Sharon Anderson and Steve Edelman, and the *Maury Povich Show*.

At a height of five feet, ten inches and an off-season peak weight of 225 pounds, Karla was well known for her mixed wrestling videos, which featured her wrestling much smaller men most of the time. But she also did work for Bill Wick, Premier Productions, Builtmore Productions, Flexible Productions, Leather & Lace, and Mass Muscle, where the men were not that small. She also wrestled women, going undefeated until her confrontation with Nicole Bass, also renowned as one of the world's largest female bodybuilders (six feet, two inches and 240 pounds). Karla is married to Al Blake (see page 48), a retired American professional wrestler known as Vladimir Petrov. (Courtesy of Karla Blake.)

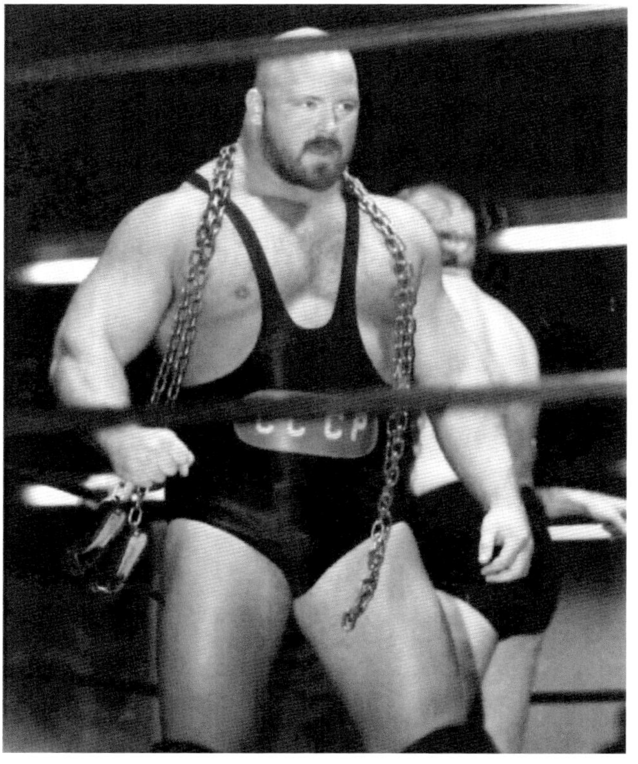

Al Blake

Better known by his professional wrestling ring name, "Vladmir Petrov," Al Blake was born in Minneapolis in 1961. He wrestled in different North American leagues including the Universal Wrestling Federation, most notably through the 1980s as a part of Russian Team and Paul Jones' Army with Ivan Koloff.

A previous bouncer, in early 1987, the six-foot, three-inch tall, 300-pound Blake was carried into the Jim Crockett Promotions as the masked Vladimir Petrov, "the Russian Assassin." Although then head-booker Dusty Rhodes was to initially have brought in John Nord, he instead had Blake group with Koloff at the last minute.

Confronting Nikita Koloff in an arrangement of Russian Chain matches, they harmed Koloff's neck with the assistance of Dick Murdoch a couple months later. They likewise had an arrangement of matches with then-National Wrestling Alliance (NWA) World Tag Team Champions Rock 'n' Roll Express, the Freebirds, and Jimmy and Ron Garvin. They lost to Ron and Barry Windham in a competition for the unfilled NWA United States Tag Team titles and were ousted in the opening round of the Jim Crockett Sr. Memorial Cup by Bob and Brad Armstrong.

Petrov additionally headed off to the Universal Wrestling Federation to fight with "Dr. Death" Steve Williams over the UWF title and additionally collaborated with the Angel of Death in a losing exertion against the NWA World Tag Team Champions, Rock 'n' Roll Express, at the Superdome Extravaganza on June 13, 1987.

He wrestled single matches against Barry Windham and Todd Champion throughout the prior year, losing to Jim and Ron Garvin in a tag group match with the Barbarian at the Great American Bash on July 4, 1987. A common finishing move for Blake was the "Bearhug."

In 1991, after his discharge, Blake started wrestling under his own name in the World Wrestling Federation. Be that as it may, he was utilized predominantly as a preliminary wrestler and left the following year, resigning to Minnesota. Blake is married to Karla Nelsen (see page 47). Together, they made female wrestling movies featuring Karla. (Courtesy of Karla Blake.)

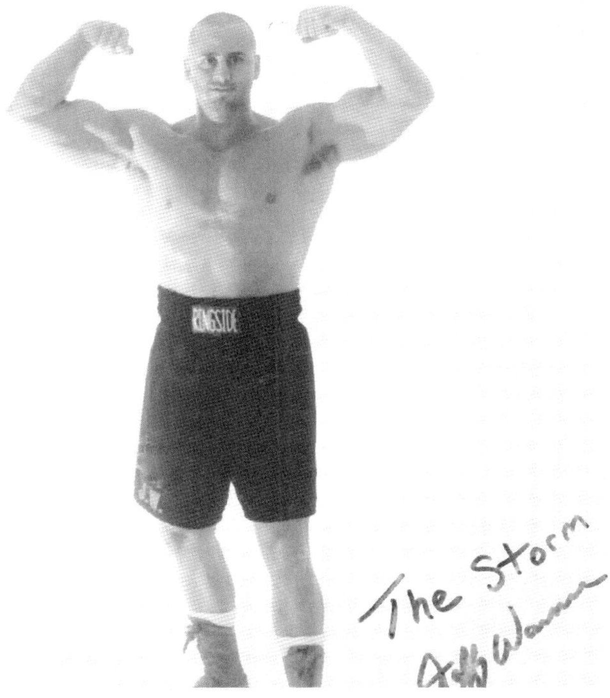

Jeff "The Storm" Warner

Jeff Warner was best known in the professional wrestling circuit under the ring name "J.W. Storm." He contended in World Championship Wrestling most eminently as a part of the tag team Magnum Force with Tim Hunt. He likewise has great stints in Pacific Northwest Wrestling and Pro Wrestling America, winning the tag-team titles in both advancements.

Warner began wrestling in 1989 in the NWA's Pacific Northwest domain. He rounded out a tag team with Art Barr, who was utilizing a "Beetlejuice" ploy called "the Juice Patrol" with Warner getting "Big Juice." They fought with Ricky Santana and Curtis Thompson, who formed the tag team "U.S. Male" until Warner was compelled to leave the advancement in a "loser leaves town" match on June 30, 1990.

He additionally wrestled in Pro Wrestling America throughout the late 1980s and early 1990s and won the tag-team titles as one-half of Maximum Overdrive with Tim Hunt, crushing Matt Derringer and Bret Derringer on June 24, 1989. Holding the titles for a year, they at long last lost them to the Steiner Brothers at Clash of the Champions XII in September 1990.

Warner, who had formerly won the PWA Iron Horse Television title April 5, 1990, guarded the title before moving to the National Wrestling Alliance in June of that year. He soon started wrestling under the name J.W. Storm, cooperating with Scotty Flamingo (who later was Raven) and wrestled against veterans including Terry Taylor and Brad Armstrong, losing to him at Halloween Havoc on October 27, 1990.

In February 1992, Storm additionally had tryout matches for the World Wrestling Federation against the Undertaker, "The Model" Rick Martel, the Warlord, and Hercules in spite of the fact that he vanquished Kato of the Orient Express a few times at house shows between February 8 and March 2.

Warner owned a gym in Pine City near the height of his wrestling profession. He credits his wife, Jennifer, with sparing his life from drug and liquor misuse. They had four children, he became a born-again Christian and, in 2002, he became an ordained pastor through the International Ministerial Fellowship. He started touring the United States with his "Ultimate Strength" show that combines lectures with demonstrations of strength, for example, breaking through a stack of concrete blocks. (Courtesy of Tom and Angela Foster.)

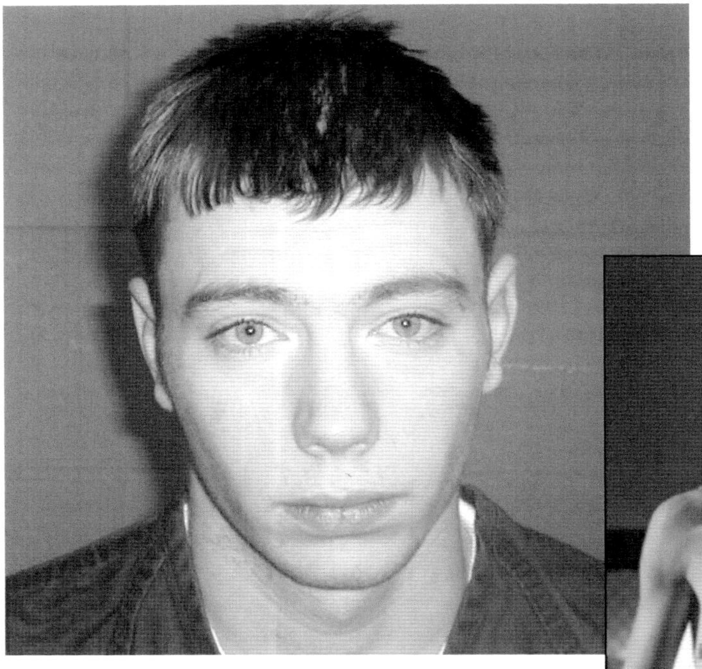

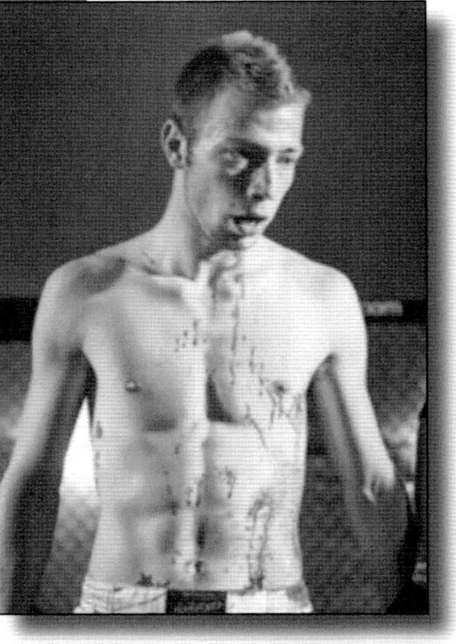

Andrew Selvig

Selvig was born on June 15, 1990. Living in nearby Taylors Falls at the time, on his 18th birthday, he helped himself to a Christmas present and found himself in big trouble. He was charged with taking a lock box containing $230,000 in cash from his grandparents' Amery, Wisconsin, basement.

Selvig told his friends he won money at the casino, but his grandfather checked on his lock box and found it missing. Officers later found the box in a truck that Selvig bought with the stolen money. He served time in jail in Minnesota for the incident, and authorities were able to recover over half of the money.

Selvig was sleeping in his vehicle in the Pine City Walmart parking lot when he found a mentor there, who has remained anonymous. This person opened his home and took in Selvig. Since Christmas 2008, he has been fighting for a second chance. He readily admits the incident inspired him to pursue a dream of becoming an MMA fighter, an aspiration he had previously left on the back burner. The dream came full-circle, and he has appeared in many professional MMA fights all over Minnesota, Wisconsin, and Iowa.

Selvig acknowledges the impact the incident caused his family. "I don't have the prettiest history, but every day is another day in progress," said Selvig. "Ever since my first fight, I fell in love with it." He uses the moniker "The Phoenix," a tattoo of which is on his left rib, signifying rebirth and a new way of life. He hopes his newfound passion, along with his strengths in muay thai, jiu-jitsu, and kickboxing, will help him move into the next chapter of his life. (Courtesy of Ashley Patterson-Selvig.)

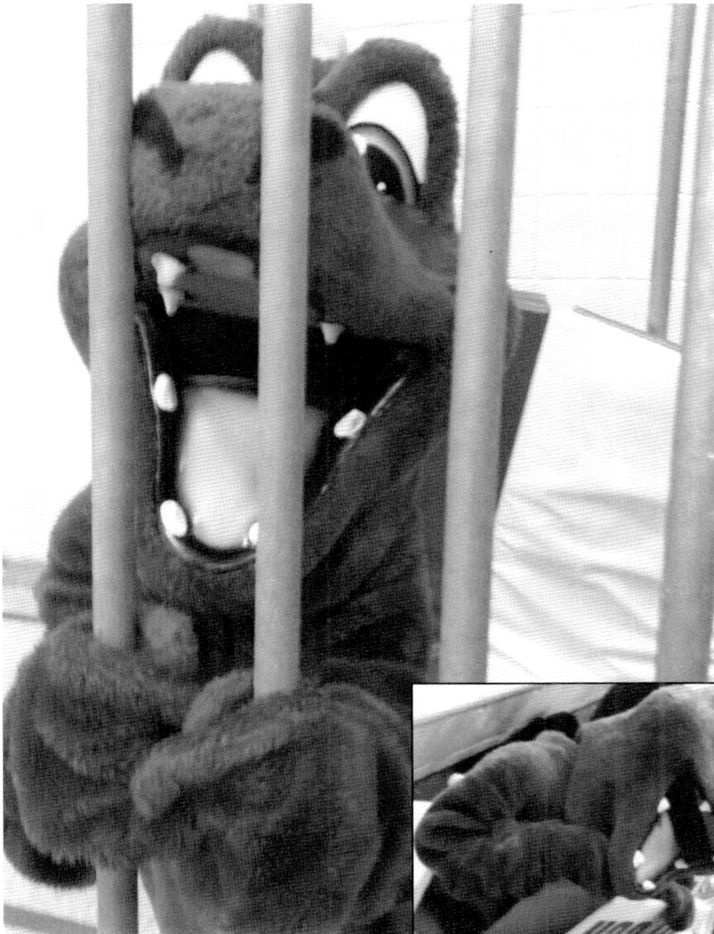

Pine City Dragon Mascot

In 1938, the Pine City Schools held a contest to come up with a mascot. Student Shirley Johnson submitted the idea of a dragon, and it was adopted. Prior to that, the term *Chengwatana* was used a lot, but it didn't really fit as a mascot. The school's former colors of kelly green and gray are now kelly green and white. (Both, courtesy of Pine City Public Schools.)

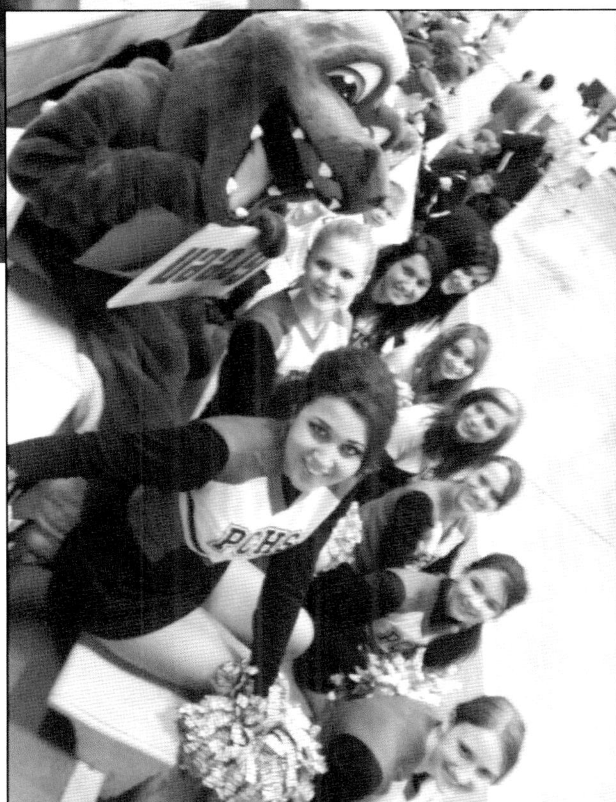

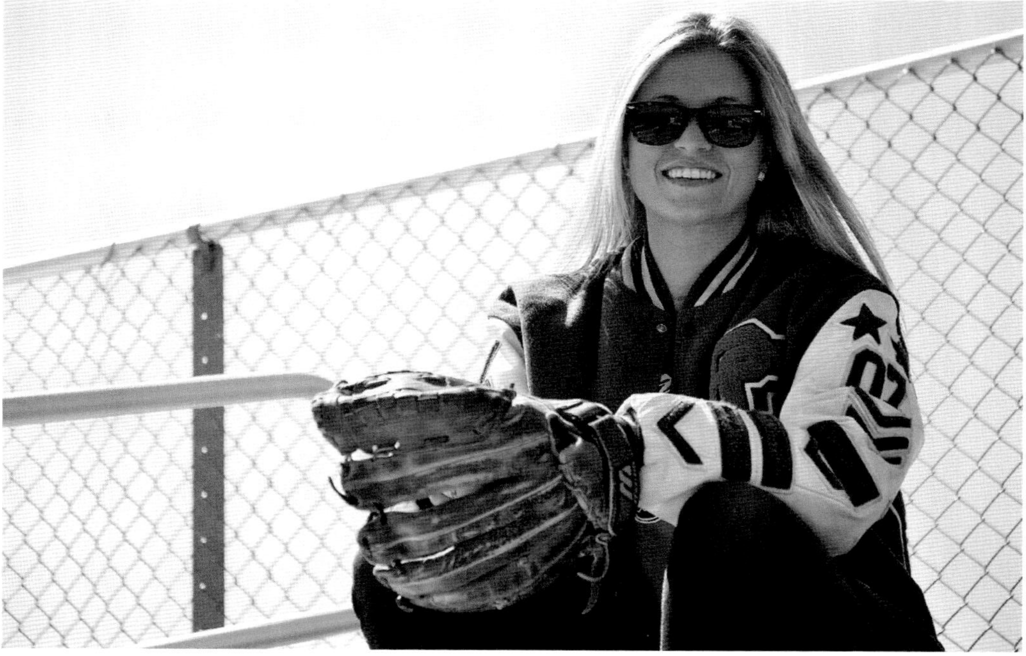

Rhiannon Sauter

Sauter was born in 1988 and graduated from Pine City High School in 2007. In her senior year, she broke the state's record with 1,084 career strikeouts. The previous record was set in 1995 by New Ulm Cathedral pitcher Stephanie Klaviter. Sauter had an ERA of .30 while pitching 186 innings and striking out 352 batters (fifth all-time). She faced 591 batters. Sauter lettered every year of high school in volleyball, hockey, and softball. In 2004, she scored the tying goal and the overtime winner to send the team to the state hockey tournament. In 2006 and 2007, she and the Dragons were state softball conference champions. The team went to state both years, placing fourth each trip. Sauter broke a state tournament record as well: most strikeouts in a regulation game, 20. She was named to the all-tournament team and to the all-state first team. Since 2008, she has served as a volunteer coach for Pine City varsity softball. (Above photograph by Noah Sikkink; right photograph by Noah Phelps.)

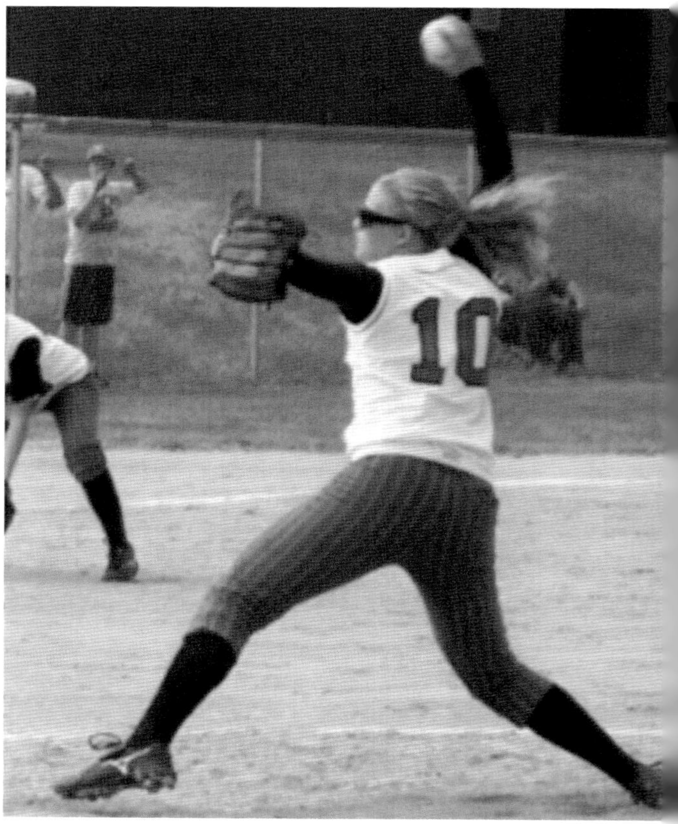

William Korbel

Bill Korbel was born on December 2, 1896, in Iowa, but he ended up living in Pine City after serving military merit first class in the military. In 1928, he married Amelia T. "Emily" Peters, the daughter of William "Bill" Peters and Catherine "Katy" Pangerl, in Pine City. The two had a daughter, Phyllis. His father-in-law became widowed and lived with the family for a time. Korbel was a part of the successful 1963 hockey squad, which had an 18-4 record, was named St. Croix Valley Champions, and went on to the state tournament, where they lost to Columbia Heights in the playoffs.

Korbel was a bookkeeper in a garage in Pine City, but he stayed involved in hockey. On March 2, 1973, the Pine City Youth Hockey Association presented Korbel with an award in appreciation for his many years of continuous efforts and devotion in promoting hockey in Pine City. The town's hockey venue, Korbel Arena, was named in his honor. In 1975, Bill Korbel was named Pine City's Citizen of the Year. He died on February 20, 1996, in Pine City. (Courtesy of the Pine City Civic Center Association.)

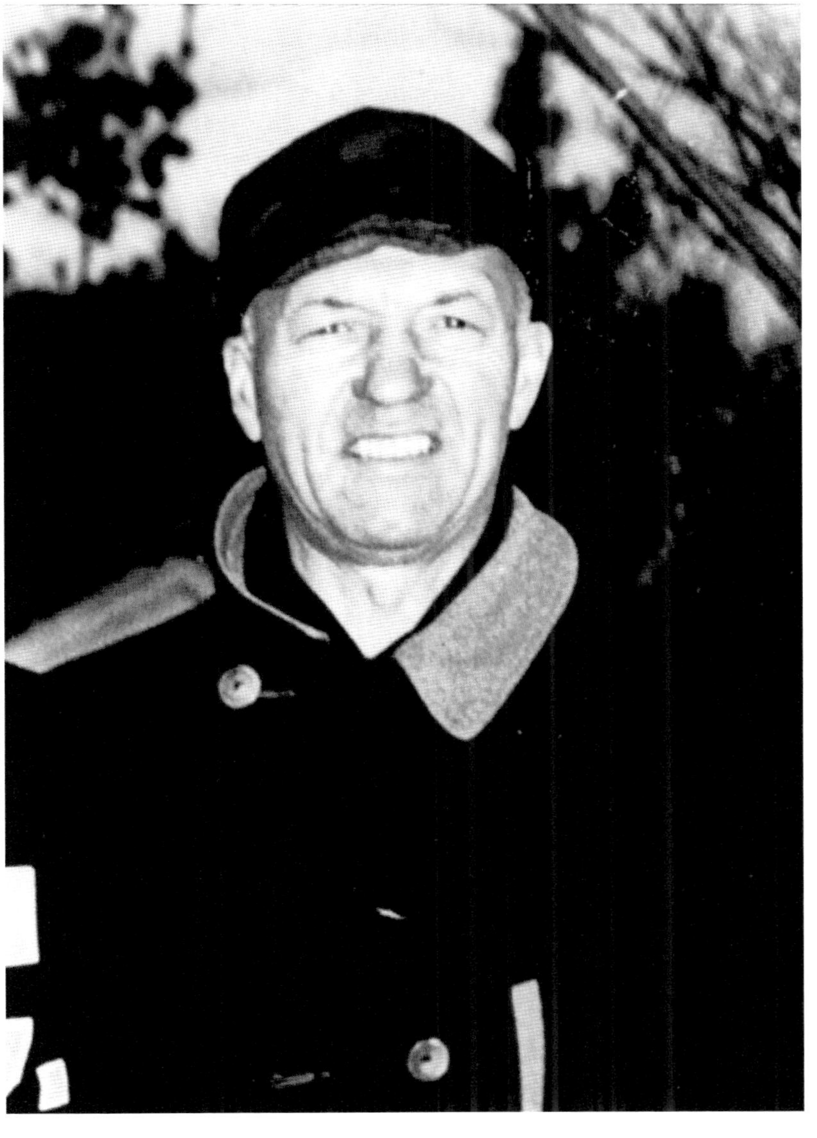

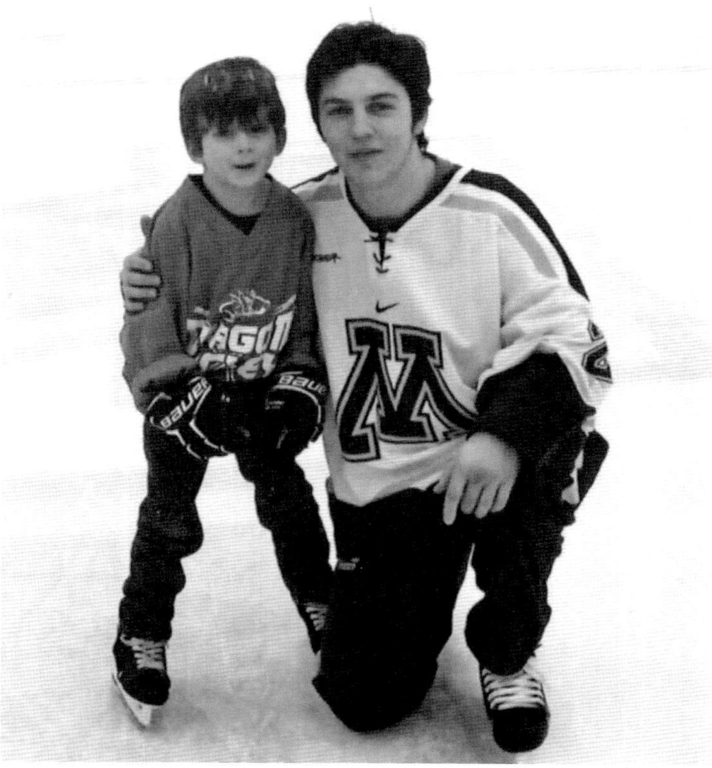

Christian Isackson

Christian Isackson was born on January 20, 1992, and as a kid he partook in Pine City Youth Hockey. He later became an NCAA player for the Minnesota Gophers, and, in 2010, he was a seventh-round draft pick (203rd overall) for the Buffalo Sabres.

Isackson played high school hockey as a junior for Minnesota's Saint Thomas Academy, scoring 18 goals with 39 assists in 27 games. He played for the United States at the Five Nations U-17 competition in Slovakia and had one assist in four games for the second-place squad.

Isackson was one of the finalists for Minnesota's Mr. Hockey award as a senior at Saint Thomas Academy, scoring 25 goals with 35 assists in 28 games. Prior to the season, he vied for Team Southeast in the Minnesota-based Upper Midwest Elite League.

For the 2010–2011season, he played for the Sioux Falls Stampede in the US Hockey League. In 58 regular season games, he scored 17 goals with 27 assists. That year, the Stampede reached the Clark Cup semifinals, thanks in part to Isackson's three goals and five assists in 10 playoff games.

Isackson appeared in 11 games as a freshman for the University of Minnesota in 2011–2012 as part of a talent-laden forward group. The Golden Gophers had 13 NHL draftees up front incorporating five seniors. The Gophers were one of the top teams in college hockey, winning the Western Collegiate Hockey Association title and earning their way to the NCAA's Frozen Four. Minnesota vindicated a misfortune to North Dakota in the WCHA elimination, crushing the Fighting Sioux in the NCAA West Regional.

A raw, offensive talent, Isackson spent his sophomore year skating for the Gophers and had a hat trick in a preseason exhibition. He skated with them again in 2013–2014 before turning professional. He has been seeing more ice time from year to year.

Isaacson shoots right, is a right winger, and is pleased and humbled when the announcer at Mariucci Arena howls, "From Pine City, Minnesota, Christian Isackson!" Pictured are Isackson and five-year-old Pine City mini-mite Merrick Johnson. (Author's Collection.)

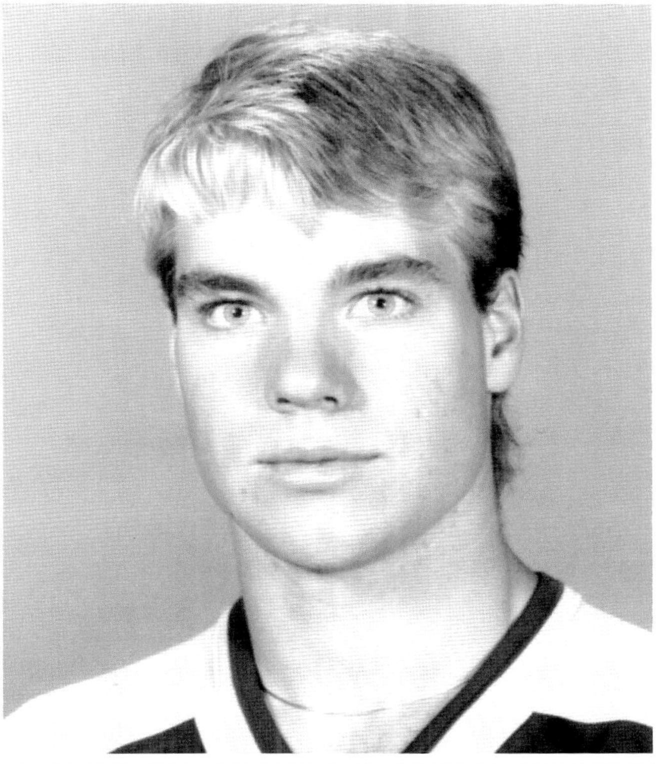

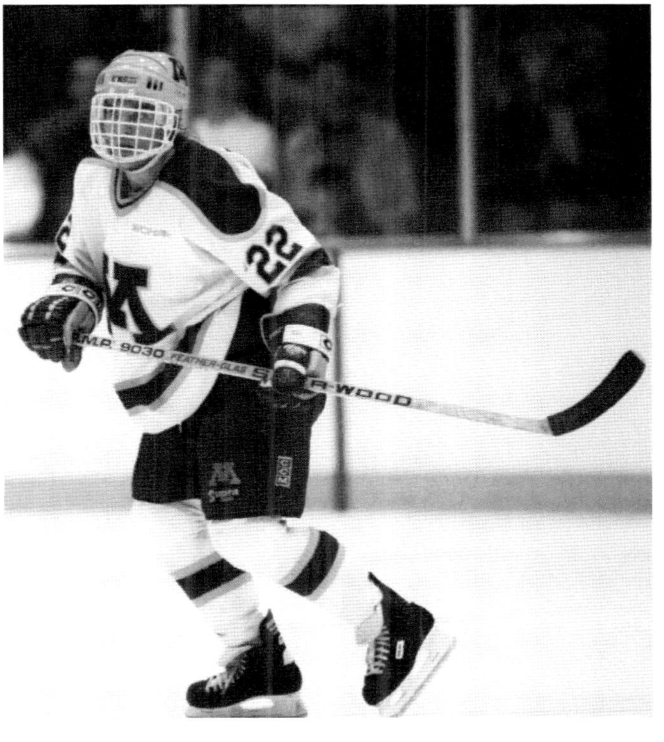

Grant Bischoff
Grant Bischoff was born on October 26, 1968, in Anoka, Minnesota. He graduated high school in 1987 in Grand Rapids, Minnesota, and was a hockey standout. Bischoff was most active in hockey from 1987 to 1993, playing the first four years for the University of Minnesota Golden Gophers and the last year for the St. Paul Fighting Saints. While with the Gophers, he improved each season. In his senior year, he scored 23 goals and had 24 assists. In his season with the Saints, he had 36 goals and 33 assists. A 5-foot, 10-inch forward, Grant was an 11th-round draft pick of the Minnesota North Stars in 1988.

Grant married Jacqueline "Jackie" Tok on July 11, 1992, in Coleraine. The two lived in Pine City for four years, and Jackie taught at Pine City schools. They had four children, two boys, Jacob and Jonah, and two girls, Tyara and Jazzlyn. Grant was a real estate appraiser. While raising the family, Jackie found some spare time to return to school and earn a master's degree in education from St. Catherine's University. For a short time, she taught in Hill City and Grand Rapids, Minnesota, and, later, she was a kindergarten teacher in Cohasset, Minnesota. She passed away on Friday, November 19, 2010. Grant's son Jacob has been following in his father's footsteps. A hockey standout at Grant Rapids High School, Jacob is expected to play for the Minnesota Gophers. (Courtesy of Grant Bischoff.)

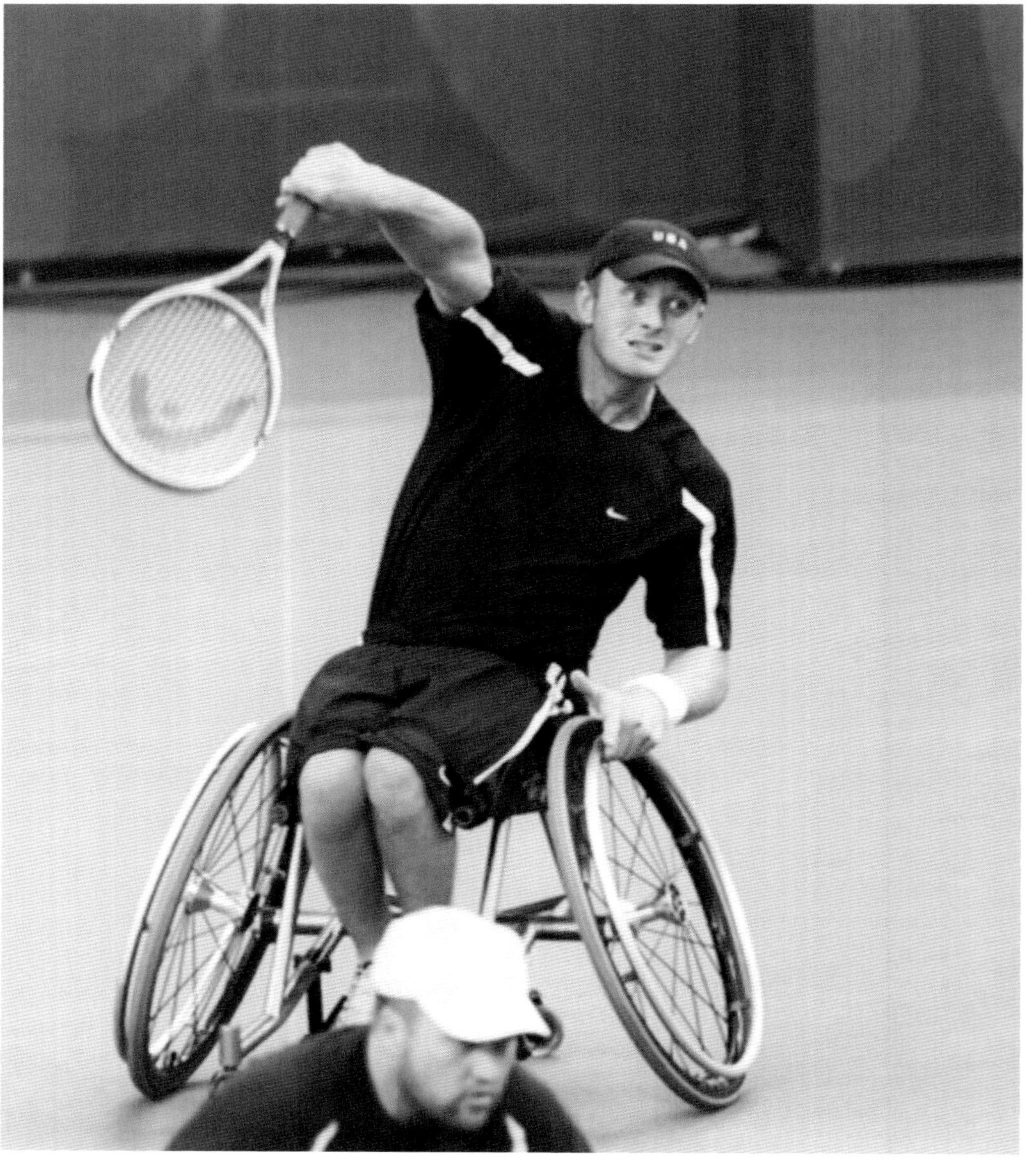

Jon Rydberg

Jon Rydberg grew up in Pine City and graduated from Pine City High School in 1996. He is a world-class wheelchair tennis player and Paralympian. He was a part of the 2004 United States Paralympic group that contended in Athens, Greece. In 2007, he became the top-ranked wheelchair tennis player in the United States.

At the 2008 Summer Paralympics, he contended in both singles and doubles. In singles, he lost in the third round to eventual gold medalist Shingo Kunieda, and in doubles he and partner Stephen Welch were bumped out in the second round.

An accomplished wheelchair basketball player as well, Rydberg helped the Rolling Timberwolves program that the Minnesota Timberwolves support. He additionally has his own clothing line, Midevil, Inc. (Courtesy of the United States Tennis Association.)

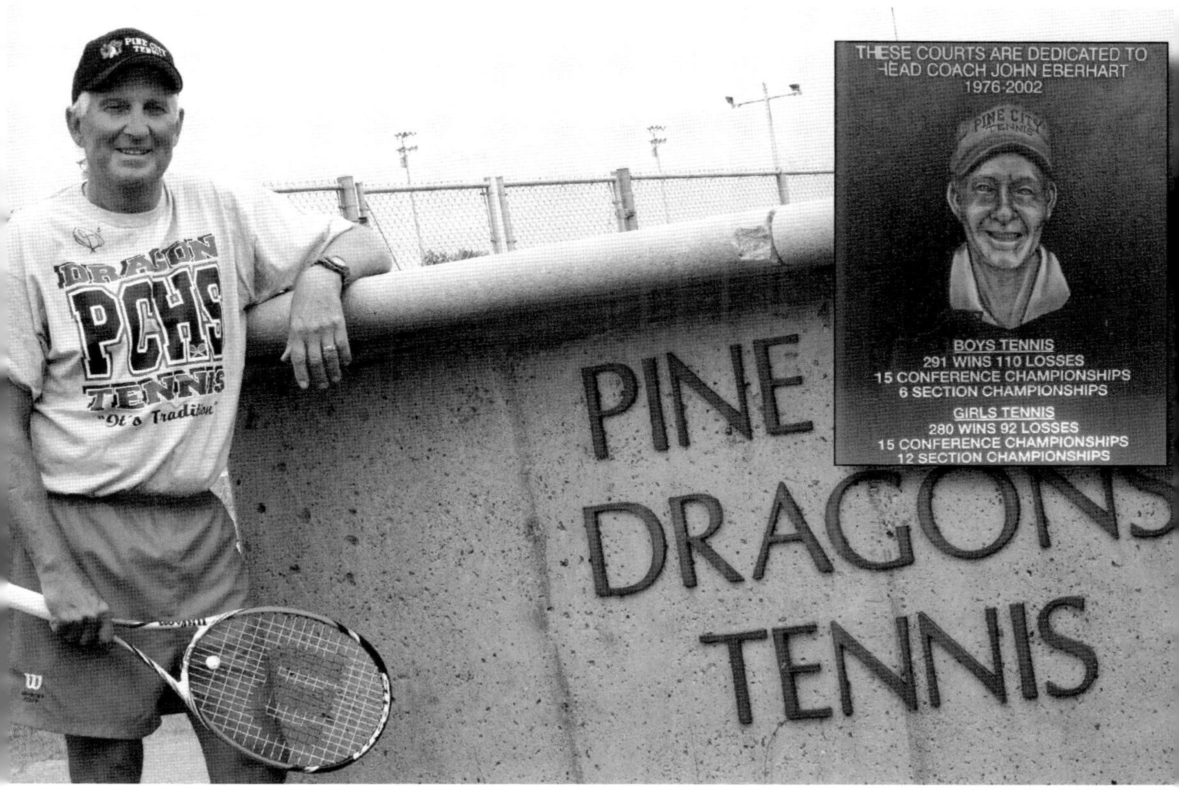

John Eberhart

Eberhart coached at Pine City High School for nearly 30 years, from 1975 to 2002. He initially coached girls' basketball (1975–1982), but he was best known for coaching tennis. He was at the helm of the boys' tennis program from 1976 to 2001 and girls' tennis from 1975 to 1982, all the while building a stellar program at Pine City.

Not many people have had a bronze replica made of themselves and courts dedicated to them while still alive. But, then again, not many have coached three ranked teams in one year, or had the success John Eberhart has had. In 1982, all three teams he coached were ranked in the state: in the spring, the Dragon boys' tennis team was ranked fifth; in the fall, girls' tennis was ranked second; and in the winter, girls' basketball was ranked fifth. State appearances were made by both the boys' and girls' tennis teams that year.

In 1992, Pine City had two doubles teams in the semifinals of the girls' state tournament: Kristen Kozisek and Jamie Fedder finished third, and Kristy Rieser and Carrie Eberhart finished fourth. In 1995, the girls' tennis team won four trophies, earned championships in the conference, section, and academically, and won fourth place in the state tournament. "We always had a total team attitude," said Coach Eberhart. "Our motto was, 'We win together, we lose together, we eat together.'" His Dragon tennis players wore T-shirts that read, "It's tradition," because year after year, they just kept winning. Eberhart's overall coaching record in boys' tennis was 291 wins to 110 losses. For the girls, his record was 280 wins to 92 losses. The boys had 15 conference championships and 6 section championships. The girls had 15 conference championships and 12 section championships. "Pine City kids were very tough," said Eberhart. "They were lots of fun to work with. I enjoyed each year. It was fun for so many kids to experience winning, and going on to state tournaments." Eberhart was named Minnesota High School Tennis Coach of the Year five times: in 1985, 1990, 1998, and 1999 for the boys, and in 1993 for girls' tennis. (Photograph by Noah Sikkink.)

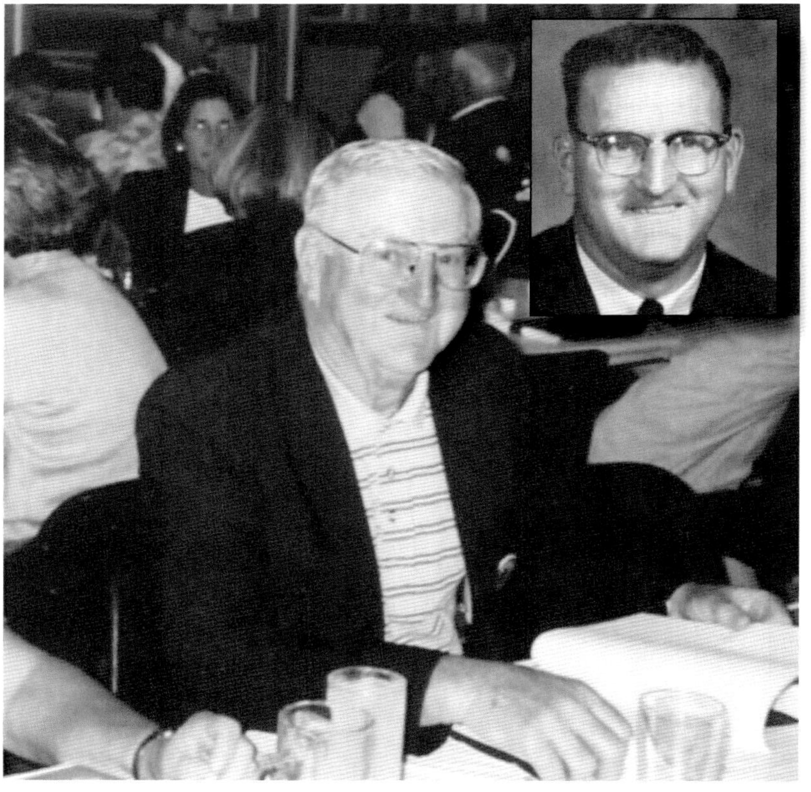

Roger Hagstrom

Hagstrom was born on October 29, 1929 and grew up in the Chisago Lakes area. He and his wife, Rita, were married on August 20, 1955, and they moved to Baudette, Minnesota, in 1957 after living in St. Cloud, where he was finishing college. Hagstrom began his teaching career in Baudette. Meanwhile, a Pine City geography and physical education teacher named Jerry Thayer was planning to leave, so Hagstrom vied for and received the position. He taught at Pine City for 34 years, retiring in 1991.

He loved every sport, especially football, basketball, and baseball. He has played, coached, or umpired for all of them, as well as other sports. As a baseball player, he made a state tournament appearance in 1962. The March 1, 1946, edition of the *Askov American* reported that Hagstrom was one of three basketball players from District 25 (which included Pine City) to make the all-star team, representing Lindstrom–Center City. The same year, Jerry Hoefler and Richard Connaker, both from Pine City, made the all-star aggregation. Hagstrom was often a leading scorer for the teams he played on.

He is most proud of coaching Tim Odegard to a state championship in boys' golf in 1980. He also had three girls' golf teams go on to the state tournament. He did not coach his own children, four boys and two girls, all of who graduated from Pine City High School. Over the years, Hagstrom has been instrumental in coaching and helping with a free summer recreational program for children begun by Hoefler. A Korean War veteran, Hagstrom was involved in the VFW and American Legion in Pine City. He was named Citizen of the Year in 2000 and was inducted into the Minnesota Coaches Association and the Dragon Athletic Hall of Fame. (Courtesy of Rita Hagstrom; inset courtesy of Wendy Johnson.)

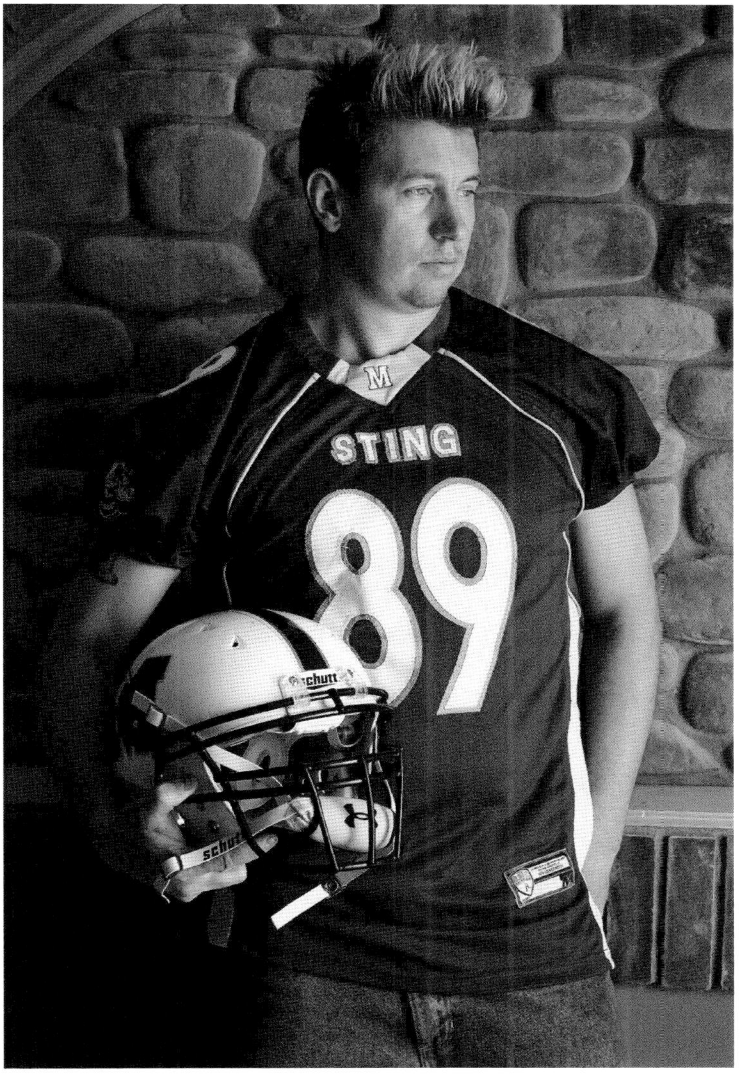

Josh Wilcoxen

Josh Wilcoxen was born on October 23, 1977. He played football in high school and attended the University of Minnesota–Crookston, playing for the Golden Eagles. After college, he wanted to stay involved in football, so he coached at Pequot Lakes High School, working alongside volunteer-coach Chip Lohmiller, formerly of the Washington Redskins. Wilcoxen then went back to school to study health and wellness. That is when he learned massage therapy.

In 2006, he bought land in the new Cross Lake Preserve neighborhood of Pine City and built a home. He liked to canoe and kayak, so Pine City's abundance of water offered a nice setting. "It almost feels like coming up to the cabin every time I go home," said Wilcoxen, who works full time in massage therapy in Roseville, Minnesota. Missing football, he coached flag football in North Branch. But, he also wanted to play, so Wilcoxen, who is six feet, two inches tall and weighs 210 pounds, tried out for the semiprofessional Minnesota Sting in 2011 and made the team as a tight end. The 2012–2013 Sting team was the winningest in the organization's history, going undefeated and being nationally ranked. (Photograph by Noah Sikkink.)

Ron Kubesh

Ronald J. Kubesh was a professional football player for the Baltimore Colts. In his senior year at Pine City High School, as a linebacker, he made 26 tackles in a 29-14 win over Duluth High School. He also played guard on the offense. In his four years at Pine City, the team never lost a football game. The Dragons were 27-0 in four years, and 36-0 over a five-year stretch.

At Pine City, he made the all-state football team as a linebacker and guard. From there, he went to the University of North Dakota, where he made Little All-American as a linebacker and guard. At the time, he could run the 100-yard dash in 10.3 seconds. From 1952 to 1954, Kubesh was involved in nearly half of all of the tackles made for the Fighting Sioux where he was named to the All Century Team. He graduated from UND in 1955. He was inducted into the University of North Dakota Hall of Fame in 1979, was a two-time All-North Central Conference selection, UND's MVP in 1954, and a four-time letter winner, missing only two minutes in his final three seasons. Drafted by the Baltimore Colts in 1954, Kubesh joined the team in preseason and played one and a half years. Because there was not as much money in the game at that time, Kubesh decided to stay in his professional field of mechanical engineering and joined Western Electric. He and his wife, Alice, had three sons, John and twins Pete and Tom. He moved to Virginia and lived there for over 40 years, but he still loved to do much of what he did in Pine City: hunt, fish, and listen to country music. He admired Bronco Nagurski, the NFL Hall of Fame fullback for the Minnesota Vikings, who he fished with from time to time. Kubesh passed away October 22, 2008. (Courtesy of UND Athletics.)

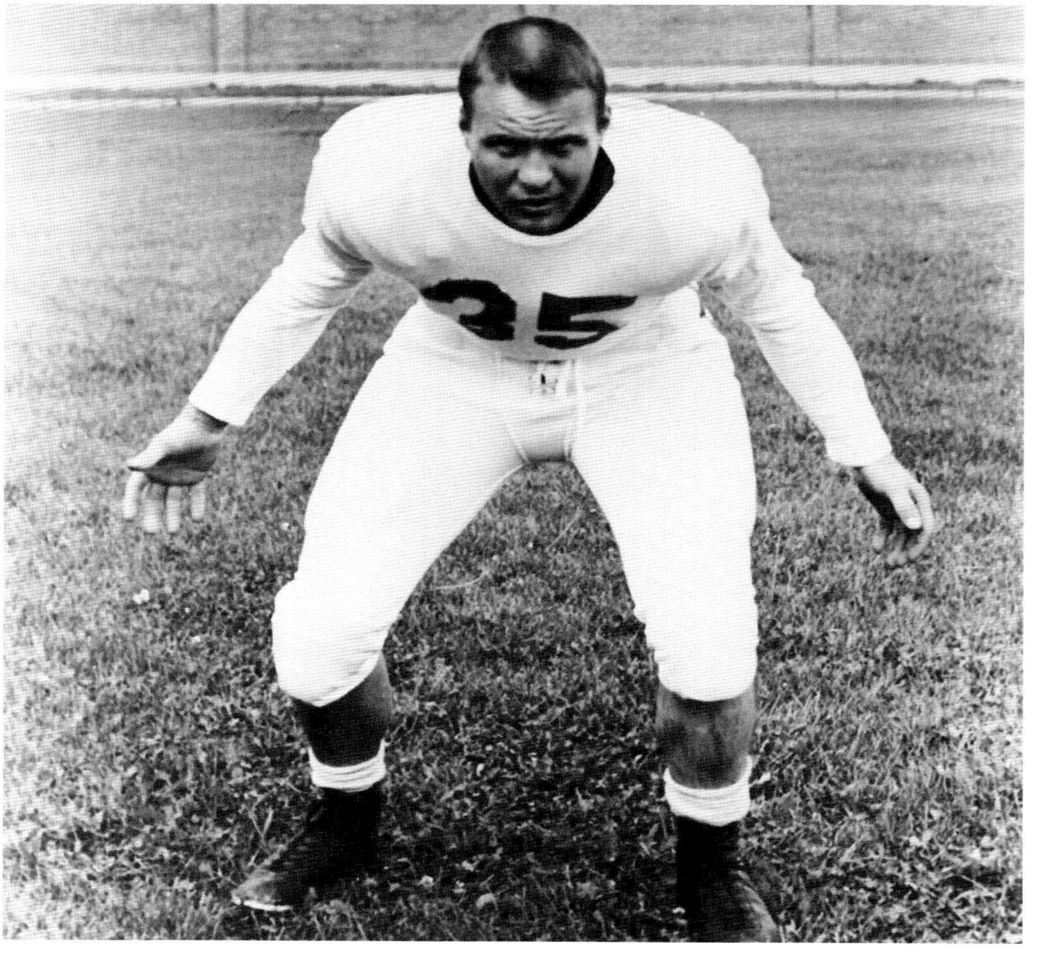

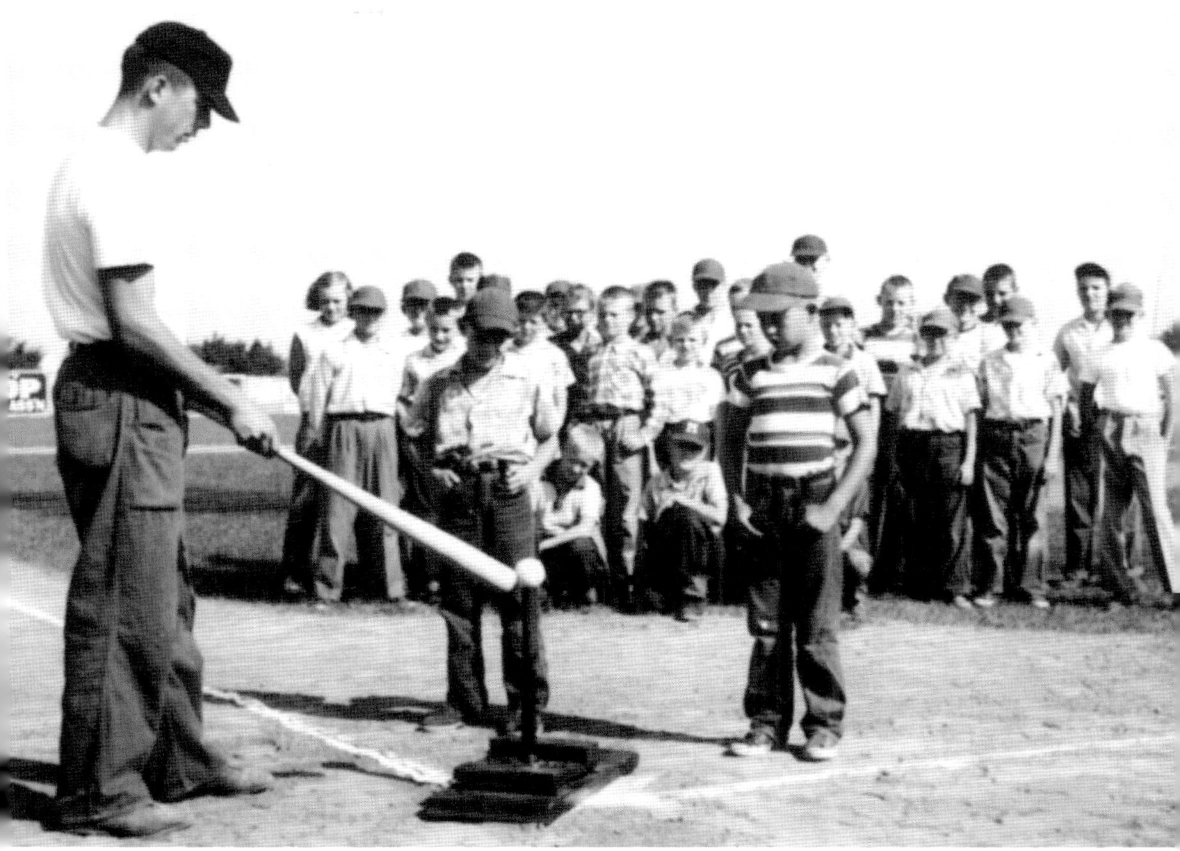

Dell Bethel

Bethel, a one-time Pine City resident, was a professional baseball player, decorated soldier, author, coach, and scout. He pitched for the New York Giants from 1950 to 1951, earning a 5-1 record to start their season. Then, Bethel was sent to Korea as a member of the US Army. He suffered a wound when a grenade entered the foxhole he was in. The injuries to his pitching hand meant he could no longer control his 96-mile-per-hour fastball.

Bethel, nicknamed "Big Bear," received two Bronze Service Stars and a Purple Heart as a result of his injuries. He continued to live a life of baseball after leaving the Army. He returned to the Giants, but his injuries affected his play, and he was sent to the minor leagues to play for the Minneapolis Millers. His next move was to become a teacher and coach in Pine City, where he lived for several years. Bethel had a 25-year coaching career, working with university, high school, Little League, and Pony League teams, taking many of them to state, regional, and district championships. Bethel held his first baseball clinic in 1955 at the old baseball diamond at the Pine County Fairgrounds. Here, he demonstrates for skeptical youngsters the use of a new baseball innovation, the "batting tee." Pictured at the tee are Rod Doft (left) and Rick Foster. Among those in the background are Stuart Clem, Wally Connaker, and Nancy Lewis. Bethel was also involved in the highly successful Pine City Pirates amateur baseball program. The Pirates had several state appearances in the 1950s and 1960s.

Bethel was a technical director for the movie *Bang the Drum Slowly*, coaching Robert De Niro and Michael Moriarty how to play ball. He even had a part in the film as the third-base coach. He was the author of *The Men of Old Baldy*, *Inside Baseball*, *Complete Book of Baseball and Instruction*, and *Coaching Winning Baseball*. More than 30 of his players have gone on to the major leagues, including Mel Stottlemyre and Vern Ruhle. Bethel died on June 26, 2008, at age 78 after a short illness. (Courtesy of *Pine City Pioneer* archives.)

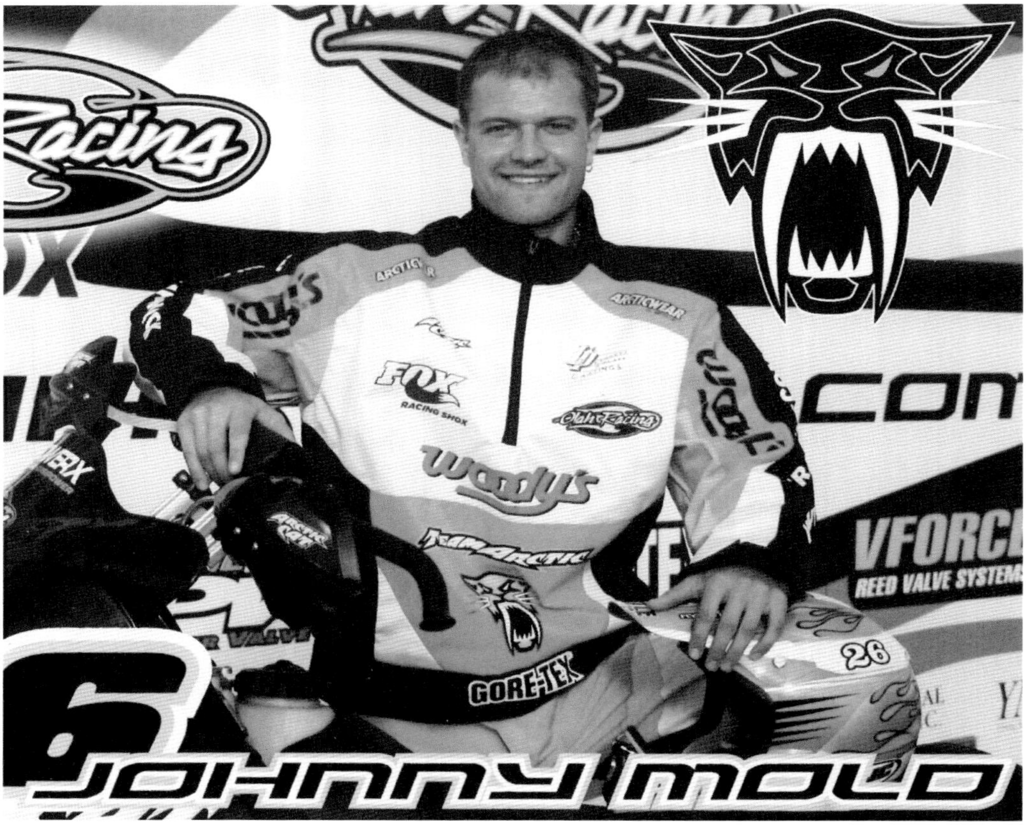

Johnny Mold

"Jammin'" Johnny Mold was a professional snowmobile racer. He grew up in Rush City, Minnesota, and lived in Pine City at the height of his snowcross career. He made eight of ten finals in the World Snowmobile Association (WSA) National Series in 2003 and 2004. According to the February 24, 2000, *East Central Post Review*, Mold always liked racing. He began racing dirt bikes and snowmobiles at a young age. Around 1997, when Mold was 16, what had been a hobby began to become a career.

Mold raced all over the country and in Canada, in two different circuits, the WSA and the American Snowmobile Racing Association (ASRA). He placed first in the Pro 440 and Pro 600 races at the Jackpot Junction Snocross in Morton in 2000. That same year, he took second in the open modified 800 and first in the Pro 600 categories at a snocross in Mora. He participated in one of the first races of its kind, an indoor snowcross event, at the Metrodome in Minneapolis, coming in first. Those top finishes helped Mold get ranked as one of the top three racers in his category. In 2001, at the WSA Regional in Thief River Falls, he took first place in the Pro 440. Mold was sponsored in his competitions by Ski Doo, which provided him with a race sled and practice sled and any parts he needed to maintain the sleds during racing season. While in Pine City, Mold became more heavily involved in the paving business and was hired as a foreperson for Prefer Paving & Ready Mix, Inc. (Courtesy of Johnny Mold.)

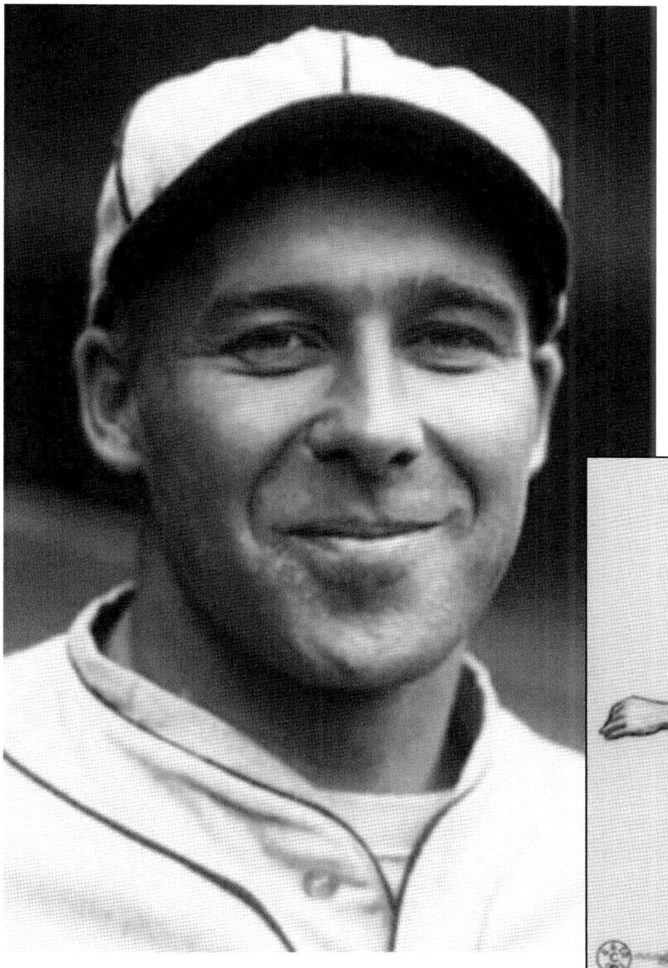

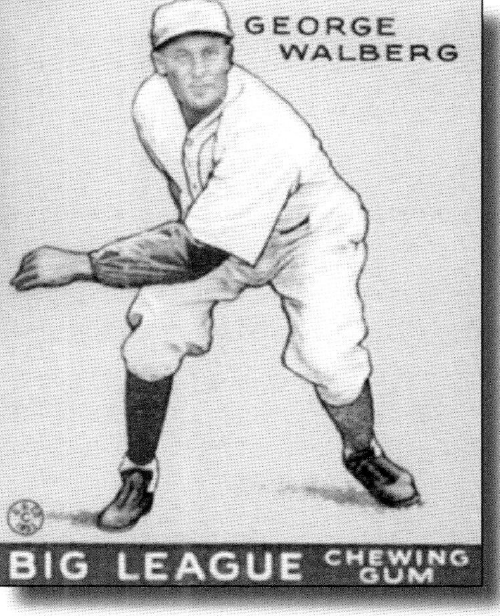

Rube Walberg

George Elvin "Rube" Walberg was a starting pitcher in Major League Baseball who played from 1923 through 1937 for the New York Giants (1923), Philadelphia Athletics (1923–1933) and Boston Red Sox (1934–1937). Walberg batted and threw left-handed. He was born in Pine City on July 27, 1896.

In a 15-season vocation, Walberg posted a 155–141 record with 1,085 strikeouts and a 4.16 ERA in 2,644 innings, including 15 shutouts and 140 complete games.

A reliable and strong pitcher, Walberg averaged 16 wins for the Philadelphia Athletics from 1926 to 1932, with career highs of 20 wins in 1931 and 18 in 1929. He likewise had a 1–1 imprint with a 1.93 ERA for the Athletics in five World Series appearances. A great hitting pitcher, Walberg gathered a .220 batting average with four grand slams and 84 runs batted in. When the Athletics were dismantled in 1933, he was sent, plus Lefty Grove and Max Bishop, to the Boston Red Sox in return for two players and $150,000. He was a spot starter and reliever with Boston throughout three seasons and pitched his last game at the age of 41. Walberg surrendered 17 homers to Babe Ruth, more than any other pitcher.

He died in Tempe, Arizona, at age 82 on October 27, 1978. In 2002, he was inducted into the Philadelphia Baseball Wall of Fame. (Author's collection.)

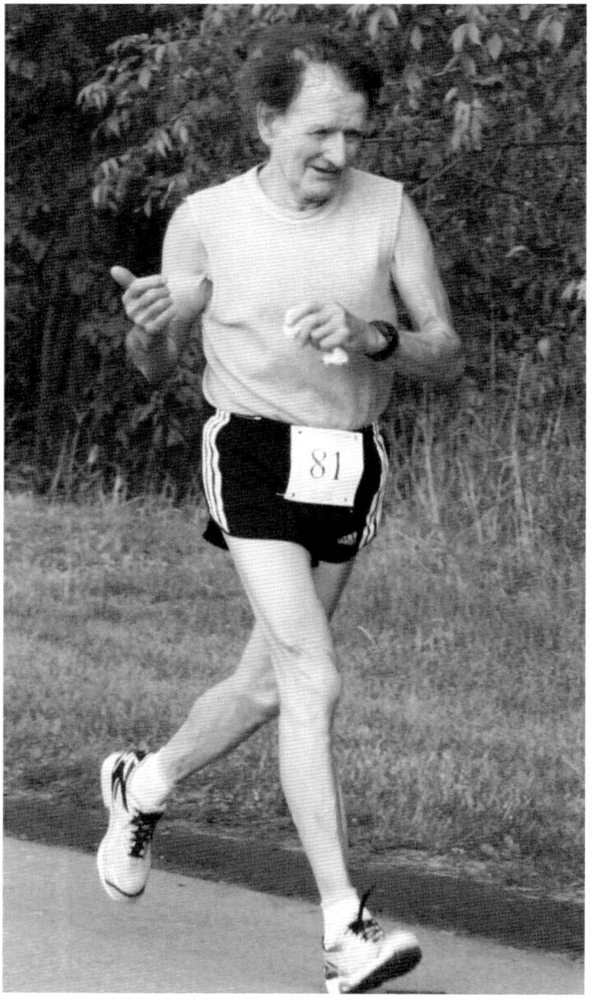

Lloyd Young

Minnesota long-distance running legend Lloyd Young died at the age of 87. Widely known to the Minnesota distance running community as Lloyd "Forever" Young, he made his mark on the running scene by setting countless age-group and single-age masters records during the twilight years of his full life. The elfin octogenarian was also known in the running community for his friendly demeanor and the joy he took from his sport. Aside from being a remarkable athlete, Young wrote poems and creative prose about his distance running.

Young was born on July 18, 1923. According to his *Pioneer Press* obituary, he spent his early life in St. Paul, often under the care of aunts. After service with the US Navy and Army, he married Daisy Rosendahl of Sandstone, Minnesota. Young's wholesale revision of the Minnesota Masters record books began in earnest in the early 1990s, when, in his early 70s, he kicked off a decade-and-a-half period as the dominant 70-plus distance runner in the state. His long list of state single-age records includes a 20:27 5k at age 70; a 35:27 8k at age 73; a 1:21:32 10-mile run at age 8; and, in one of his final races, a 5:00:35 marathon at age 85 at the 2008 Medtronic Twin Cities Marathon. Young was twice named US Masters Runner of the Year in his age group and was repeatedly the Minnesota Runner of the Year among his peers. A 2003 poem of Young's captures his youthful spirit: "The soul of a runner is not found on a shoe but deep within lives the other you where desire is akin and motivation is true." (Courtesy of Bob Higashi.)

CHAPTER SIX

Artists, Entertainers, Journalists, and Pageantry

Pine City has had its share of sisters in the Miss Pine City Princess Court: Carly Weinholzer (Little Miss Pine City 1995–1996, Miss Pine City 2006–2007) and Jenny Weinholzer (Princess 2002–2003); Lacey Pixley (Miss Pine City 2004–2005) and Laura Pixley (Princess 2004–2005); and Chelsey Koppen (Miss Pine City 1993–1994) and Niki Koppen (Miss Pine City 1991–1992). But, the most royal family to have made its way into the court was the Davidsons, with three pageant winners. Trudy Davidson was princess in 1993–1994; Cindy Davidson was Miss Pine City in 1989–1990; and Sherry Davidson Rootkie was Miss Pine City in 1985–1986. The annual contest has been a tradition since 1984, when Cheryl Fix was crowned the first Miss Pine City. Jim Dennison, executive director of the Pine City Chamber of Commerce, wanted to encourage more youth involvement, so he organized the first such coronation. In 1992, the first Little Miss Pine City was crowned, Stephanie Skalicky. The primary role of Miss and Little Miss Pine City has always been about self-improvement, volunteerism, and being an ambassador for the community and to make appearances in various parades throughout Minnesota.

This chapter not only covers pageantry and the Pine City Princess Court but also artists and entertainers who have ties to the community.

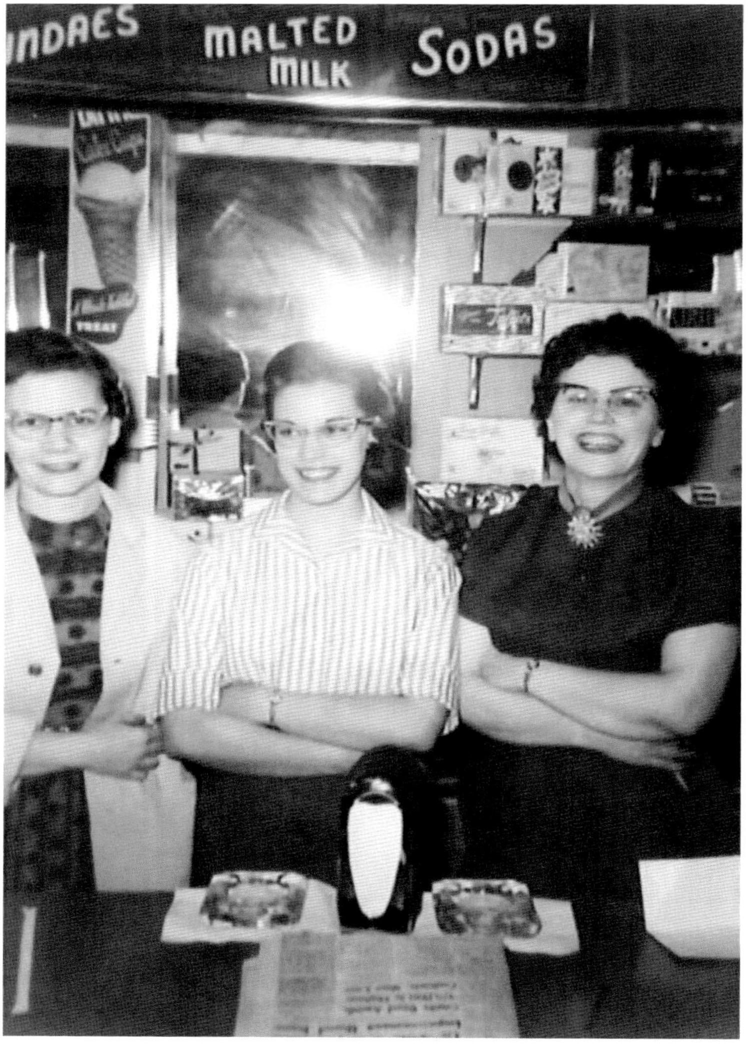

Geneva Olson

Geneva Olson worked as a soda jerk at the town drugstore from 1957 to 1972. It was her first job out of high school at Willow River, in Northern Pine County. When her sister moved to the county seat, Pine City, to work at the courthouse, Geneva stayed with her and found the job at Pine City Drug. The store was owned by Hoyt Haycock, who purchased it in the early 1950s. Olson was known for being innovative and friendly, and she mixed up flavored soda water or ice cream sodas to perfection.

"Hoyt Haycock was a very wonderful boss and I enjoyed working for him," said Olson, who started out working for 75¢ an hour and, by the time she left, $2.10 an hour. After school, kids from town would come in and have their nickel bags of potato chips and their nickel or dime Cokes, with their favorite flavors, cherry, lemon, lime, and more. "Sometimes some of them wanted a 'Rainbow Coke', or 'Graveyard,'" recalled Olson, who masterfully crafted a plethora of drinks. "That's where you would mix four or five flavors together. One of [the customers] would be Mike Sauser and his brother and two sisters." She met her husband in 1959, and they were married in 1960. She worked on the family farm after she finished at the drugstore. Shown here are, from left to right, Elaine Kubat, Geneva Olson, and Millie Hyland, the town's main soda jerks. (Courtesy of Geneva Olson.)

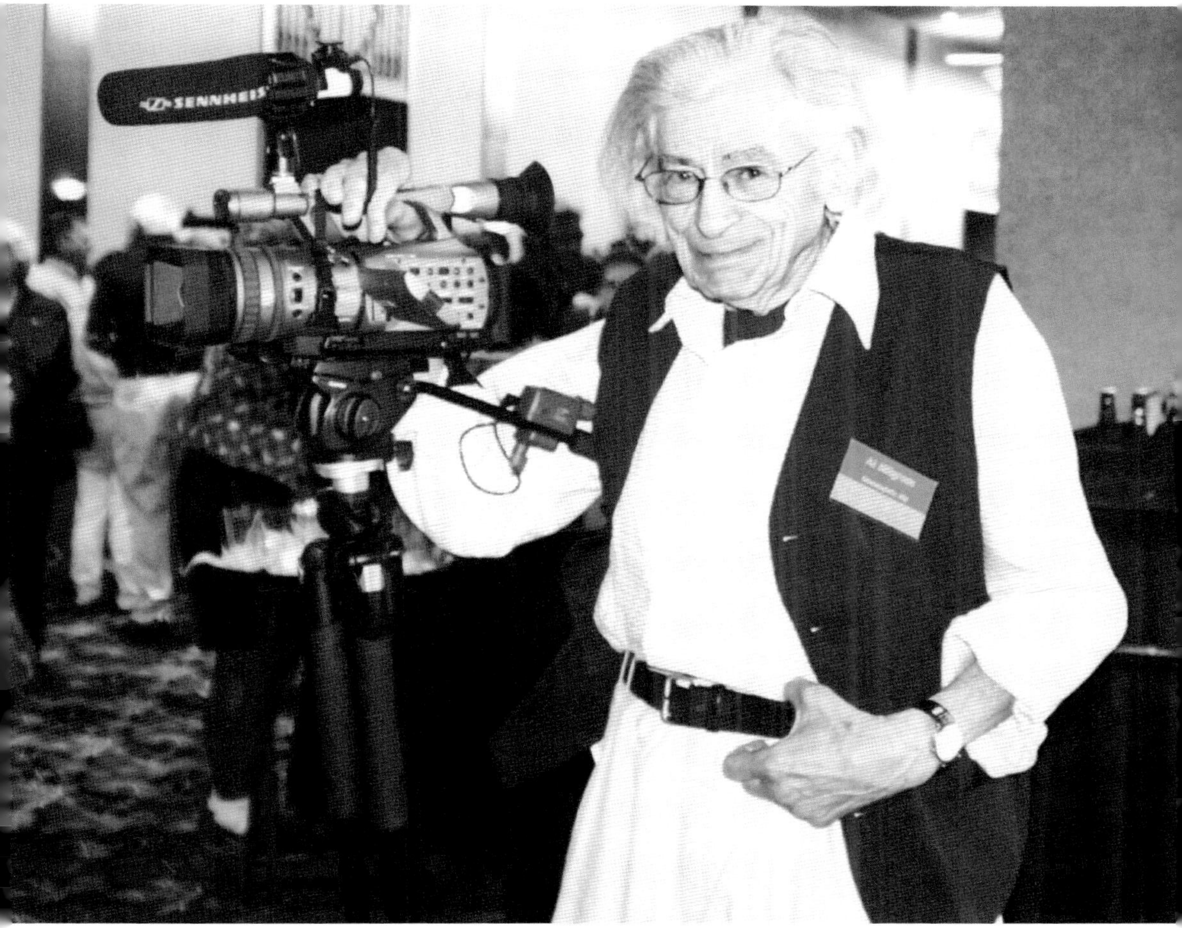

Al Milgrom

Al Milgrom is a respected name in the international film community. He was founder of Rivertown Film Festival in Stillwater, Minnesota, in 1983. It later moved to Minneapolis and was renamed the Minneapolis–St. Paul International Film Festival.

Milgrom, born in Pine City in 1921, was involved in sports and band in high school. After graduating from Pine City High School in 1940, Milgrom joined an Air Force photographic unit and served in Japan from 1943 to 1946. He then returned to the University of Minnesota to finish a degree in journalism. He worked as a newspaper reporter and editor from 1947 to 1960 for the *Stars and Stripes* in Europe, and he worked for stretches at the *Pioneer Press*, the *Washington Post*, and the *Star Tribune*. In the mid-1960s, he began teaching at the University of Minnesota, and he founded the University Film Society in 1962.

According to an October 11, 2012, article in the *Pine City Pioneer*, Milgrom said his love of film started at age three in Pine City, where he would see Charlie Chaplin films with his father. He viewed the downtown Family Theater as an important social center of the community. In 2007, Milgrom received the Ordway's Sally Award for his service to the arts community. In a 2007 interview with *City Pages*, Milgrom said of his continuing efforts to bring great, diverse films to Minnesota: "If the question is, 'Why do it?' then the answer is . . . Mount Everest. Why climb that? Because it's there." On April 14, 2012, the Minneapolis–St. Paul International Film Festival declared Al Milgrom Day. The honoree was presented with a Lifetime Achievement Award. He returned to Pine City in October 2012 for the second annual Highway 61 Film Festival to share some of his favorite films. (Courtesy of the *Pine City Pioneer* archives.)

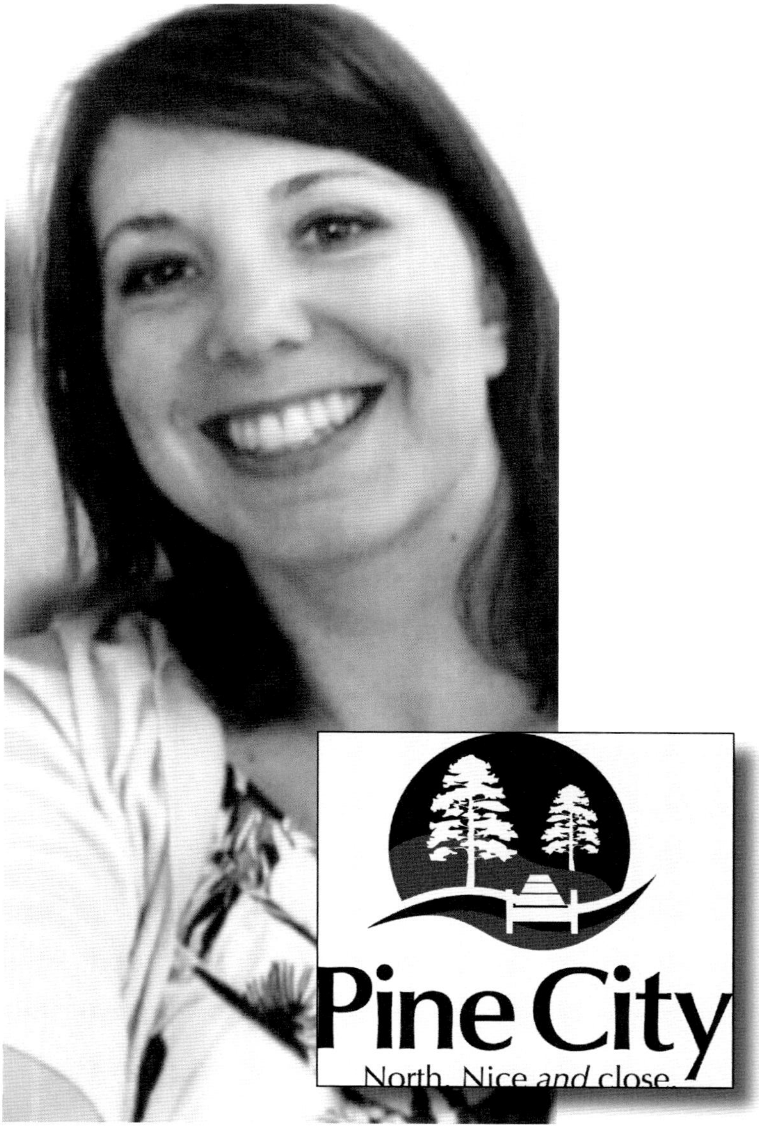

Julie Stumne Nelson

In 2009, residents formed a branding committee and made a pitch for the city to adopt an official logo. It included former 3M marketers Lynn Denn and Shirley Schmidt, graphic designer Jake Abbott, Pine Technical College director of marketing Dani Chandonnet, chamber of commerce executive director Becky Schueller, and city staff. The group was fortunate to have another graphic designer, Julie Stumne Nelson, come up with the final design for the logo, featuring two native pines, the Snake River, and a dock, with the tagline, "North. Nice *and* close."

Nelson was born on April 9, 1979. She works as a designer at Ackmann & Dickenson, Inc. in the Twin Cities. Previously, she had worked for other agencies, including The Nerdery and Creative Arc. She graduated from Pine City High School in 1997 and attended Hamline University (1997–2001) and Minneapolis Community and Technical College (2006–2008). (Courtesy of Julie Nelson; logo courtesy of the City of Pine City.)

Jayme Osterdyk Meyer

Jayme Meyer was raised in a household in which her dad was a sheet rocker and her mom was a wallpaperer; so interior design was the norm. According to *Spaces* magazine (November 23, 2010), Meyer "grew up changing her room's walls just about as often as she changed clothes." Her artistic nature and love for design was set free at the Flower Box, where she worked from 2000 to 2002. She worked for the family business, Osterdyk Painting and Drywall, from 1997 to 2000. It only made sense that she would hone those skills and go on to be named senior interior designer at Martha O'Hara Designers in Minneapolis and be recognized and honored with design awards in 2010 and 2012 by the American Society of Interior Designers. She earned those awards in multiple categories, including bedroom, bathroom, kitchen, and multiple function rooms. She has come to be known as an expert in the Twin Cities area for the latest colors, trends, and room fashions.

Meyer is inspired by architecture, fashion, and technology, according to her company's website. "By transposing her inspirations into her design, all facets of Jayme's interiors are thoughtfully constructed," it says. Those designs have allowed her to work for many NHL and NFL players, including Steve Hutchinson, Chad Greenway, and Brett Favre (Minnesota Vikings); Lawrence Tynes (New York Giants); Scot Fujita (Cleveland Browns); and Matt Carle (Tampa Bay Lightning). (Courtesy of Martha O'Hara Designers.)

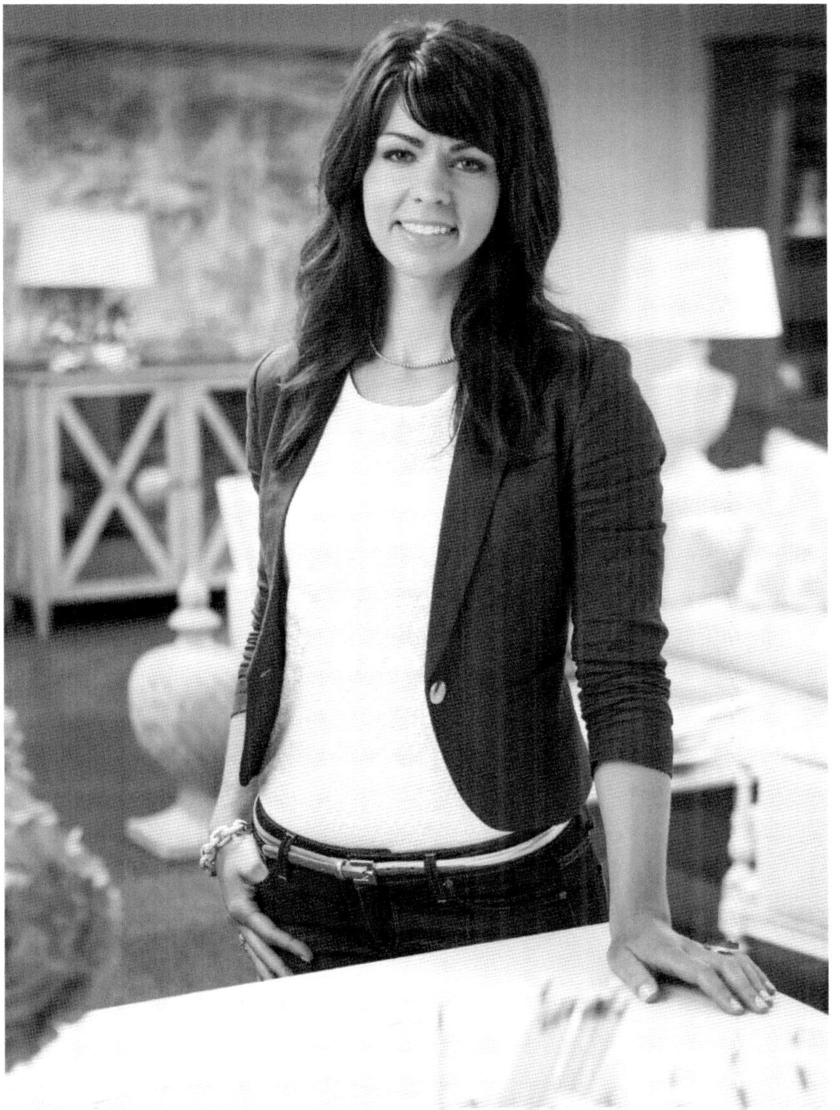

THE PINE CITY
Pioneer

PINE CITY, MINNESOTA 55063-1504 • 629-6771 • FAX 629-6772 THURSDAY, DECEMBER 29, 2005 • 75¢

En Vogue

Pine City woman enters the modeling world in a big way

by C.J. Gustafson
Freelance writer

Look closely at the Christian Dior ad in this month's issue of Vogue magazine and you're likely to see a familiar face.

Looking beautiful and stylish in a black velvet jacket and platinum blonde hair extensions is 20-year-old Michelle Hecht, who graduated from Pine City High School in 2004.

The Vogue ad marks the culmination of four long years of training, competitions and auditions for the daughter of Tom and Penny Hecht.

While still in high school, Hecht was paging through Seventeen magazine when she came across an ad for Barbizon Modeling and Acting Centers. The ad included a cutout card to send in for more information. The aspiring model sent the card off, not knowing what to expect.

She eventually received a letter inviting her to attend auditions being held to screen for new Barbizon students at the school in Minneapolis. Hecht decided to give it a shot and was one of 17 girls

At that point, her true commitment to modeling, and the support of her parents, was tested. She learned she would have to pay several thousand dollars to attend classes and drive to the Cities every other weekend. Although Hecht's parents both live in Pine City, they are no longer together.

Because of employment circumstances, her father, Tom, was in the best position to devote time and money to her modeling career, but Hecht says her entire family, including her two older brothers, Rich and Chris, have been amazingly supportive.

This commitment was pushed even further when, after three months, the Barbizon classes moved to Des Moines to incorporate the large group of students in that city.

"Because I was under 21, I needed a parent to accompany me," Hecht explained. "Every other weekend, my dad drove me to Des Moines."

At the school, Hecht studied all aspects of modeling, from makeup application to model stance, presentation to

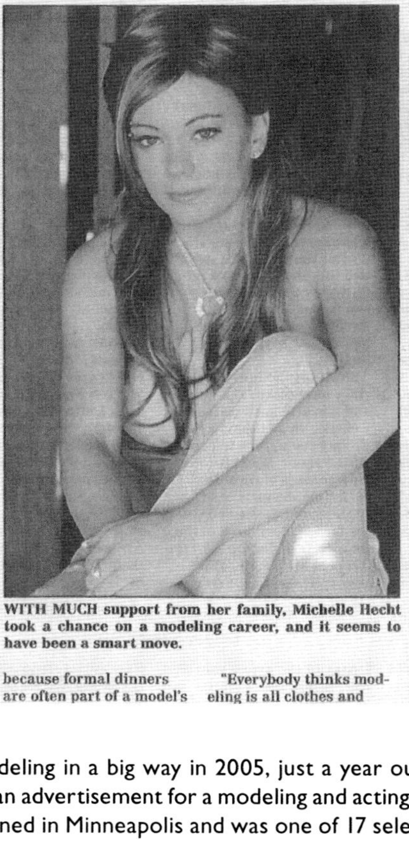

WITH MUCH support from her family, Michelle Hecht took a chance on a modeling career, and it seems to have been a smart move.

because formal dinners are often part of a model's

"Everybody thinks modeling is all clothes and

more to it," she said.

As part of the preparation to enter the world of modeling, the school also had a well-known fashion photographer take headshots of Hecht and the other students. They also helped her put together a portfolio and prepare her resume.

When Hecht completed her schooling, she sent her headshots and resume to about 100 agencies from a list supplied by Barbizon. About five months ago, she was contacted by SA Model Management, who invited her to audition to represent the agency at a one-week, International Modeling and Talent Association (IMTA) event in New York City.

Hecht auditioned and was selected to participate. Although the modeling agency paid for many of the expenses, she and her father had to pay for their own airfare, and she also needed a formal evening gown for a dinner part of the event.

Hecht described the IMTA event as the opportunity of a lifetime.There were over 300 modeling agencies there, looking for new talent. Each day

Michelle Hecht

Michelle Hecht entered the world of modeling in a big way in 2005, just a year out of Pine City High School. It all began when she came across an advertisement for a modeling and acting agency while paging through a *Seventeen* magazine. She auditioned in Minneapolis and was one of 17 selected from 500 girls. She then entered training, studying all aspects of modeling, from makeup to stance, presentation and runway to etiquette. SA Model Management selected Hecht to represent the agency while she was in New York City at an International Modeling and Talent Association event.

At the pinnacle of her modeling career, she was featured in *Vogue* magazine in a two-page Christian Dior advertisement, holding a handbag, wearing a velvet jacket, and with platinum blonde hair extensions. (Author's collection.)

70

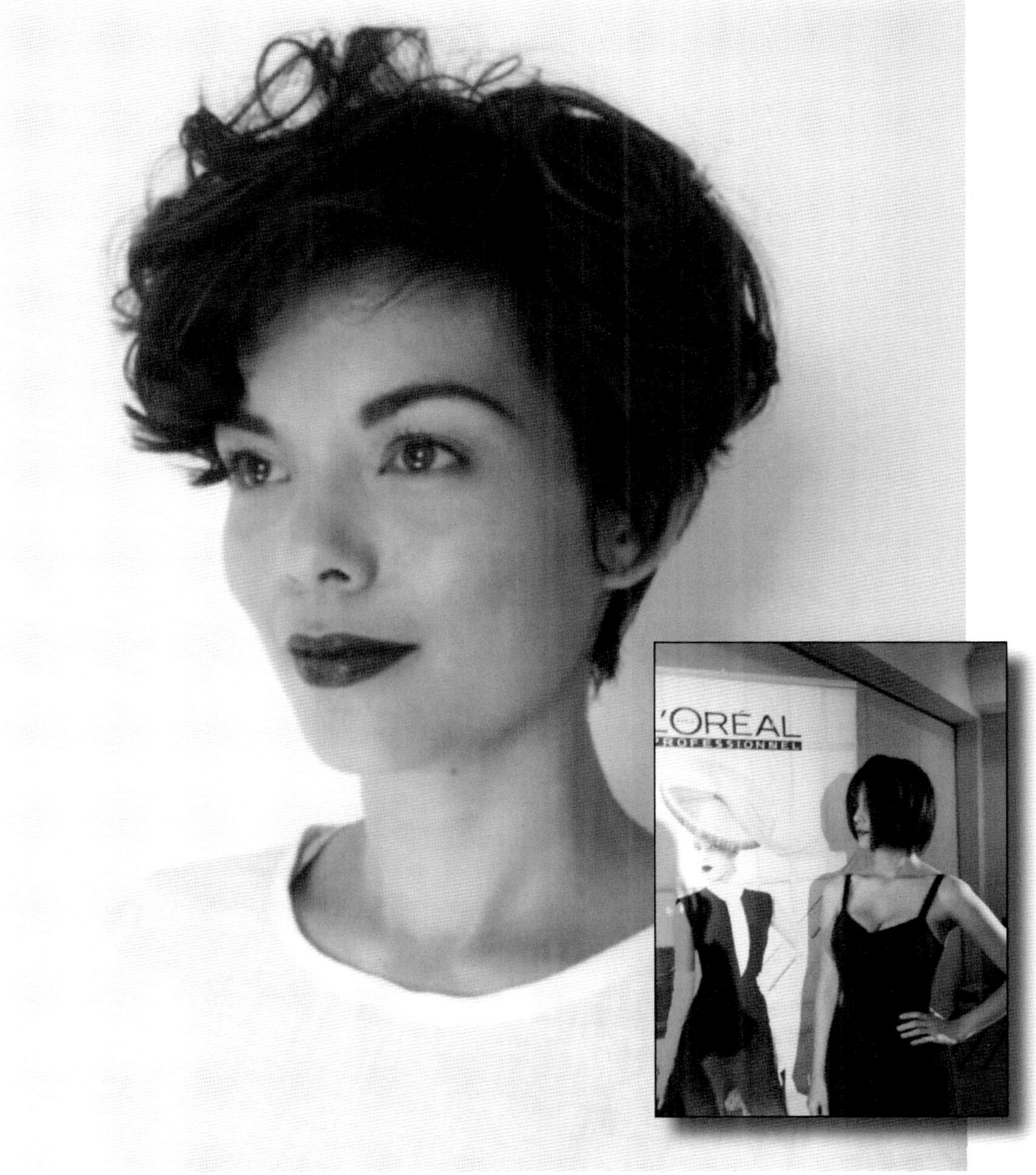

Junko Molitor

Stephanie Junko Molitor, a model, and her husband, Mark, moved north of Pine City to start a hydroponic farm called Junko's Garden in 2008. The couple grows lettuce, herbs, and greens from organic, non-genetically-modified seed. Together, they have one daughter, Tazuko Meridian, named after her Japanese grandmother.

Junko's modeling has included work with L'Oréal and the Mall of America (MOA). She was featured on many MOA billboards along interstates, including one during the 2009–2011 recession that read, "The ECONOMY LOOKS better in a NEW OUTFIT." (Both, courtesy of Junko Molitor.)

Jeremy Voigt

Jeremy Voigt was born in Texas to his mother, Sharon Voigt Sachs. When he was little, they moved to the Twin Cities, where he began modeling and acting as a preteen. That led to national commercials for HGTV, the US Postal Service, Bacardi Limited, and the Black Eyed Peas. He has also acted and helped cast music videos from several big names, like Lil Jon, E-40, Lil Wayne, Fabolous, Big Sean, Pusha T, and The Game.

When he was in seventh grade, Voigt and his mom moved to Pine City, where she married Terry Sachs, and Jeremy became one of five siblings. "Growing up in Pine was a lovely experience in my life," says Voigt. "When I hear people out here say you got that Minnesota nice personality, I can't help but think of my upbringing." After high school, he moved back to the Twin Cities and went to Dunwoody College of Technology. After a few side jobs, his mother encouraged him to go back into acting. He contacted his childhood agency, Caryn International Model and Talent Agency, which was excited to get him started doing photo shoots and runway shows and even a few commercials around Minnesota. In 2008, Caryn entered Voigt in a convention called IMTA (International Model and Talent Association), held twice a year, in Los Angeles and New York. He was given the opportunity to audition for over 500 agents and managers from all over the world. Following the five-day convention, he was given offers to sign and move to Los Angeles, New York, and even Milan, Italy. In March 2009, he made his choice for the sunny West Coast.

Voigt has begun producing and acting in his own Web series, which features everything from guitar covers to a sketch show called *Two and a Half Black Men*. He also has written two television shows and a feature film that he is trying to sell to studios. He lives by the following mantras: "Make moves" and "Don't count your days, make your days count." (Courtesy of Jeremy Voigt).

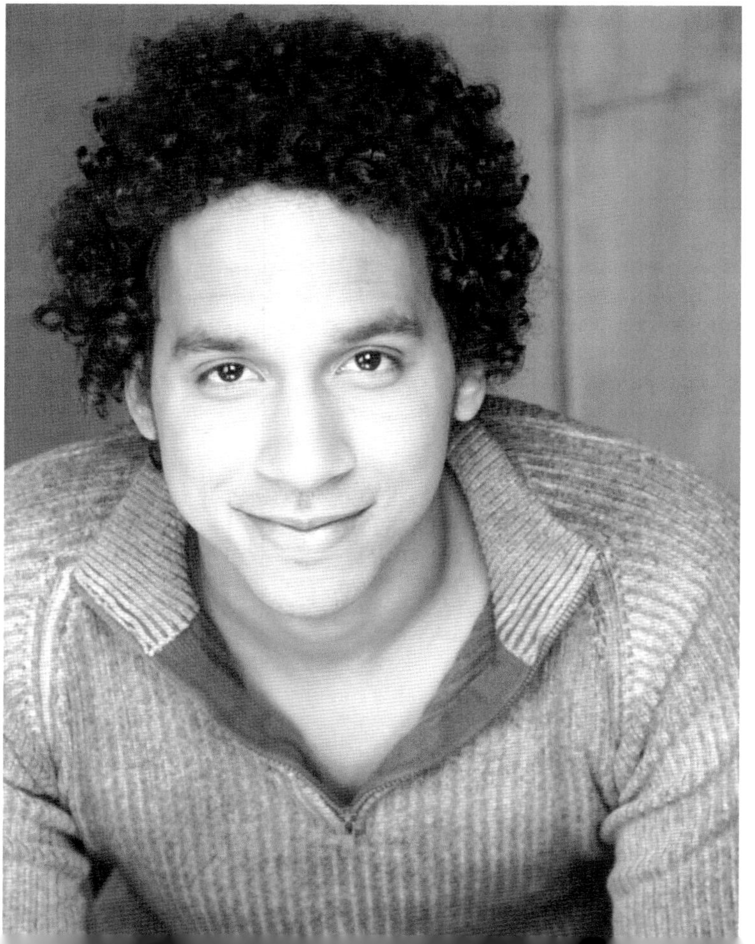

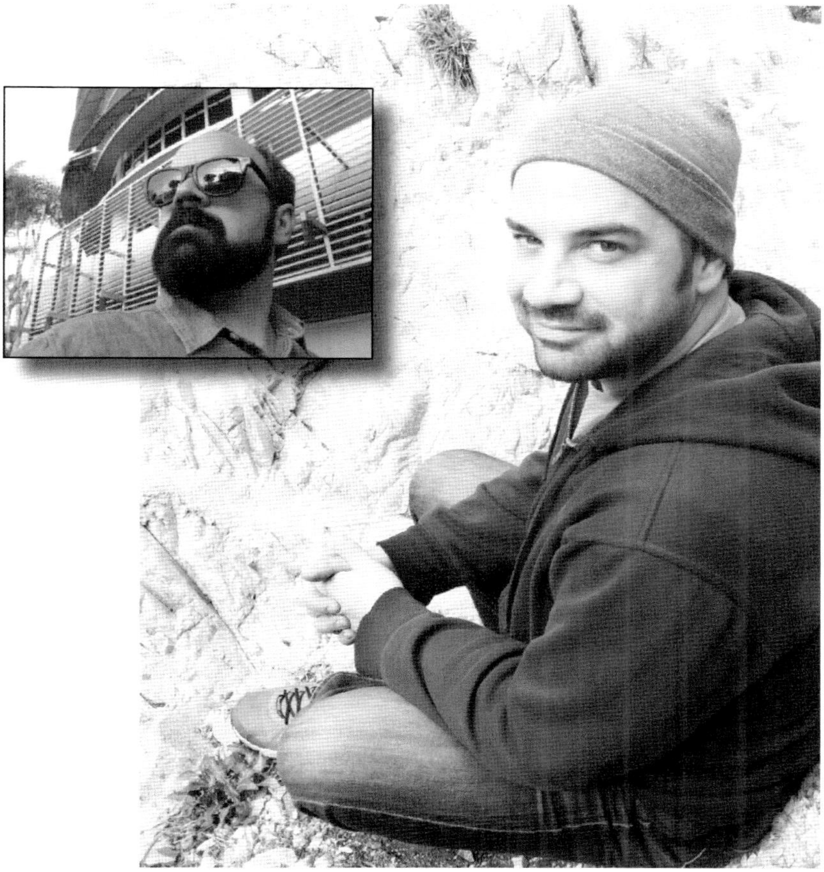

Zach Hammill

Pine City native Zach Hammill is now a Los Angeles–based director and screenwriter. Born in Rush City, Minnesota, Hammill's family moved to a small Pine City farmhouse near Chengwatana State Forest when he was five. Homeschooled at first, he started public school in second grade in Brenda Schuler's class. She was an exponent of the arts, and Hammill was into cartooning. He began to perfect his acting skills in the fourth-grade class of Elizabeth Olson. In fifth grade, he wrote, directed, and starred in his own play about monsters. The first play he acted in was *Tom Sawyer*, directed by Tom Larson, later his speech coach. At first, Hammill had no idea what a movie script looked like, so he wrote movies in play-form. Throughout high school, he wrote about one script a year. An avid movie watcher, Hammill found the perfect job at the Video Vault in Pine City. He was also cast in the Heritage Players' production of *Brigadoon*.

After high school, he flew to New York to attend acting school, at the American Musical and Dramatic Academy. He eventually moved back to Pine City, then to Minneapolis and, later, to Los Angeles, all the while pursuing his dream. He won a major fellowship on a film called *Balance*. Aside from the financial gain, it was the first formal validation that he should continue on this path, so he wrote a feature-length script. Hammill was an art department assistant on an exercise video and reality show; he worked on a Culver's commercial; and he was involved in Fox television's *Terra Nova* (2011), a one-season show that Stephen Spielberg coproduced.

He made his homecoming to Pine City in 2010 when a school auditorium in town was transformed into a movie house for an evening of showings of his various films, including the comedy *Five Bucks 'Til Friday* and *Mickey vs. the Snowman*, a film about a 1940s bare-knuckles boxing match. The film was produced by Marty Doogin Arts. (Both, courtesy of Zach Hammill.)

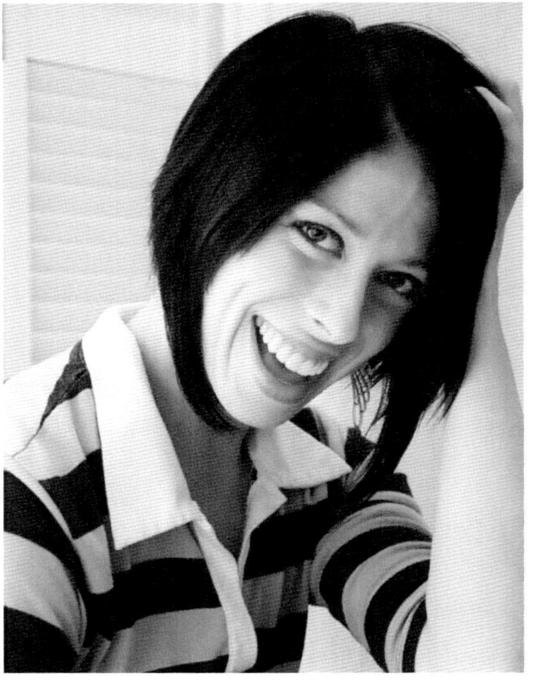

Jessica Schoper

Actress Jessica Schoper was born on May 14, 1981. She attributes her formative years in Pine City as helping her pursue her dream of acting. Her father, Wayne, became a Pine County extension agent and so the family moved to Pine City. Soon after, Jessica's mother, Becky, began teaching for Pine City schools as a music teacher. While there, she started Pine City Youth Singers.

Schoper auditioned for the Heritage Players' production of *Annie* at the request of her mom. Through that play, cast as Molly, her inner actress was born. "I had the opening lines of the play," Jessica recalled. "Next to Annie, I had the biggest part of the orphans."

Pine City shaped the next 22 years of her life. She went on to star in the short film *Calling the Shots* and landed a lead role in the feature film *Rock House*, working with former Pine City alumnus Zach Hammill. The film was shot, in part, in the lavish Jimmy Jam and Terry Lewis home, complete with a swimming pool under one of the floors. Right after shooting that film, Schoper relocated from Minnesota to Los Angeles to hone her acting abilities. She literally hopped off the bus in Hollywood and immediately poured her passion into acting. She wrote, directed, and starred in the film *LA Girls*. Schoper has done everything from sketch and improvisation to Kraft Macaroni & Cheese commercials and stand-up comedy at the Candy Store on Sunset Boulevard. She was even in a pilot for the WB Television Network. (Both, courtesy of Jessica Schoper.)

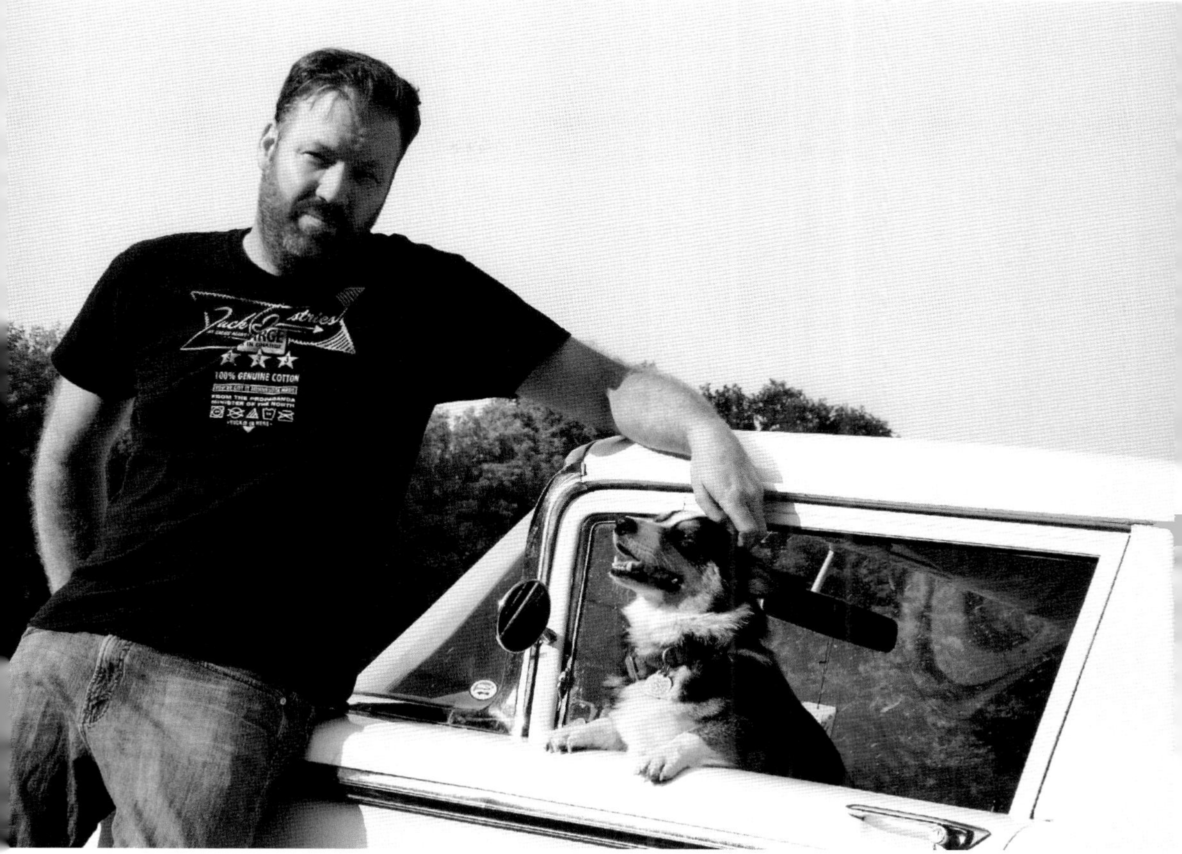

Jeff Tuckner

Jeffrey Tuckner, known as "Tuck," was born on March 21, 1974, and graduated from Pine City High School, where he was voted most artistic. He attended the University of Wisconsin–Stout, where he studied graphic and industrial design. Today, he helps to redress worn-out vehicles to make them anything but lackluster. At age 15, he bought a 1949 Ford that he saved up for by selling sweet corn. At age 16, Tuckner built a rare 1934 Ford Ranchero and drove it to Chicago. His love for cars was apparent. "Everything I do, I do my best," said Tuckner, whose reputation is as a masterful restoration expert and graphic artist. He travels to shows around the nation.

Tuck made his debut television appearance on the Discovery Channel's *Jesse James: Outlaw Garage* on April 9, 2012. Tuck had an interest in traditional 1960s show rods. He bumped into a friend through an online hot rod community called the Jalopy Journal. Someone with a similar interest helped put him in touch with the garage where the show was filmed. Tuck went to South Austin Speed Shop in Austin, Texas, and was in the first of six episodes that season. He said he was scared to move to Austin because of his mother's health concerns. "We wrote down all the pros and cons," said Tuck, who opted not to take up the offer to continue in the show but rather be with his wife in Pine City. He helps others learn his skill as an industrial technology teacher at East Central High School. He even works part-time at Perry's Auto Body, doing automobile restoration. His brother, Deejay Tuck, mixes tunes at a downtown nightspot called Froggie's. (Photograph by Noah Sikkin.)

Amy Olson

Actress Amy Olson was cast as Miss Pine City in the motion picture *Drop Dead Gorgeous* (1999), staring Kirsten Dunst. While the film was set in the fictional town of Mount Rose, Minnesota, all of the other cities mentioned or represented by pageant contestants, including Burnsville, Forest Lake, and Pine City, were real. The ironic thing about Olson being cast as Miss Pine City was that she was actually from Pine City, where she was adopted as a child into a loving household. Director Michael Patrick Jann was unaware of the connection. "The director just gave me a sash and appointed me that role," she said. "[It was] total luck of the draw." About Pine City, she remembers most her wonderful family and friends. "I thank my lucky stars for them every day," she said.

Since graduating from Pine City High School, she has mainly done print modeling and had her acting start in commercials, both nationally and internationally. Among the companies she has worked for are Target, Wells Fargo, and Nike, as well as television episodes of *Nash Bridges* and *Law and Order*. She said she loves being able to travel and meet many wonderful people. (Courtesy of Amy Olson.)

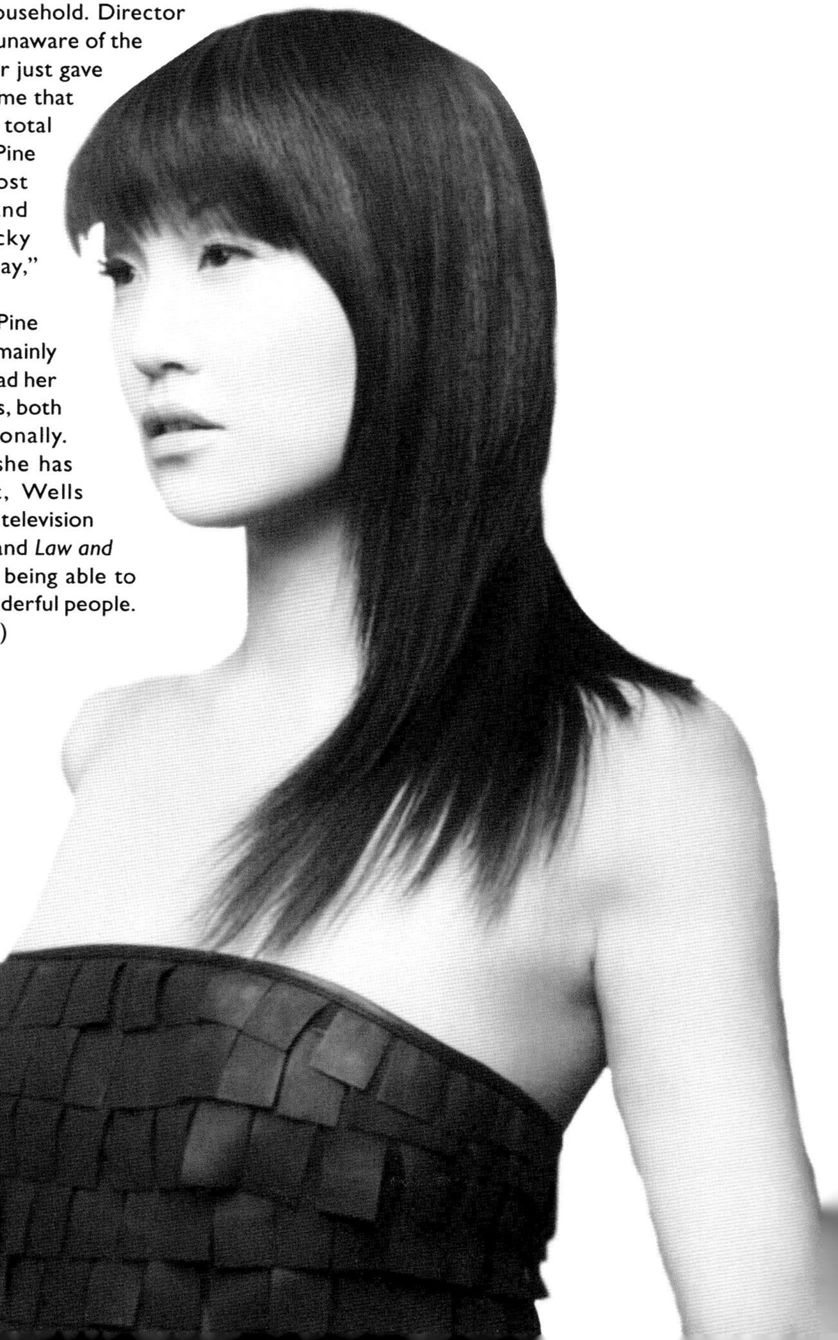

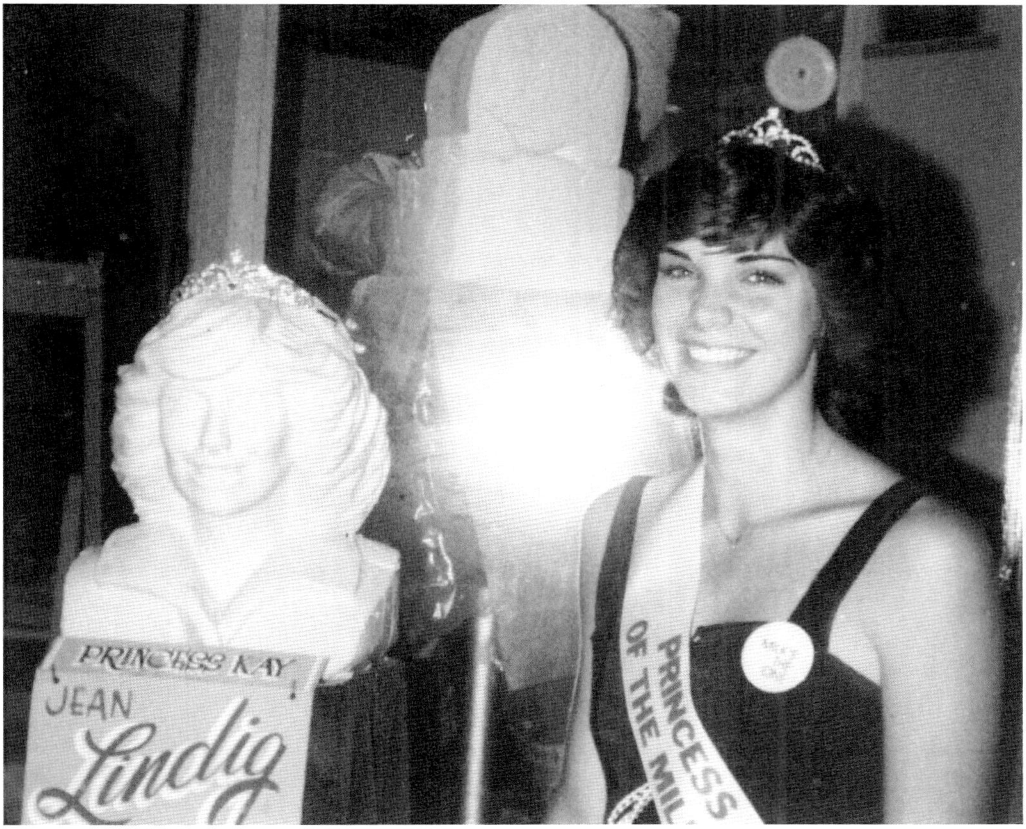

Jean Lindig Kessler

The year was 1980, and Jean Lindig Kessler was crowned Princess Kay of the Milky Way, the title awarded to the winner of the statewide Minnesota Dairy Princess Program, an annual competition organized by the Midwest Dairy Association. Kessler was raised on a farm in Pine City Township, just east of town. Her communication skills, personality, and general knowledge of the dairy industry and its products are what carried her through the competition. During her one-year term, she served as official goodwill ambassador for the Minnesota dairy industry. She was crowned the night before the 1980 Minnesota State Fair opened, and received a scholarship as well as statewide and national media coverage.

Pine County selected Kessler as a dairy princess, and she was among 12 of 100 princesses competing to advance to the Princess Kay of the Milky Way competition. She was then required to take on public relations roles at the Minnesota State Fair. A butter sculpture of Jean was carved out of a 90-pound block of Grade A butter by sculptor Linda Christensen. It was housed in a walk-in, glass-walled refrigerator. It took about seven hours to perform the carving. Kessler was able to take the butter sculpture home with her at the end of the fair, and she has it to this day. (Courtesy of Richard Lindig.)

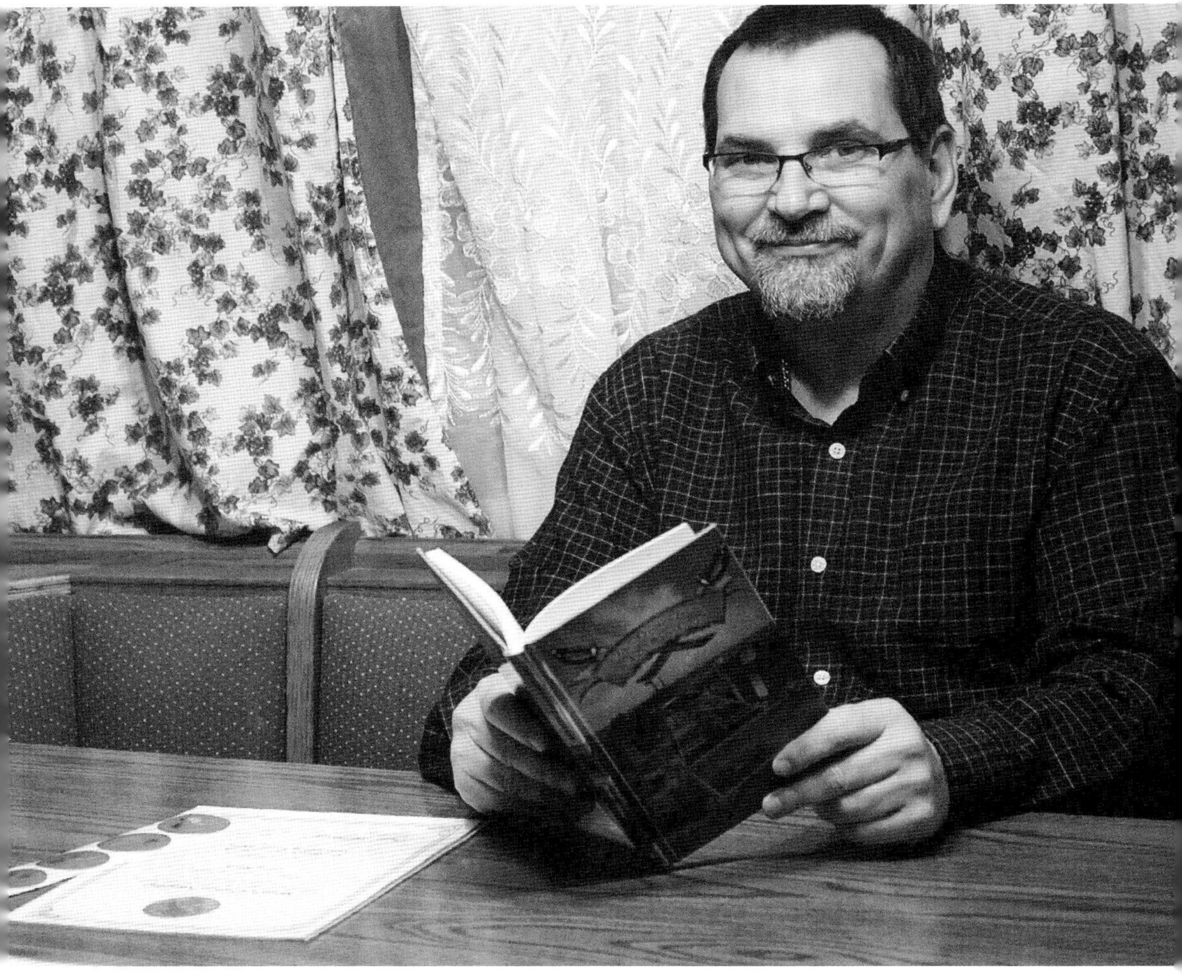

Michael Willert

Michael "Mike" Todd Willert was born in 1962 on a small cattle ranch in Rush City, Minnesota. He is the award-winning author of several children's fiction titles. His book *Long Neck*, which uses zebras and a giraffe to describe a familiar childhood predicament, is about teasing and getting along with all types of people. Because of its storyline, dealing with acceptance, and its illustrations, the book won three awards. The Mom's Choice Awards announced on January 28, 2010, that Willert won their award for being among the best in family-friendly books. The program recognizes authors, inventors, companies, parents, and others for their efforts in creating quality media, products, and services. Willert used the revenue from his books to start a nonprofit organization. He is a supporter of many causes, including the Children's Miracle Network. (Photograph by Noah Sikkink.)

Andy Greder

Andy Greder was born on July 12, 1983, in Minneapolis. Besides living there and growing up primarily in the suburb of Maple Grove, he also lived in Illinois, Iowa, and even Yugoslavia for a time. His first job was in Duluth, but he also traveled to South America, including Ecuador and Argentina, to work on organic gardens and reforestation projects. His love for the outdoors, nature, and agriculture helped him decide to settle in Pine City and gave him a chance to sustain his parents' farm, raise chickens, and have a large garden.

Greder, who played sports and loved the subject of athletics, wanted to bring a sports page to his junior high school's paper. Today, he is a journalist, having written primarily for newspapers in the state's two largest media markets, the *St. Paul Pioneer Press* and *Star Tribune* (Minneapolis), as well as the *Duluth News Tribune*. Other outlets he has written for include Reuters, the *Pittsburgh Post-Gazette*, and various magazines. He writes hundreds of stories a year, some breaking news, but his passion is for travel writing.

In 2013, Greder was bestowed the Business Writing Award from the Minnesota Society of Professional Journalists. Much of his writing is done in a newsroom or in his home office, but the gazebo on his picturesque family farm on Pokegama Creek, just west of Pine City, is where he reads, edits his first drafts, critiques, learns, and reflects. About his work, Greder said, "I try to be as broad of a generalist as possible and be as kind as possible." He said about his warm welcome to Pine City, and his involvement in the community through the local farmer's market, "It has deepened my appreciation and belief in the human character." With a younger brother and sister, Greder has been looked to as a leader in his family. (Photograph by Noah Sikkink.)

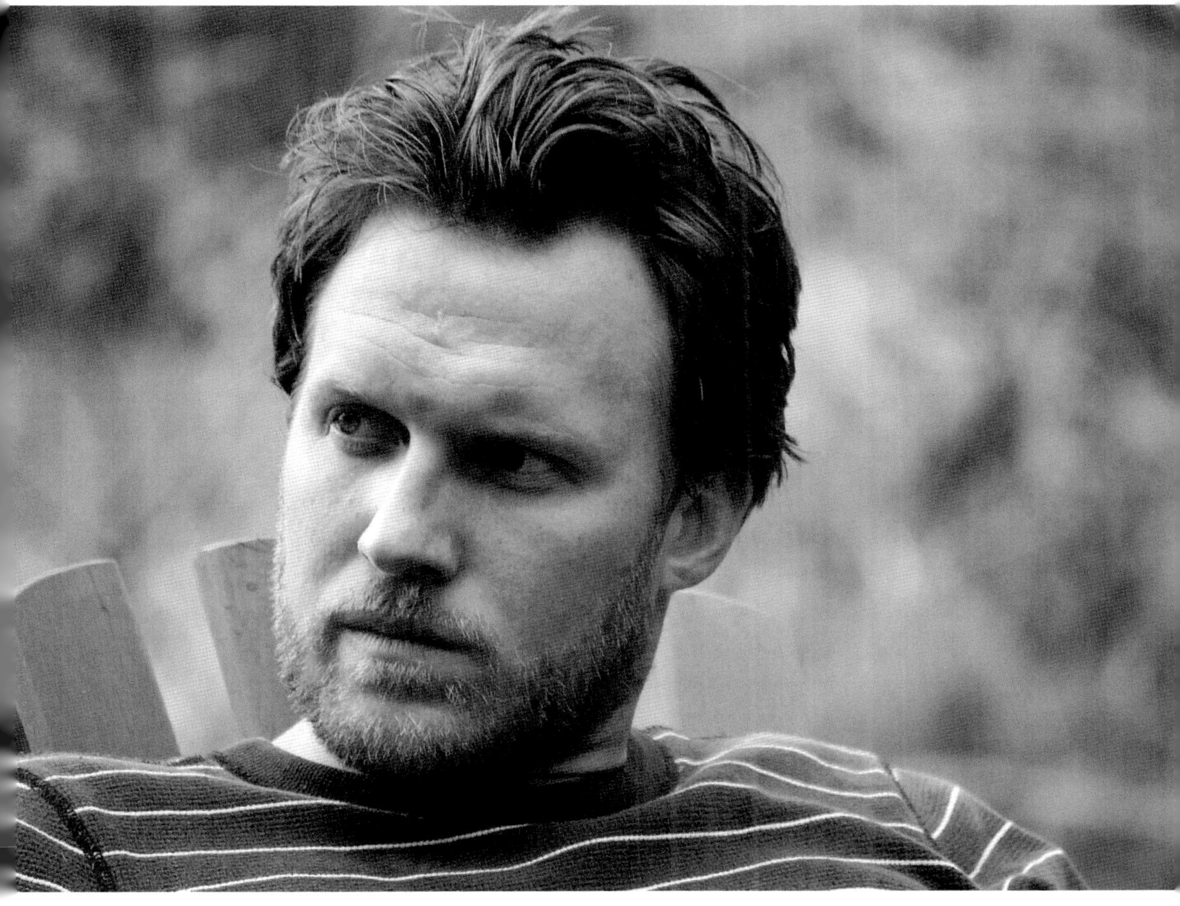

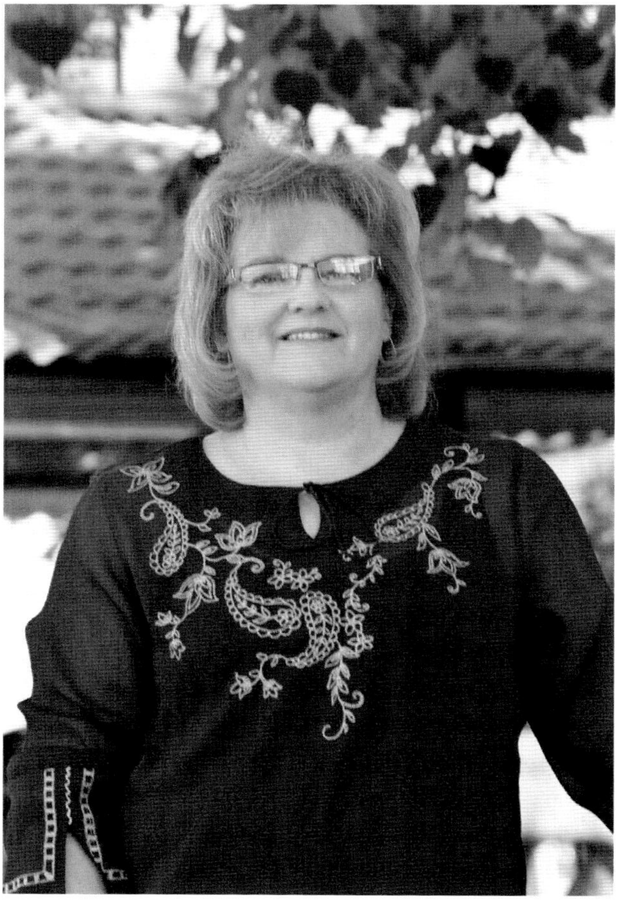

Angela Foster

Angela Foster is a poet and a memoirist who has a fondness for rapper Eminem and reminiscing about farm life. In 2004 and again in 2006, she received the Carol Bly Award in Creative Nonfiction from Bemidji State University. She also received a grant from the East Central Arts Council and was a 2006 and 2009 finalist for the Loft Mentorship program. In 2010, Foster won a hand-carved chair and the title "Bard" at the Cambria Eisteddfod competition in New Ulm, Minnesota. Foster also served as "Pie Poet Laureate" for Braham, Minnesota's Pie Days. Her memoir piece "Brat" was performed by the Petaluma Readers Theatre in California. A haiku written by Foster was selected for Poetry on the Sidewalk at the Pine City library.

Her work has been published in *Minnesota Literature*, *Talking Stick*, *Dust and Fire*, *Otter Tail Review*, *Tiny Lights*, *Poetry Midwest*, the *Drum Literary Magazine*, and *Lake County Journal*. Her poetry and creative nonfiction have received awards from Brainerd Writer's Alliance, National League of American Pen Women, Cup of Comfort, New Orleans Study Abroad Competition, Lucidity, The League of Minnesota Poets, National Federation of State Poetry Societies, and others.

Foster has taught memoir at the Loft Literary Center in Minneapolis and throughout Minnesota. She served as coeditor of "County Lines: 87 Minnesota Counties, 130 Minnesota Poets" and holds a master of fine arts degree in creative nonfiction from Pine Manor College in Boston. *Farm Girls*, a book of poetry and essays written with her sister, Candace Simar, was released in January 2013. A Minnesota dairy farm girl herself, Foster grew up near Pequot Lakes and ended up in Pine City after marrying her husband, Tom. She is the mother of four, all boys. (Photograph by Noah Sikkink.)

Jack Jasperson

Jasperson was an accomplished student of all things, whether in the classroom, flying, hunting, or reading. Born in 1937 in Bagley, Minnesota, he was the oldest child of Ernest and Clara Aldrich Jasperson. Jack earned a bachelor's in art education from Bemidji State University and a master's degree in art education from the University of Minnesota, Duluth.

He was an art teacher at the public school in Pine City for 27 years. A certified flight instructor, he shared his love of flying by helping others to attain their small-aircraft license. In addition, Jasperson captured the joy of others through his photography business. After his retirement from teaching, he moved to Cave Creek, Arizona, where he continued to enjoy flying, especially radio-controlled model airplanes, painting, traveling, and deer hunting trips back in Minnesota. He passed away suddenly at his home on December 21, 2010, at the age of 73. (Courtesy of Helen Foster.)

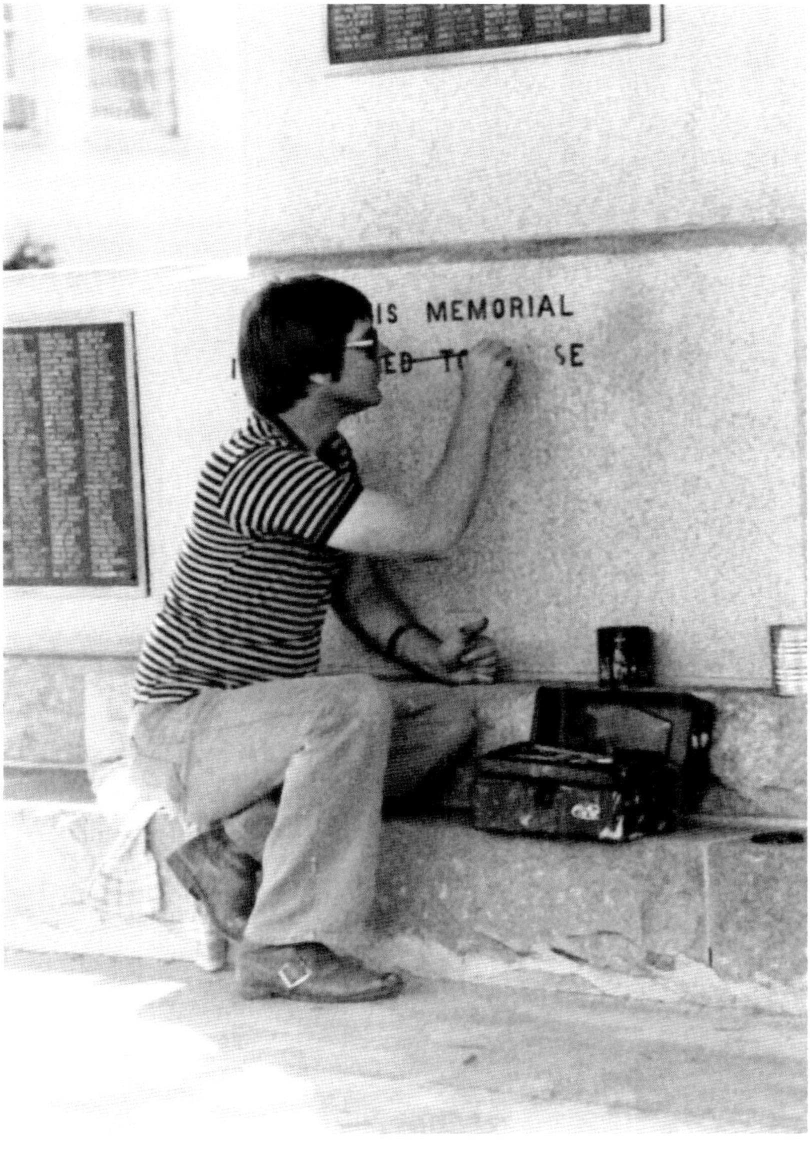

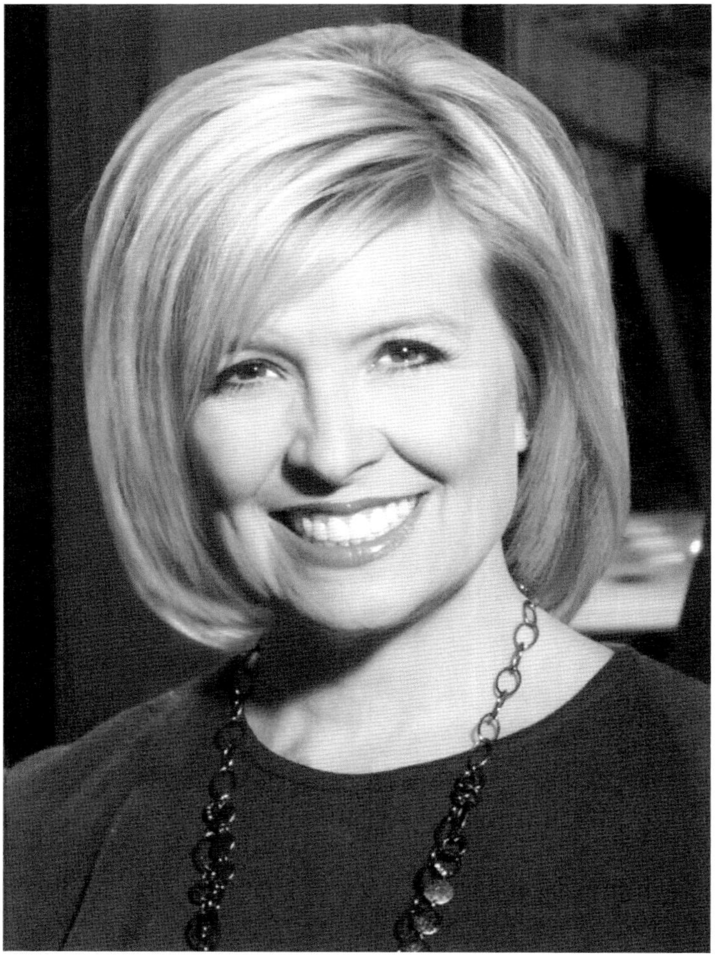

Allison Rosati

Most people in the Midwest know Allison Rosati as the news anchor for WMAQ-TV in Chicago. She was born in Delaware and came to Pine City at the age of nine, where she grew up. "We had moved to the 'country' from the Twin Cities, buying a farm just outside of town," Rosati said. She attended Gustavus Adolphus College, where she studied speech and communications, graduating cum laude in 1985.

Rosati started her career in Rochester, Minnesota, in 1985. KTTC-TV hired her as a general assignment reporter and, less than a year later, promoted her to producer and co-anchor of the 6:00 p.m. and 10:00 p.m. newscasts. She later went to WGRZ-TV in Buffalo, New York, and anchored the evening newscasts at WGRZ. She was host of *First Thing in the Morning* when she first came to WMAQ. She volunteers for many Chicago-area organizations, and over the years, she has received many awards and Emmys.

"I have such fond memories of growing up in Pine City," Rosati said. "Looking back now the streets of Pine City in my mind seem like something out of a movie. The clean streets with big trees and well-kept businesses. . . . I remember the cool air in the bank, the sweet smell of the bakery, the buzz of the Café, the quietness of the drugstore and the excitement of the Pizza Pub, especially after a sporting event."

"Maybe it was my youth, but the days seemed endless in Pine City. People took time to talk to each other on the sidewalk, there was time to breathe and for me time to dream. Pine City gave me a strong sense of community, and that has helped me in all the places I have called home since leaving." (Photograph by Charles Shotwell; courtesy of NBC Studios.)

Mesa Kincaid

Mesa Kincaid, born Cheryl Holm on September 23, 1956, was known best as a talk radio host in the Minneapolis–St. Paul broadcast area. She was raised in Minneapolis and attended Minneapolis Edison High School, where classmates voted her the one with "wild wit." After high school, Kincaid wore many hats behind the curtains of the old Cricket Theater in Northeast Minneapolis. During her time there, she also attended Brown College for radio. She got her break and sprung into the Minneapolis market in a relatively short amount of time. Kincaid worked in the 1970s and early 1980s at numerous stations, including KQRS-FM, WCCO-FM (now KMNB), and KSTP-FM. She is best remembered as "Cheetah" or "The Fox that Rocks" on U100, which later became KDWB-FM.

Kincaid also worked on KQRS-FM in the morning with Tom Barnard, on the *Cat and Kincaid Show.* A pioneer in a male-dominated industry, Kincaid was known for her sparkling on-air presence and, on a more personal level, her deep compassion and sacrifice for those she cared about. She was so popular, several parents named their female children after her. She had an exciting and wild ride during her years in radio. With the birth of her daughter, she added more professional voiceovers and consulting to her work in order to spend more time with her daughter. During that time, the late 1980s and early 1990s, she also worked briefly as a marketing consultant for the Old West theme park Mission Creek, in Hinckley, Minnesota.

She lived with her husband, Donald Hoeft, and their son in Pine City until her death on September 6, 2009, from an apparent heart attack at the age of 52. (Courtesy of Donald Hoeft.)

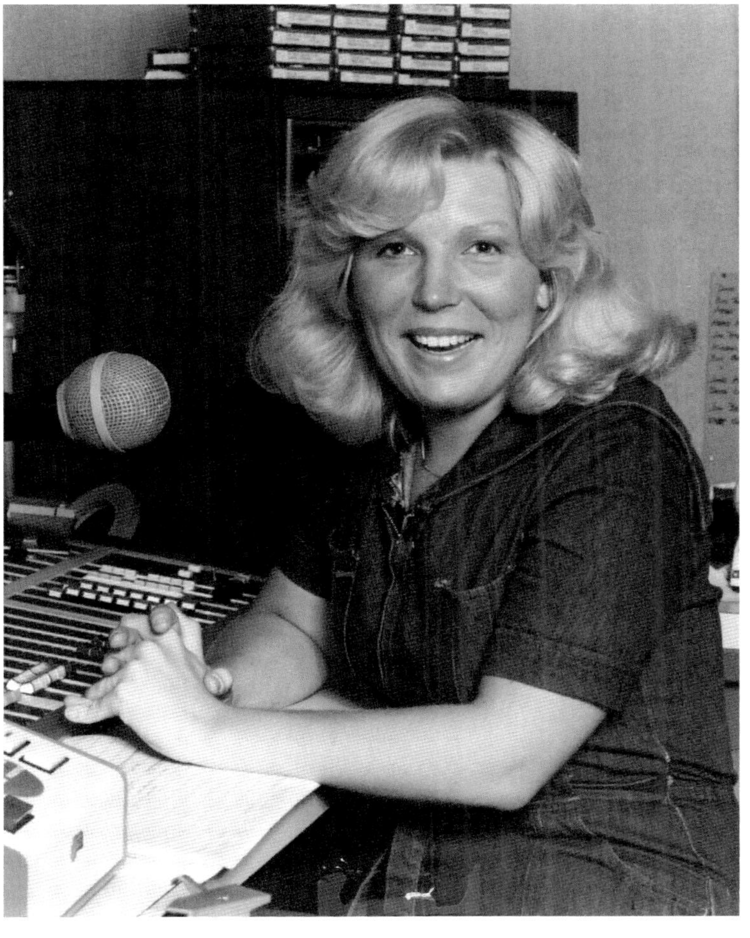

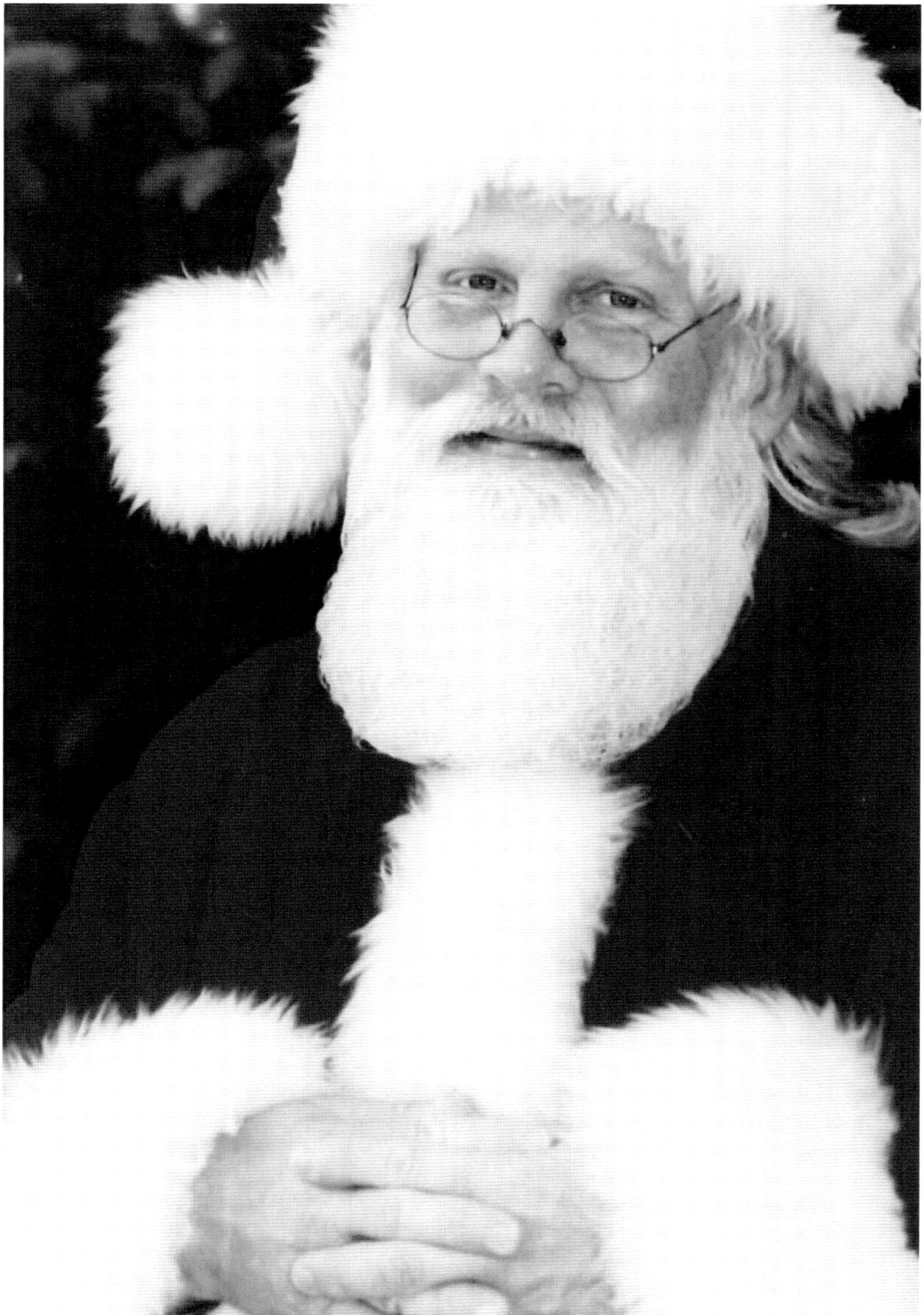

Bob Haedt (BELOW AND OPPOSITE PAGE)

Bob Haedt is a Santa Claus right out of the pages of a Christmas story. His blue eyes have a big twinkle; his cheeks are red; his beard is white; and his heart is golden. Many people have put on the Santa suit, but few have had the spirit of Santa live through them the way it did through "Santa Bob." Haedt was born on November 9, 1945, in Montana, and he moved to Pine City at the age of six. He graduated from Pine City High School in 1964, then enlisted in the Navy, following in the footsteps of his military father.

Haedt was the resident woodworker in Park Rapids, Minnesota, where he met his wife, Mary. He brought two children to the relationship, and so did she. After delivering beer for a living in Pine City, he took a job at the University of Minnesota Hospital, where he grew out his hair and beard. In 1969, he was asked by a nurse to play Santa Claus for the first time. He has played the part thousands of times since then and has become known as one of America's finest Santas. His beard was red when he started, and he whitened it with powder. Eventually, his natural white hair was perfect. In 1995, his Santahood became official when he was hired by a mall on the outskirts of Philadelphia, Pennsylvania. He spent six-week stints there but kept his full-time residency in Pine City.

Haedt has had his photograph taken with hundreds of thousands of people across the United States. He has held snakes and an alligator, and at least two couples became engaged next to him. It is no surprise that this Santa also had a workshop at his home. As a woodworker, he has bestowed gifts upon many blind children, making toys and dice suited for them. His wife's longtime teaching career sensitized him to the needs of disabled children. He often wore his teddy bear shirt to work to make kids feel less intimidated. Besides as Santa, Haedt gave gifts in other ways, teaching Pine City students about beekeeping and saving the town's train depot when it was set to be torn down; he purchased it for a dollar and restored it. He also helped with the 2011 Pine City library renovation. (Both, courtesy of Bob Haedt.)

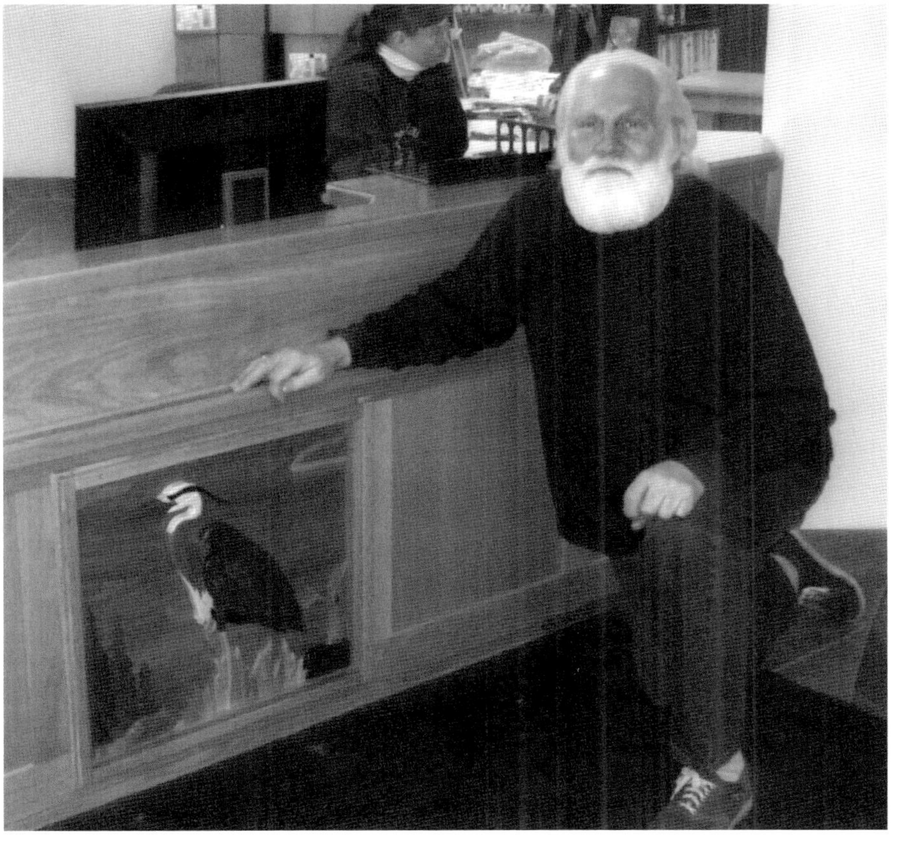

Lee Swanson

Lee Swanson is a former executive news producer for KGTV, San Diego. He was the news director at KATU-TV in Portland, Oregon, and has also been a television news producer in Houston, Greenville, South Carolina, and Waterloo, Iowa. A Pine City native, Swanson began his television career as a reporter in Sioux Falls, South Dakota. He is a graduate of the University of Minnesota.

According to the May 23, 1969, edition of the Pine City High School (PCHS) *Chengwatana* newspaper, Swanson was also the first PCHS student to go to state in speech. He participated in the category "Serious Interpretation," reading from the play *The Rainmaker.* (Photograph courtesy of Lee Swanson.)

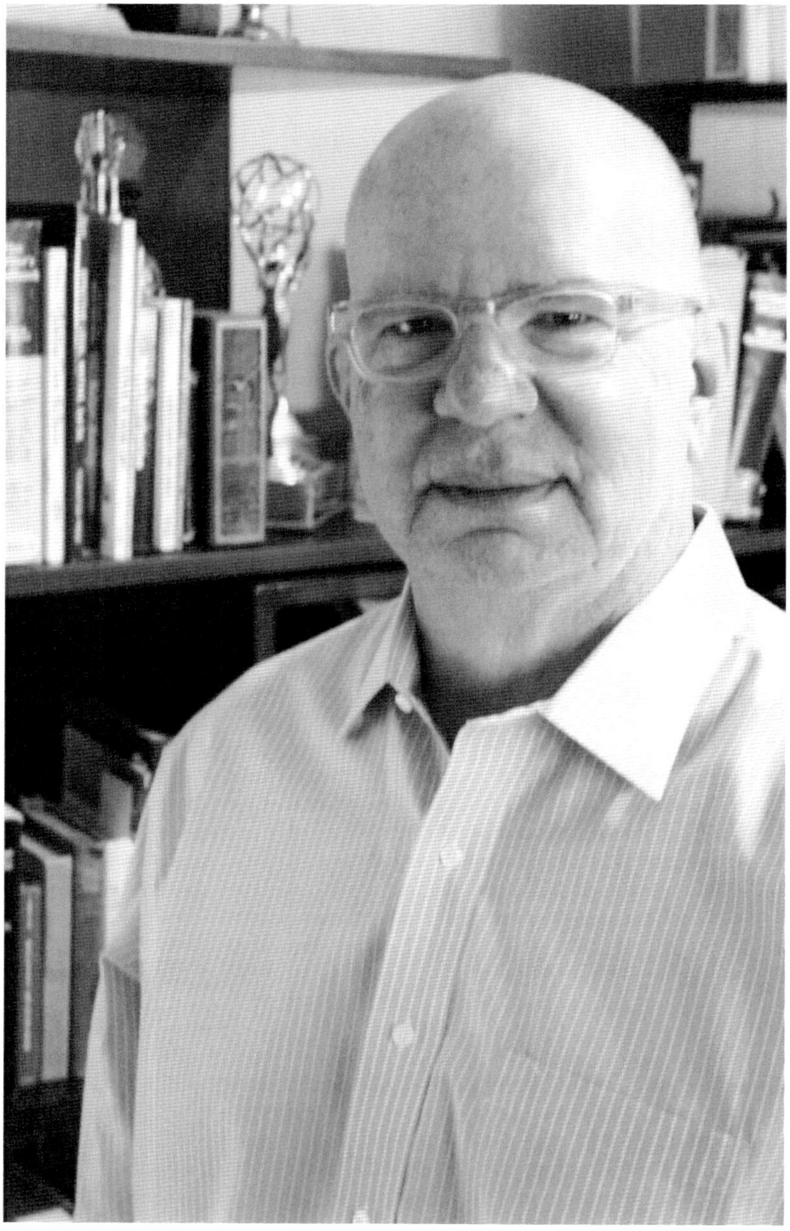

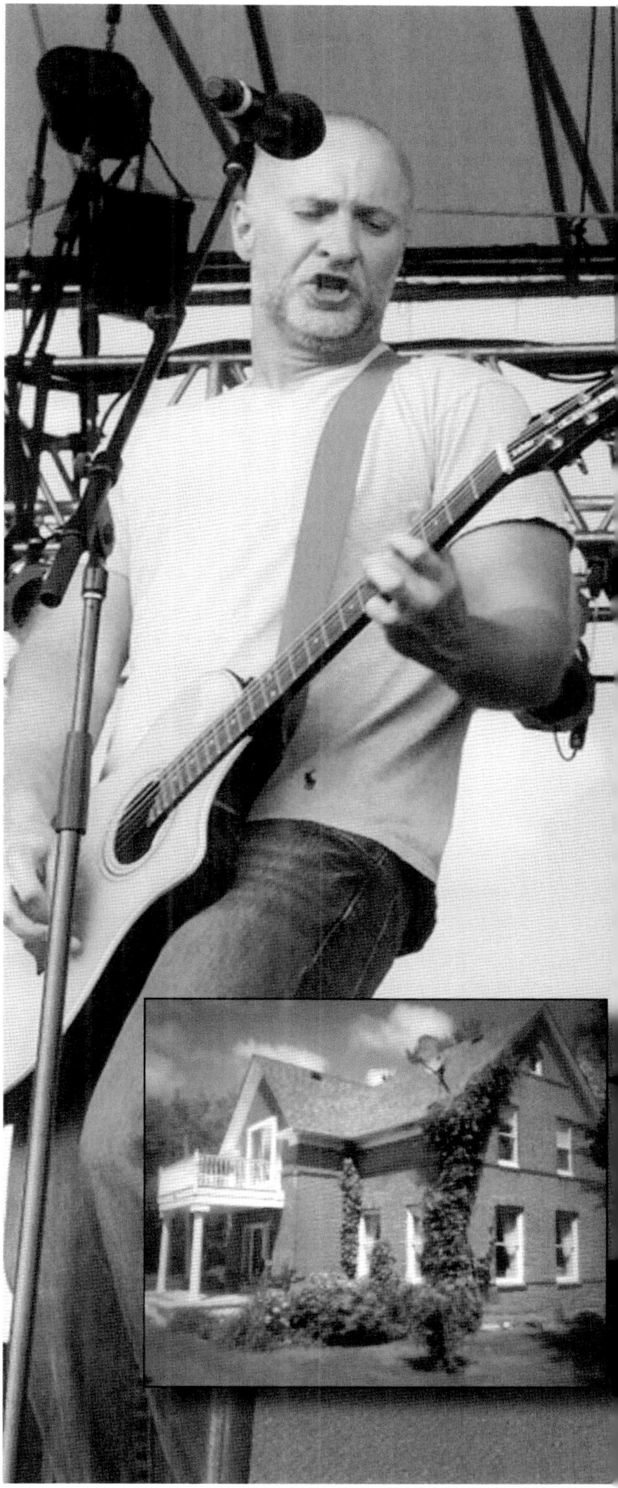

Bob Mould

Robert Arthur "Bob" Mould, born on October 16, 1960, can be described as a singer, rocker, songwriter, guitarist, and author. The musician was best known as the lead singer for the groups Hüsker Dü and Sugar.

"See a Little Light" is a song Mould poured out in 1988, during a burst of creative sequestering at his home near Pine City following the breakup of Hüsker Dü. The song has been described as shimmery, upbeat, folkish, and an influence on the course of popular music. Having quit drinking and drugs, Mould bought a remote farmhouse from a teacher. It was here, at Rural Route 1, Box 253, that he was left to his own devices to come up with a new sound. He isolated himself to do small-town things like feed chickens and mow the lawn. Mould was on a journey to try to find a sound that had nothing to do with his past. There, he wrote the songs that would make up his first solo album. Mould grew up in a small town in New York called Malone. Pine City had a slower pace, more like home to him than the hustle and bustle of Minneapolis, where he escaped to after growing up with his "drinking dad, quiet mom . . . [and] fights on the weekends."

"I was essentially a hermit. I would go to the grocery store and go home, that was about it," Mould recalled about his time in Pine City. He said he owned the farmhouse from November 1987 until June 1989. His partner used the large outbuilding on the property for his artwork. Mould had the inaugural reading of his autobiography, *See a Little Light: The Trail of Rage and Melody*, in early summer 2011 at Magers & Quinn bookshop in Minneapolis. The 75-minute reading dealt a lot with his reflections on coming out as a gay man. Despite having a live-in boyfriend, even when his band Hüsker Dü was making a name for itself, Mould said his gayness was an "open secret," a trait he neither advertised nor hid. After he and his partner's time in Pine City, Mould moved back to his home state of New York, emerging as a solo act with critically acclaimed albums such as *Workbook* and *Black Sheets*. (Right, courtesy of Gaelen Hadlett; inset, author's collection.)

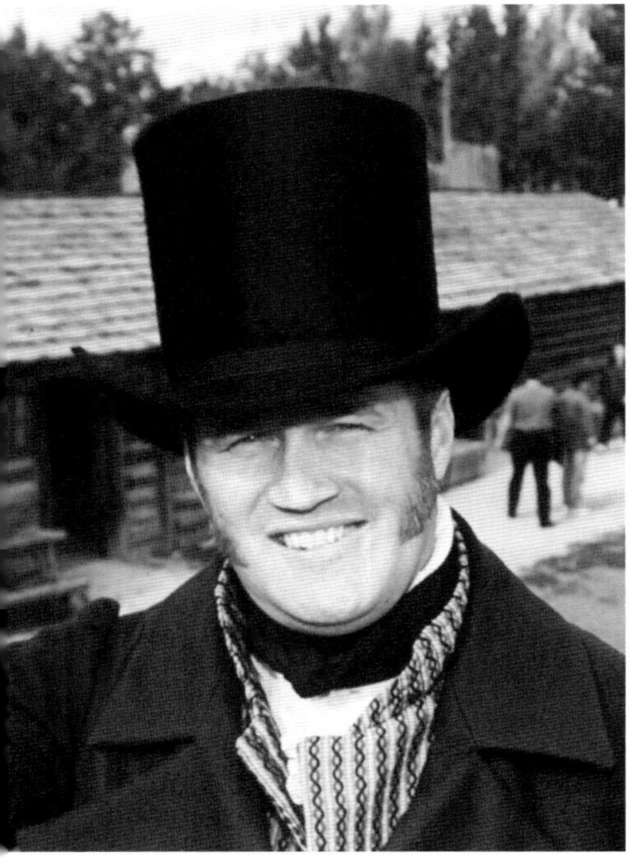

Patrick Schifferdecker

John Sayer and Thomas Connor were said to have established the North West Company Post. Patrick Schifferdecker is the figurehead that helped later generations enjoy it. A knowledgeable historian, Patrick, who graduated from Johnsburg High School in McHenry, Illinois, in 1981, came to manage the site when its numbers were floundering. Over the years, the site has been on the brink of closure, but he helped work to increase the range of audience and to increase visitor numbers. He oversaw construction of a new interpretive center, complete with a gift shop and meeting facilities.

Patrick even portrays a voyageur guide at the historic site and has helped create an environment that allows visitors to step into the recreated world of 1804, stop at the Ojibwa encampment, and learn how the seasonal living of the Ojibwa changed when Europeans arrived. While there, visitors can meet a fur trade clerk, who explains the system of barter that moved beaver fur from the hands of Indian hunters and onto the heads of fashionable Europeans. (Left, courtesy of the Minnesota Historical Society; below, author's collection.)

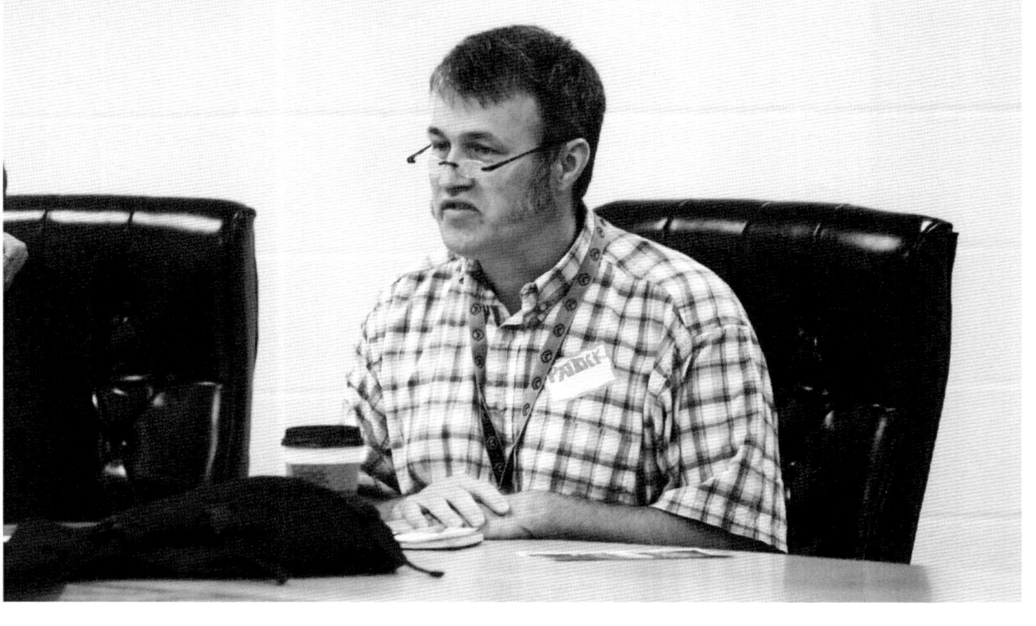

CHAPTER SEVEN

Time-honored Businesses

Businesses are an important part of any community, and Pine City has long been a town devoted to its commercial sector. Before Interstate 35 ran through town, Old US Highway 61 was the main thoroughfare between St. Paul and Duluth. The businesses, in large part, catered to highway traffic, and included restaurants, service stations, and motels. Pine City had the first 24-hour service station on the 150-mile stretch between the state's two largest cities. The town had lodging, such as the Schwartzwald or the Gail Motel fixing rooms, for travelers from near and far, and there were plenty of good places to eat.

Today, a few businesses remain that have been part of the fabric of the community for generations. Some of them are highlighted in this chapter. Others, like Atscott Manufacturing, have celebrated 50 years in the community and have seen much growth. There is reason to celebrate the success of business in Pine City.

Today, there are more than 200 members of the Pine City Area Chamber of Commerce. There are some 500 businesses in the community. However, they are not restricted to Main Street (Old Highway 61). Businesses have sprouted on one of two developing freeway interchanges as well. That change, coupled with a large recession from 2009 to 2011, had many downtown business owners worried. Some began to diversify: a bait-and-tackle store began renting U-Hauls, and Sauser's Hardware began to display more gifts and knickknacks. Other businesses, such as Cabin Coffees and Sprouts Hometown Market, began to use technology as a means to increase business. What sets Pine City businesses apart from others is their treatment of customers. In a small town, word spreads quickly among customers. One bad experience with a Pine City merchant can be told and retold all over town in no time. The best businesses have learned to thrive in this environment by treating all customers well, respecting them as individuals, and by being part of the community. And it has worked very well.

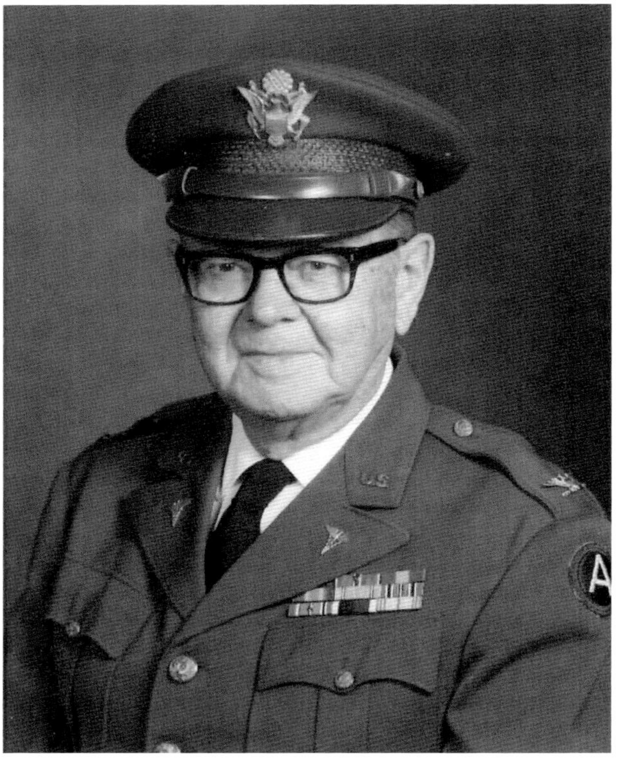

Dr. A.K. Stratte

Alf Kenneth Stratte grew up in Dawson, Minnesota, the sixth child of Norwegian immigrants. He attended Carlton College for one year and then transferred to the University of Minnesota School of Pharmacy. His schooling was interrupted in 1917 when he joined the Army during World War I. Following the armistice, he was discharged and continued his education at the U of M School of Medicine.

Following a courtship that lasted nine years and long-anticipated marriage, in 1924 Stratte married Margret Alma Schwirtz of Wabasha, Minnesota, whom he met as a freshman at Carlton College. Dr. Stratte then opened his own medical practice in Pine City in October of that same year. The couple had three kids, Margery, Alf Jr., and Jon, and seven grandchildren. Proud of being Norwegian, Dr. Stratte often prepared traditional dishes for his family, such as *lefse* and *lutefisk*.

Office visits were $1 when he opened, and $3 at the time he retired, in 1973. Stratte was often paid with a load of wood, eggs, chickens, potatoes, garden produce, or fish. In the early years, he braved the muddy or snowy roads to make calls to patients who lived on farms. The farmers often met him on the main road with a tractor and, once, a manure spreader. Several times a week, he was called out in the middle of the night to see a sick patient. He had an affinity for children and would charm them with magic tricks, taking nickels and dimes from their ears. In 1938, he organized a citywide kite contest.

Stratte's service was interrupted for five years as he was called to active duty during World War II. The Pine City National Guard was stationed in Louisiana. Following the war, Dr. Stratte reopened his medical office in the Rybak Building. He served on the Pine City School Board for 28 years, and he was a member of the Pine City Development Corporation and State Medical Association. Colonel Stratte was awarded Minnesota's highest award, the Medal of Merit, by Gov. Orville Freeman. He was also honored by WCCO Radio with the Good Neighbor Award. Stratte was Citizen of the Year in 1974, Pine City's first citizen to receive the honor. He retired the year before after practicing medicine for 50 years. He died on November 12, 1991, and was buried at Birchwood Cemetery, next to his wife. (Courtesy of Margery Swanson.)

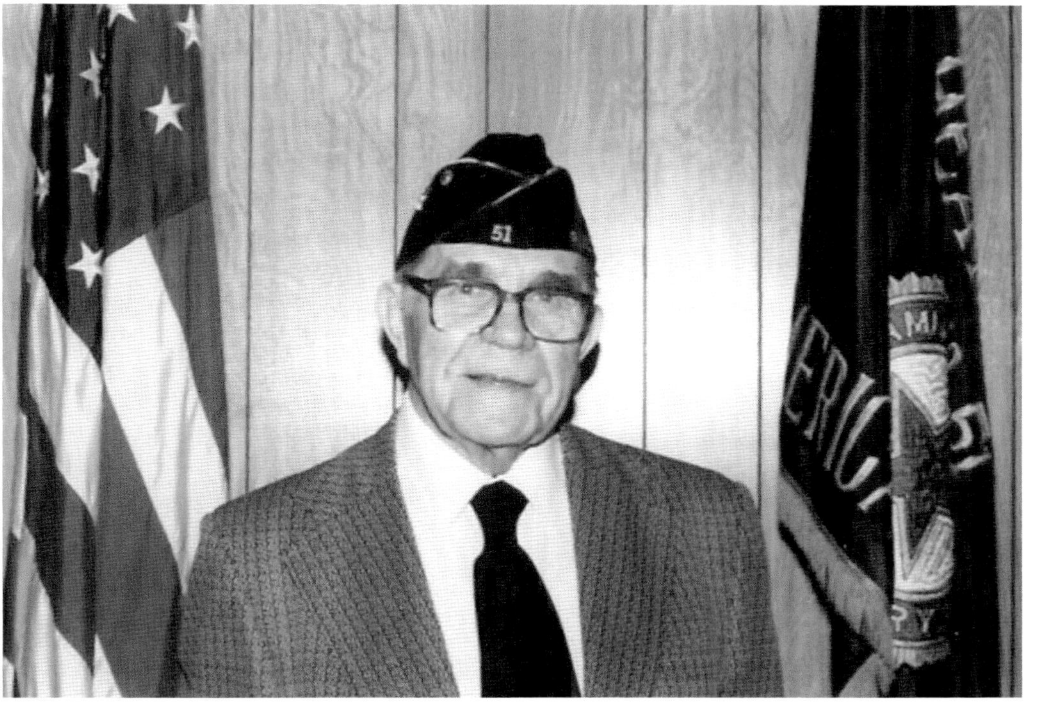

Dr. George T. Olsen

George T. Olsen was born on December 8, 1898, in St. Paul to Theodore and Ida Olsen. He attended St. Paul schools and was baptized and confirmed at Good Sheperd Lutheran Church in St. Paul. He attended the University of Minnesota Dental School, with time out to serve in the US Armed Forces during World War I. Following his discharge, he returned to dental school, graduating in 1922. That same year, he married Lillian Gjerdahl, and the couple moved to Pine City. Dr. Olsen started his practice in an office over the Family Theater, a place he occupied for 50 years. He retired in 1972 to enjoy gardening and ice fishing. Dr. Olsen was a past member of the Pine City School Board, and he was a charter member of Heath-Perkins American Legion Post No. 51 in 1919. He also belonged to the Minnesota Dental Association. Olsen was Citizen of the Year in 1976. He died on September 15, 1988, at the Lakeside Nursing Home at the age of 89. (Above, courtesy of Jody Karas; below, courtesy of *Pine City Pioneer.*)

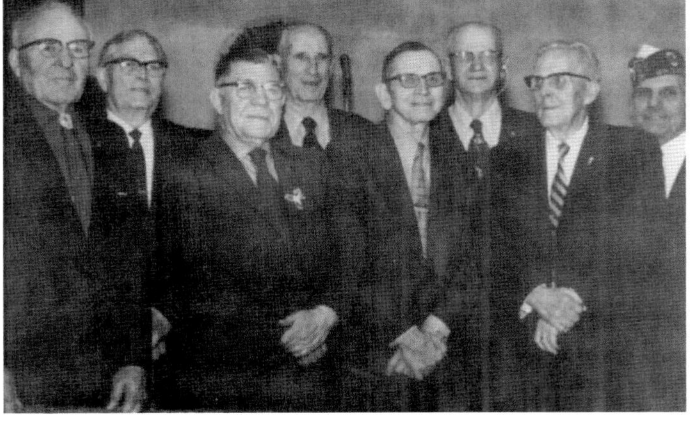

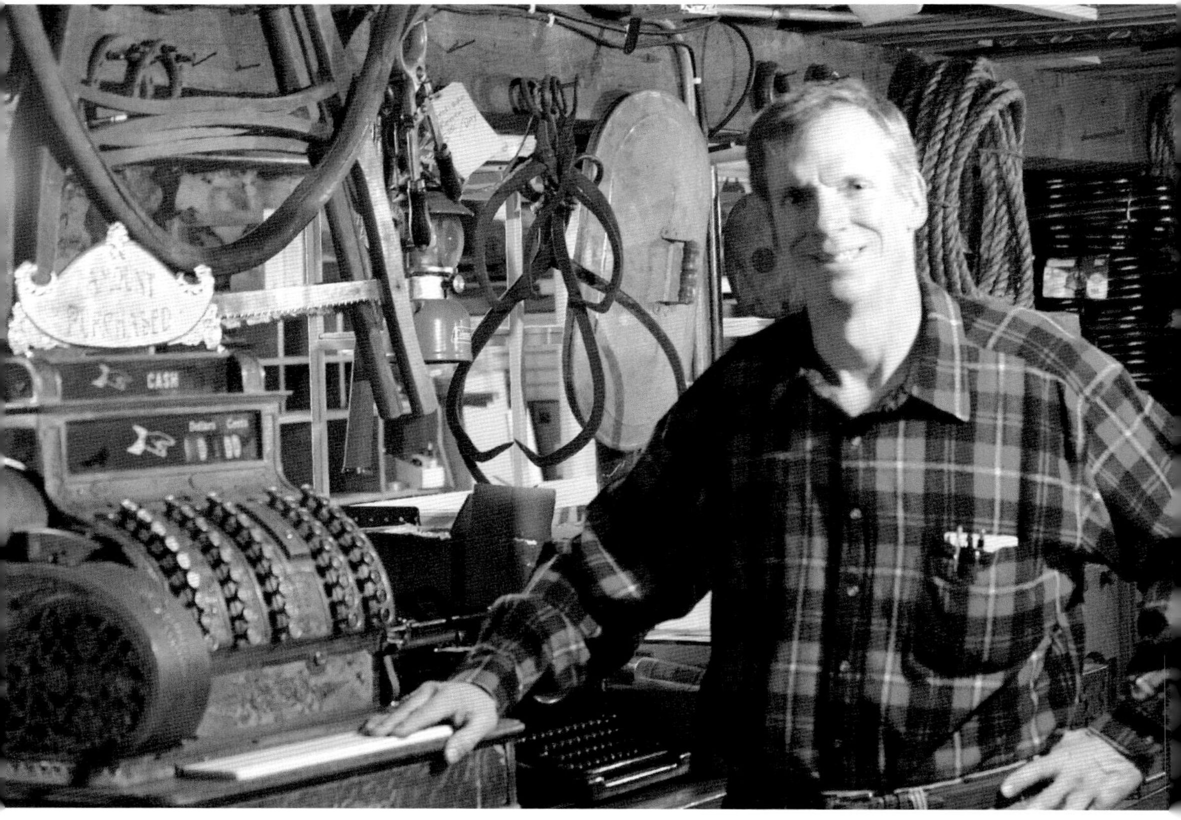

Mike Sauser

Sauser's Hardware is Pine City's longest-running business. Owner Mike Sauser is the third generation of Sausers to operate what is a kind of living history museum. William Sauser was walking the streets of Pine City one day in 1909, on his way to have a beer, when he saw a building that was for sale. It later became the iconic downtown has-it-all retailer Sauser's Hardware. A century after opening, 800 people came out to Robinson Park, across the street from the store, to celebrate and honor the business.

In its time, Sauser's has seen 16 US presidents, two world wars, the big-box era, and economic ups and downs. The most recent struggle was the recession, but Mike Sauser said the store is at its best in the face of challenges. Sauser claims his store has something the bigger stores cannot offer, a personal relationship with its customers.

Sauser has run the family business for over 30 years. It has extended from just the Sauser family to the Pine City family. Five generations of Pine Citians have relied on the hardware store for all types of tools, advice, and just good conversation. Some employees, such as Karen Kozak, have worked at the store for decades and still enjoy coming to work.

Mike Sauser was also one of the leaders of the Pine City Lions Club that raised the funds to turn the swampy land next to the VFW building into a city park. He said the park was originally intended to be a kind of marina, but those plans were scaled back to create the current park. The Pine City Area Chamber of Commerce honored Sauser as the 2010 Citizen of the Year. (Photograph by Noah Sikkink.)

Art Nelson

Arthur E. Nelson was born on March 10, 1907. In 1926, in Wittenberg, Wisconsin, his father, Albert Nelson, learned the soda-pop business and trained his sons Art and Vern in the business. Later that year, the Nelson family purchased a one-person pop factory owned by Frank Melsha, called Pine City Bottling Company. The Nelson men delivered beverages to 13 customers on gravel roads. A year later, the entire Nelson family moved to Pine City. At that time, there were no franchise drinks. The plant made its own cream soda, strawberry, blackberry, and grape sodas. It was also handling Grain Belt Near Beer, since that was a part of the original purchase of the plant.

In 1927, Soderbeck's Ferry was enlarged. As a result, the territory of the business was enlarged, too, into Northwestern Wisconsin. At the end of Prohibition, the Nelsons took on a beer franchise, Schmidt, and retained it until the early 1960s. The first franchise of Coca-Cola came in 1934, followed by the Nelsons' acquisition of a 7-Up franchise the next year. A Dr. Pepper franchise was added in 1971, and Sunkist in 1979.

Art married Mildren Maxine Therrien, daughter of Joseph and Jennie MacDermaid Therrien. They had a son, Bill, who operated the Pine City Coke Plant with him after Art's father passed away. According to the *Pine City Pioneer*, in 1937, Art, Bill, and Albert entertained employees on an outing. Traveling in a pair of 40-passenger chartered buses, they left Pine City for Ashland, Wisconsin, where they toured a plant, had lunch, and boarded a chartered boat for a two-hour lake trip around the Apostle Islands. They returned to Ashland for dinner at the Elks Club, and returned to Pine City about midnight.

In 1940, the Nelsons purchased the Coca-Cola Bottling Company of Rice Lake, which was run by Art's other brothers, Harold and Earl. Art served on the Pine City School Board until 1963. In 1982, he was named Citizen of the Year. In 1984, the Nelsons' plant celebrated 50 years. In 1986, the Coca-Cola Bottling Company was purchased by Viking Coca-Cola of St. Cloud. Art died on January 11, 1995, at 87 years old. In his honor, each year, the Art Nelson Classic tennis tournament features some of the best Class-A teams around the state of Minnesota. It is widely regarded as the best tournament outside of the state contest. (Courtesy of Ericka Nelson.)

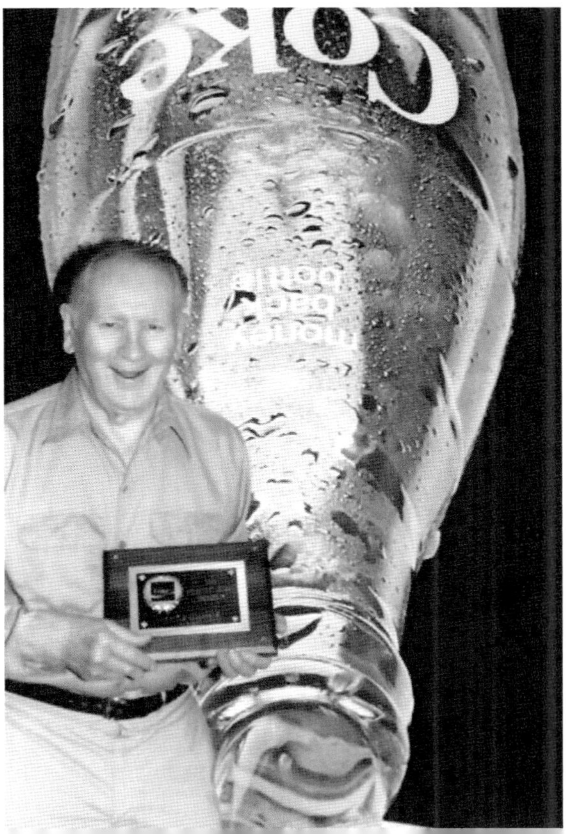

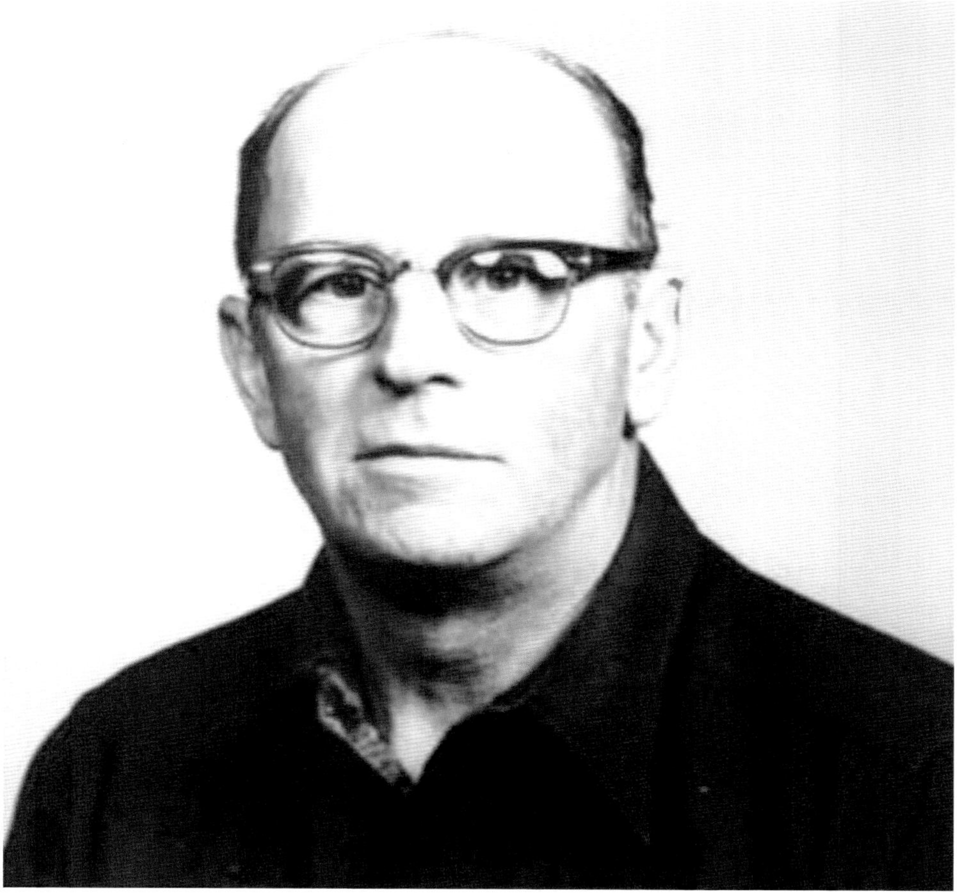

Albrecht Erhart

A longtime dairy farmer in the community, Albrecht Erhart was born in 1915. On June 17, 1940, he married Deloros Elisebeth Kraft. The two had met in 1934 at a dance at the Crystal Palace during the Depression, and they went together for six years. Their wedding day started out with rain, but the show went on after Albrecht brought a canvas to protect the ceremony and guests from the rain. After the wedding, they returned to their home for dinner and enjoyed wedding cake and fruitcake with their guests. They also had a dance to celebrate.

The couple purchased Albrecht's parents' farm and became full-time dairy farmers until 1977. During that time, they raised three sons, Dan, Tim, and Bill, all of who graduated from Pine City High School and the University of Minnesota. Dan served as an Anoka County commissioner for over 30 years. In the late 1970s, Albrecht and Deloros decided to retire from farming. They auctioned off their cattle and machinery and moved from the farm to a new house they built in Pine City in 1981. The couple loved to travel, visiting five different continents and all but three states. The first vacation they took after being married was to Spain. On their 25th wedding anniversary, they went to Boston.

Albrecht, who gave many hours to the betterment of Pine City, was voted 1987 Citizen of the Year. Good deeds come naturally to him. His leadership abilities were recognized in every organization he belonged to. Albrecht, together with Ben Sauter, was instrumental in starting the demolition derby in Pine City. He once had a paper 25¢ piece in his possession, though he didn't take great care of it for many years because he did not think about its possible value. The date on the back was 1864. (Courtesy of Liz Erhart.)

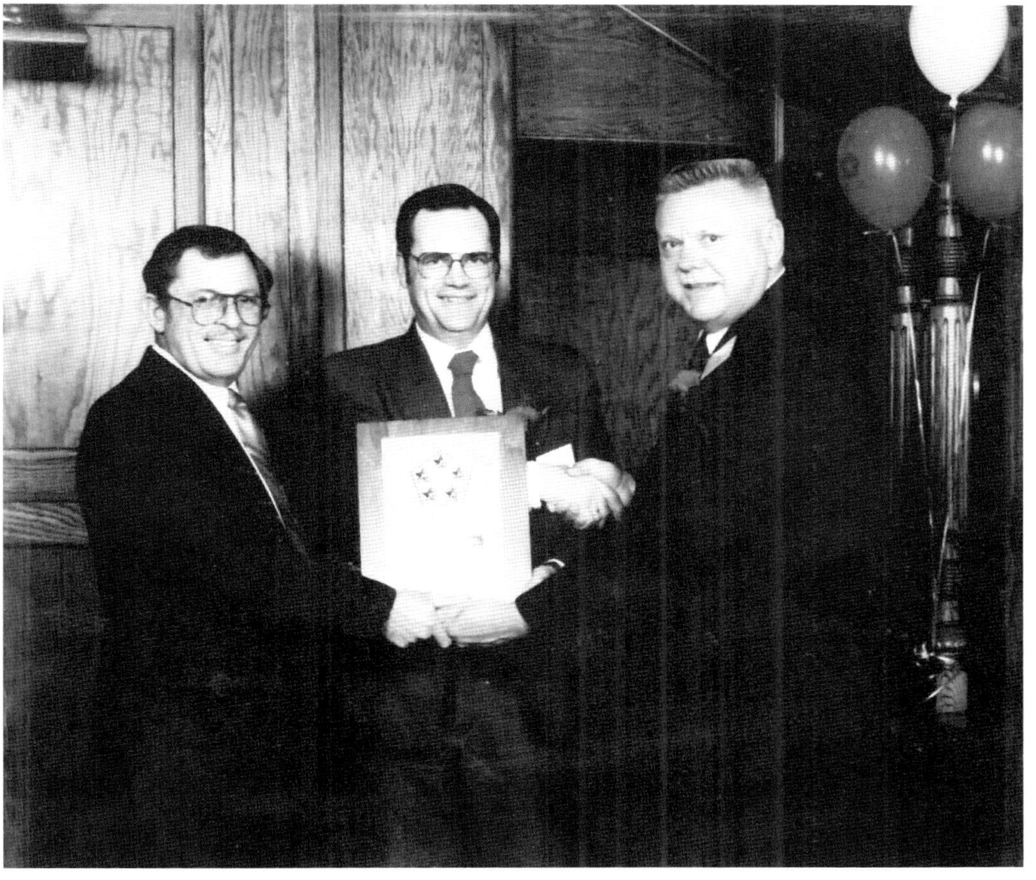

Roger Cummings
On December 12, 1973, Roger Cummings opened Cummings Chrysler-Dodge in Pine City. He sold many cars with a handshake and a smile, and the town started calling him "Smilin' Rog."

Prior to this, in 1964, he opened Skelly Oil Station in nearby Rock Creek, where he lived, and had his first Chrysler and Dodge delivered at the station in November 1973. Cummings quickly moved into the former Cavallin Ford building, where he would remain for the next 29 years in downtown Pine City.

He ran for mayor of Rock Creek and was elected to the office on November 2, 1976. He served four consecutive, two-year terms, until 1984. That year, he won a seat on the Rock Creek City Council, serving in that capacity from 1985 to 1988. An entrepreneurial mind, Cummings was 20 years old when he started his first business. Through the years, he has had nine different businesses in Pine City. He sold Cummings Chrysler-Dodge in 2002 after building a new dealership by Interstate 35 and County Road 11. The above photograph was taken on April 6, 1990, when the dealership received its five-star award. Pictured here are, from left to right, Neil Werner, a Chrysler representative; Roger Cummings, owner; and Bob Wendt, warranty manager. (Courtesy of Roger Cummings.)

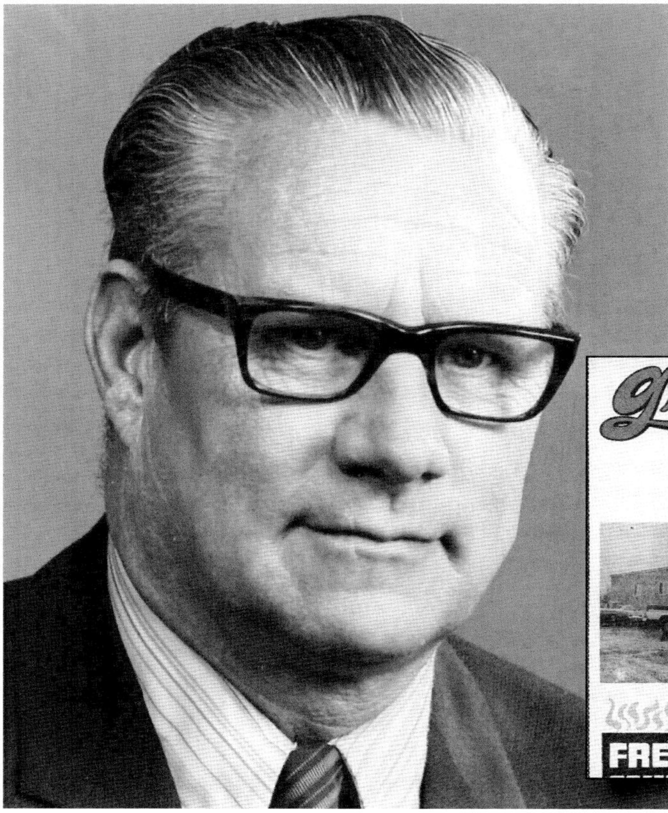

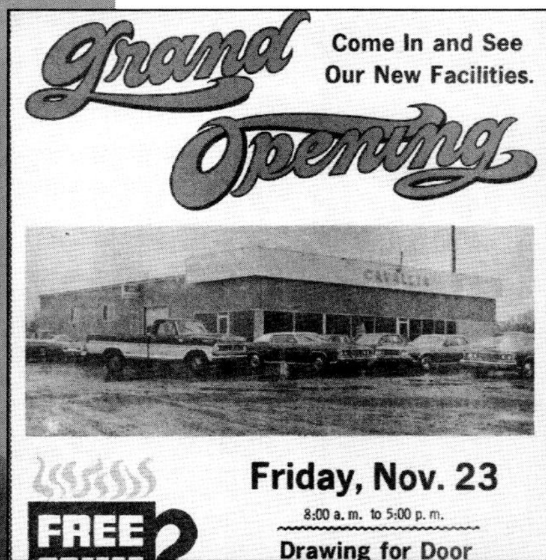

Lib Cavallin

Caleb "Lib" Bertrum Cavallin was born on July 9, 1917 in Waldo, Minnesota. His parents emigrated from Sweden, and he was extremely proud of his Swedish heritage. Caleb went to Virginia Junior College, then enrolled in the US Army and was stationed in Danville, Kentucky.

He married Mary Ann Burke on September 14, 1943; they were wed for 65 years. Mary Ann was an Army medical caretaker. Lib was sent to the Panama Canal until after World War II (1945). He then returned to Mary and their son, Richard, who was 15 months old at the time, in Nebraska City. After a couple of weeks in Nebraska City, they headed for Minnesota where Lib worked with his siblings in Two Harbors, then managed a Standard gas station.

In 1957, the Cavallin family moved to Pine City, and Lib began his own business that year, Cavallin Ford. The couple had six kids altogether: Richard, John, Carol, Thomas, Nancy. and Ronald.

At the time it opened, the telephone number for Cavallin Ford was only two digits, 94. Ford released an advertisement for the new Ford dealership that said, "Ford Motor Company is happy to welcome this new dealer to the nationwide Ford dealer family. And there's a warm invitation for you to stop in and get acquainted with this friendly group of automobile men." In 1973, the business moved from downtown Pine City to close to I-35.

Lib delighted in hobby farming, John Deere lawn tractors, Billy Graham, Gospel music, angling, swimming, and boating. He cherished family get-togethers at the farm and at the island on Snake River. He and Mary shared 17 years as winter Texans.

Lib was an active part of the Methodist church, American Legion, VFW, and Pine City Area Chamber of Commerce. When asked how he was, Lib usually answered, "Good." He was exceptionally respectful and always thanked individuals for coming to visit him. He passed away on November 9, 2008, in Pine City at the age of 91. (Both, courtesy of the Cavallin Family.)

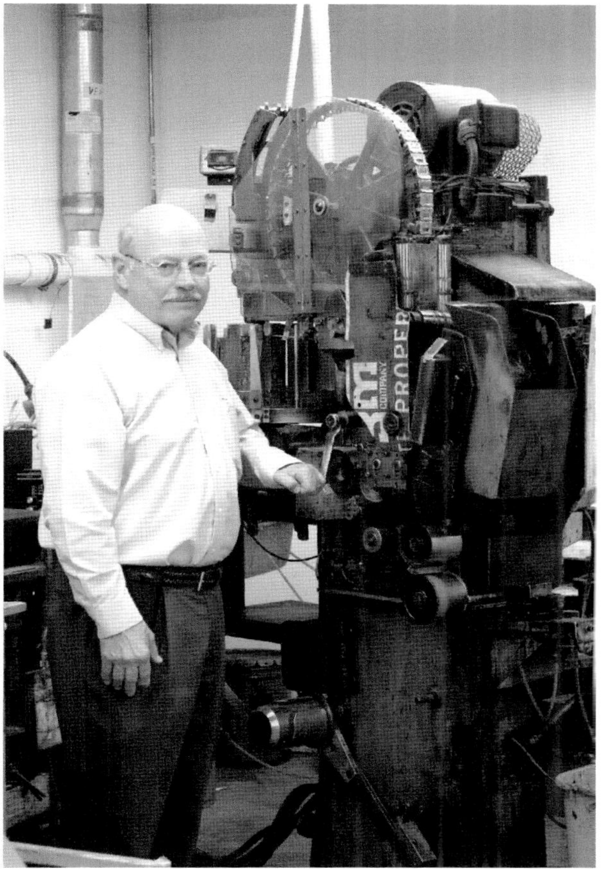

Bob Thompson

3M began operations in Pine City in 1968 to manufacture microfilm aperture cards for a global market. Since that time, the facility changed its name and ownership, but has remained one of the city's largest employers.

In 1998, one of the company's own employees, Robert "Bob" W. Thompson, was hired as the plant manager. He remained in that post through 2002 and the sale of the 3M/Imation plant to an information-technology company based in Philadelphia. In 2005, Thompson purchased the plant and assets to form MINPACK, Inc., which is now one of the top contract packaging companies in the Upper Midwest. Bob and his wife, Teddy, live in the community and are a part of its fabric. They can often be seen patronizing a local establishment or attending a community function.

Thompson is the man who saved 100 jobs in Pine City at a time when it needed them most. He was preparing for the plant's inevitable closure for years when he decided to purchase it and retool it as MINPACK, Inc. "My primary motivation to create MINPACK was to retain one hundred-plus jobs," Thompson said. The plant not only retained its employees during a deep recession, but it became one of America's largest high-tech manufacturers of microfilm and a key supplier to household names like 3M, NASA, and Boeing. It was this economic success that led MINPACK, Inc. to be named the Initiative Foundation's 2007 Outstanding Enterprise, and Thompson to be named Pine City Citizen of the Year in 2009. Thompson has helped shape Pine City, not only as the owner of MINPACK, but also through a staffing agency called 4Staffing and as an active member of the Pine City Area Early Childhood Coalition, Pine City Lions, and Pine Center for the Arts. Thompson holds two US patents as well. (Photograph by Noah Sikkink.)

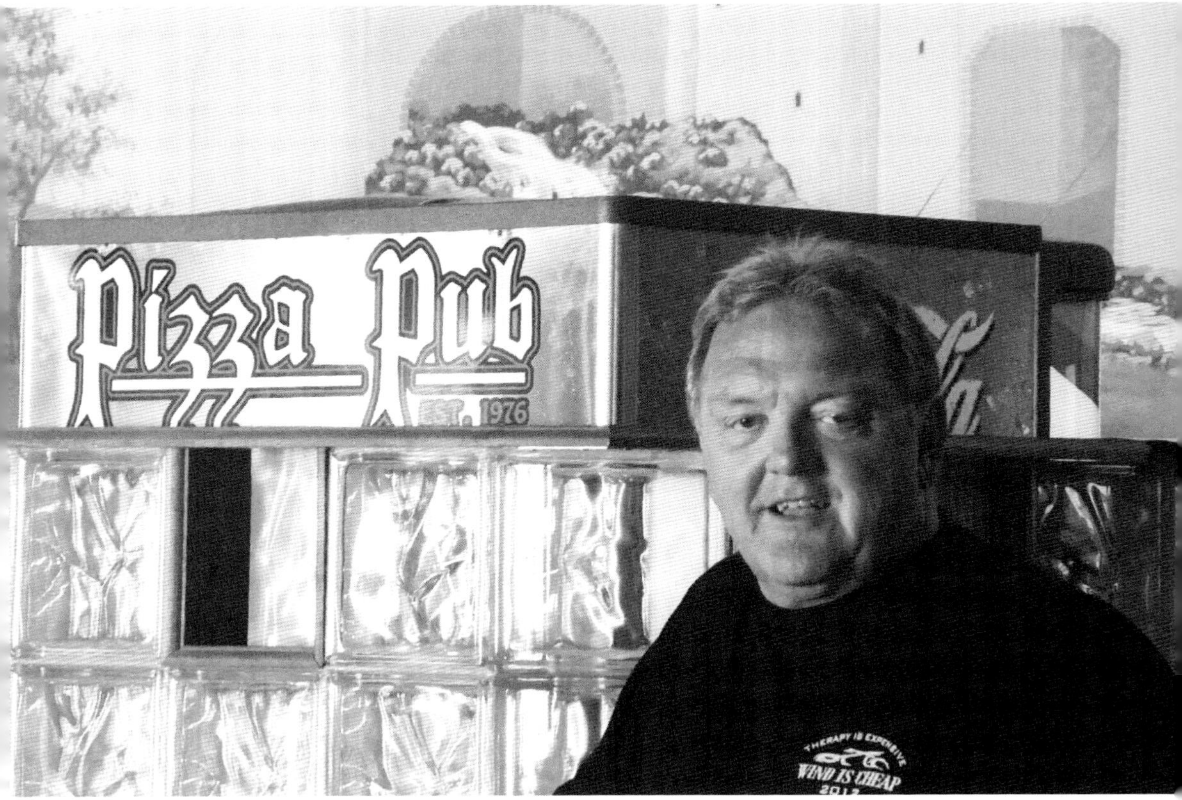

Rick Herzog

Rick Herzog was a traveling salesperson in the United States and Canada for about 10 years. He moved to town in the fall of 1976 and played softball for the Pizza Pub and attended Pine Technical Institute (now Pine Technical College) to take up welding. He was Kevin Anderson's first employee at DAKA Corporation.

Herzog bought the Pizza Pub in October 1990 from Barb Saari, who had started the business in 1976. He kept the business at the same location for about five years. Then he bought the former Alpine Inn from Bob Hunt and was there for about five years while business doubled. When Doug and Suzie Fore bought Herzog's building, he moved the Pizza Pub back downtown to a building he bought from Bob Mullins of Cambridge. The building was formerly leased to Ben Franklin.

In the fall of 1991, *Pizza Today* magazine suggested that Herzog offer a $2-off coupon for returned pizza boxes. He objected, saying it would add to his garbage. So, over the next year and a half, he invented the "Boomerang Box," a returnable pizza box. Herzog claimed that the Minnesota Office of Waste Management told him that he was ahead of his time with this invention, but he took a leap of faith and did it anyway. CNN and other news media reported on the Boomerang Box. Pizza chains, including Godfather's Pizza, began to use them. In 1996, the Herzogs opened a store in North Branch and, subsequently, independently owned Pizza Pubs opened in Cambridge, North Branch, Blaine, Braham, and Big Lake. In 1997, the Pizza Pub was awarded the Best House Special in five states at an Upper Midwest Hospitality, Restaurant and Lodging Show. The cook for that was Jerry McConnell, who, along with his brother, Matt, later opened their own Pizza Pubs. (Photograph by Noah Sikkink.)

Bob Hunt

Robert "Bob" John Hunt was born in 1939 in Anoka, Minnesota, and grew up there. He ended up in Pine City because he bought a school bus company in 1982. He bought a cabin that year, then eventually sold his operation in Spring Lake Park and made a permanent move to Pine City in 1993. The first people Hunt met were school board members, whom he liked very much. A bachelor, Hunt owned Hunt's Bus Company, which later became R.J. Hunt Bus Company.

At one time, Hunt had 250 buses among his fleets in Anoka, Spring Lake Park, Sandstone, and Pine City. Kenny Bible managed the Pine City location. Hunt later sold the Pine City bus company, but continued to live there and stayed in the business. He had a fleet in Lindstrom, Minnesota, as well, for the Chisago Lakes School District. He is seen here with his dog, Lucky. (Courtesy of Bob Hunt.)

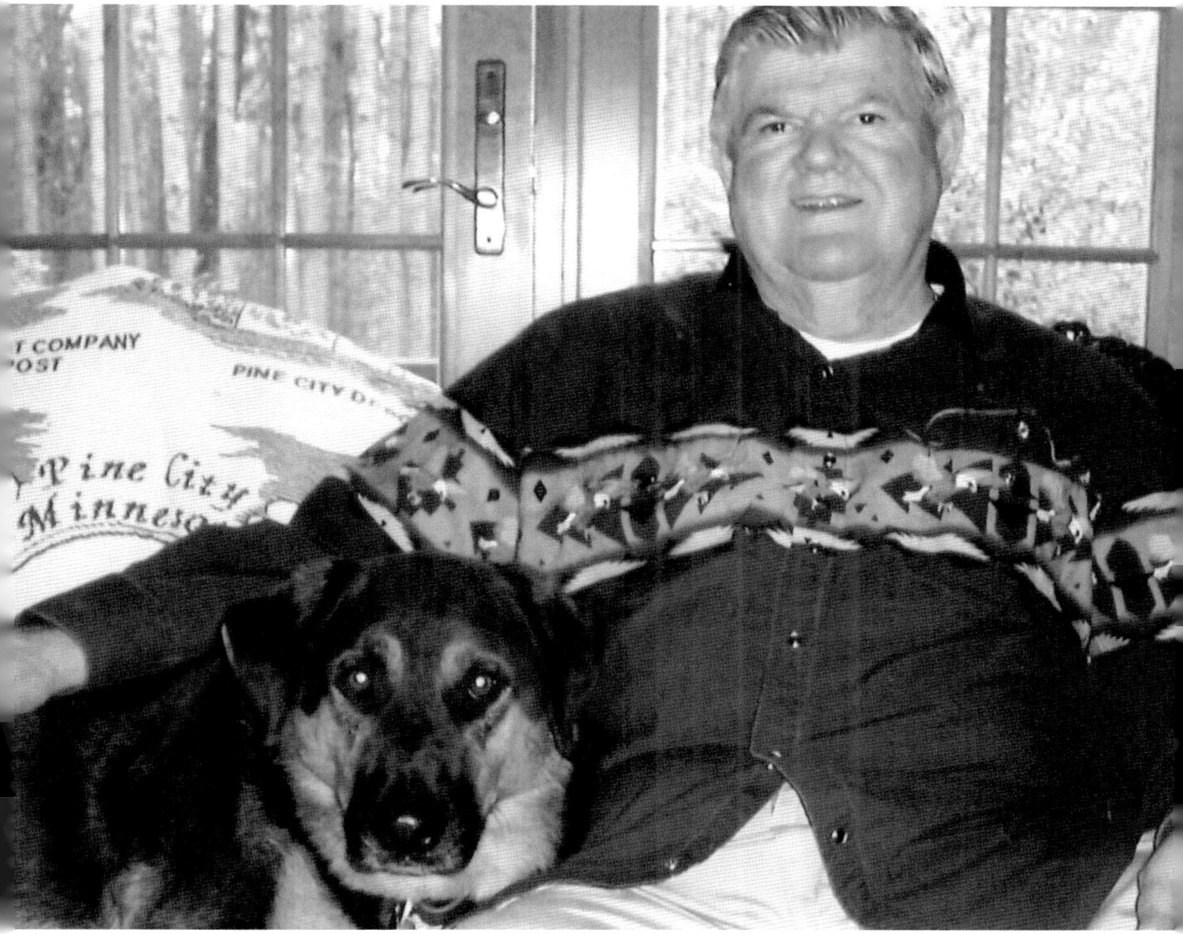

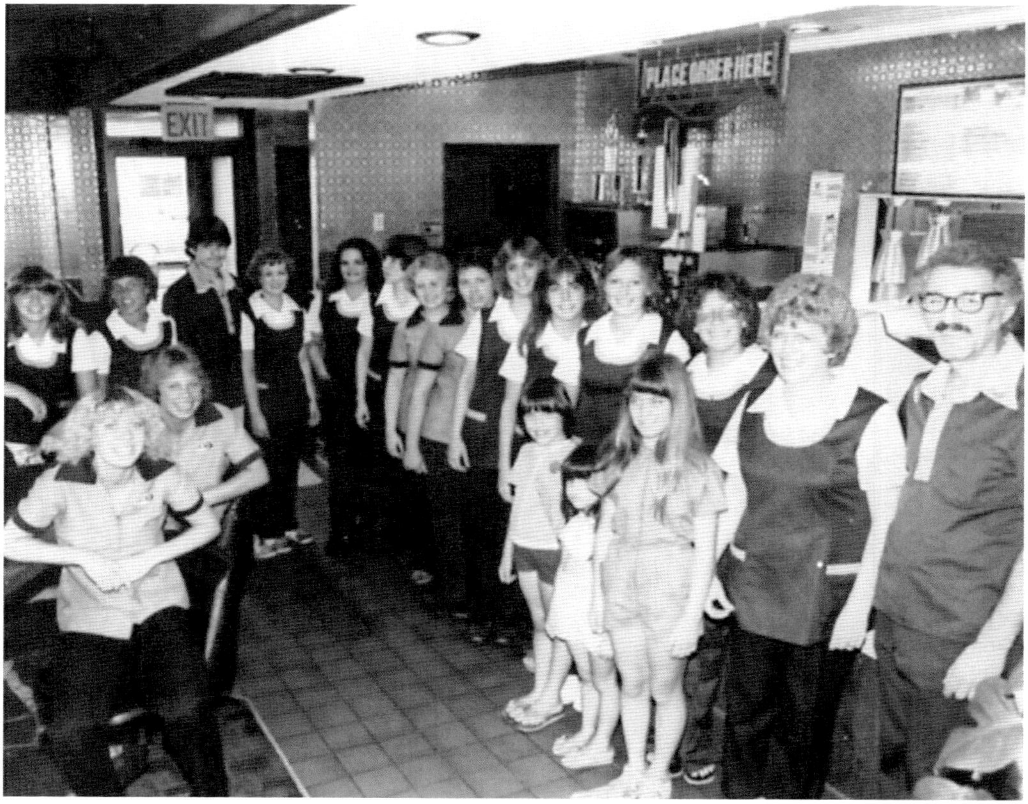
EXIT
PLACE ORDER HERE

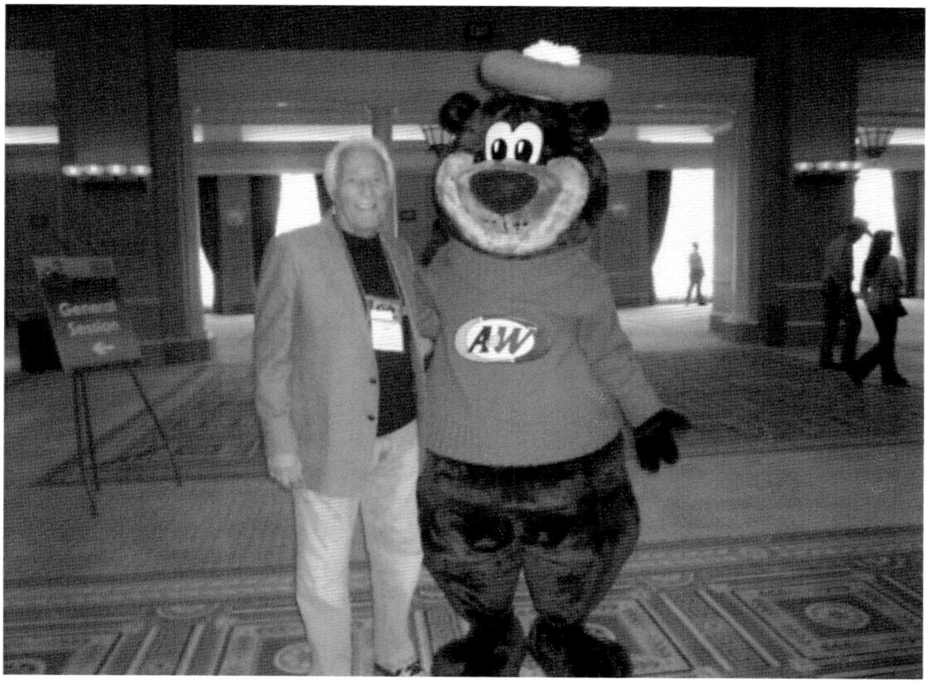
A&W

Nick and Sherrie Berchin (BELOW AND OPPOSITE PAGE)
Nick Berchin was born on August 29, 1937, in Hibbing, Minnesota. His wife, Sherrie, was a native of Glendale, California. While negotiating the purchase of a different business, the A&W in Pine City came up for sale, so the Berchins purchased it. It was June 1980, and Nick was a teacher and coach at nearby Chisago Lakes High School. The couple found a suitable house in Pine City to fit their large family; they had seven children, two of whom were born after the move.

As a coach, Nick had stopped at the Pine City A&W numerous times. It seemed like fate. Neither he nor Sherrie had any business experience, but both had a strong work ethic. Nick took a leave of absence while learning the business, and the couple worked from open to close. The Berchins had two big jobs: raising a family and running a business. Their oldest daughter, Tracy, began working at age 12. Nick returned to teaching three years into the business, but he still operated the A&W, with the burden of the management falling on Sherrie.

Nick retired from teaching in 1999. He and Sherrie are still active in the business, and their son Steve is the general manager. All seven children have worked at the A&W, and three still did as of 2013. Additionally, two of the Berchin grandchildren have worked there, as have two sons-in-law and one daughter-in-law. All seven of the Berchin children have completed college.

In his Chisago Lakes days, Nick was named Coach of the Year, Teacher of the Year, and went on to become athletic director and a representative to the State Coaches Association. He was secretary-treasurer of the East Central Athletic Conference, and he spent 24 years of his life officiating basketball, football, and track. In Pine City, he became a member of the small-business committee at Pine Technical College, was chair of the Pine Plaza Association, and a member of the Pine City Area Chamber of Commerce. (All, courtesy of Nick and Sherrie Berchin.)

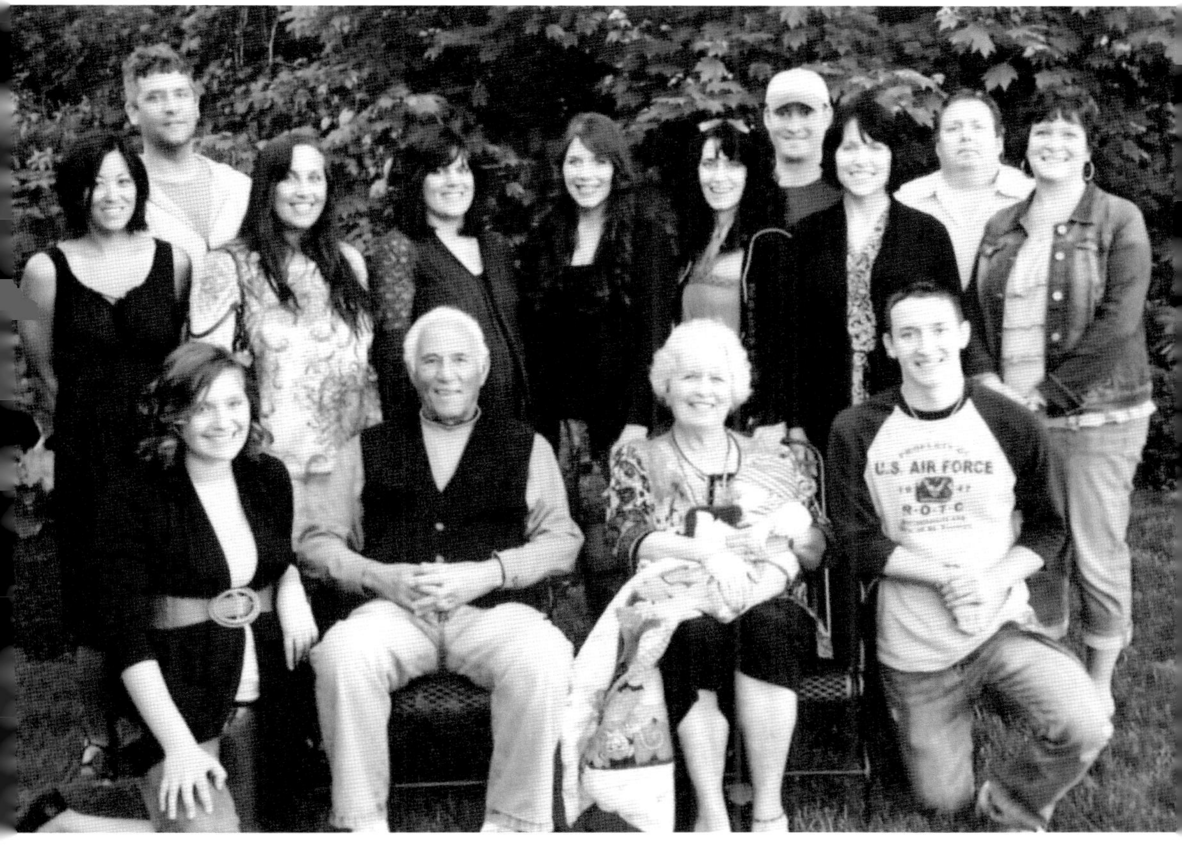

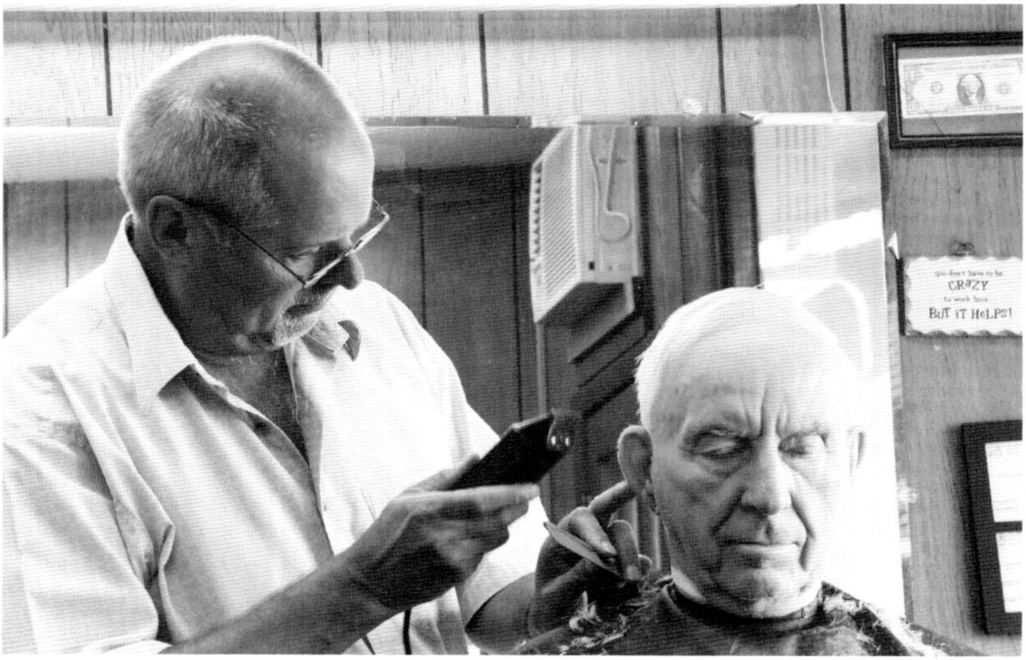

Ed Montbriand

Ed Montbriand was born in Stillwater. In 1978, he moved to Pine City, looking for a small town in which to raise his kids. There, he opened an old-fashioned, Main Street barbershop called Pine City Barber Stylist. Having cut hair for 43 years, Montbriand became aware of the issues of the day. He later ran for the county board in Pine County District Two. He served on the board for 12 years, dealing with difficult issues, such as whether to split the county and the building of a new courthouse facility. He has been credited with working diligently to get automated external defibrillators in all Pine County sheriff cars. He was also involved in the Pine City Lions Club. (Photographs by Noah Sikkink.)

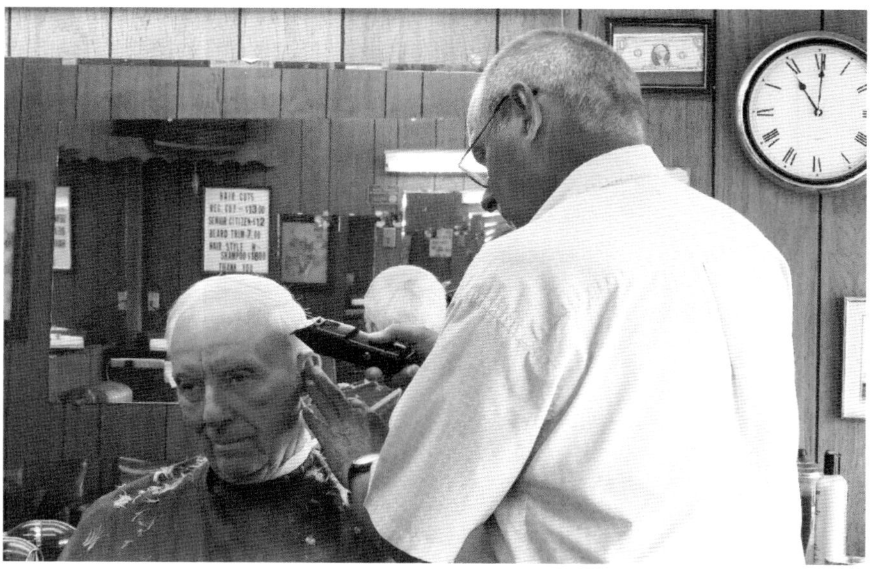

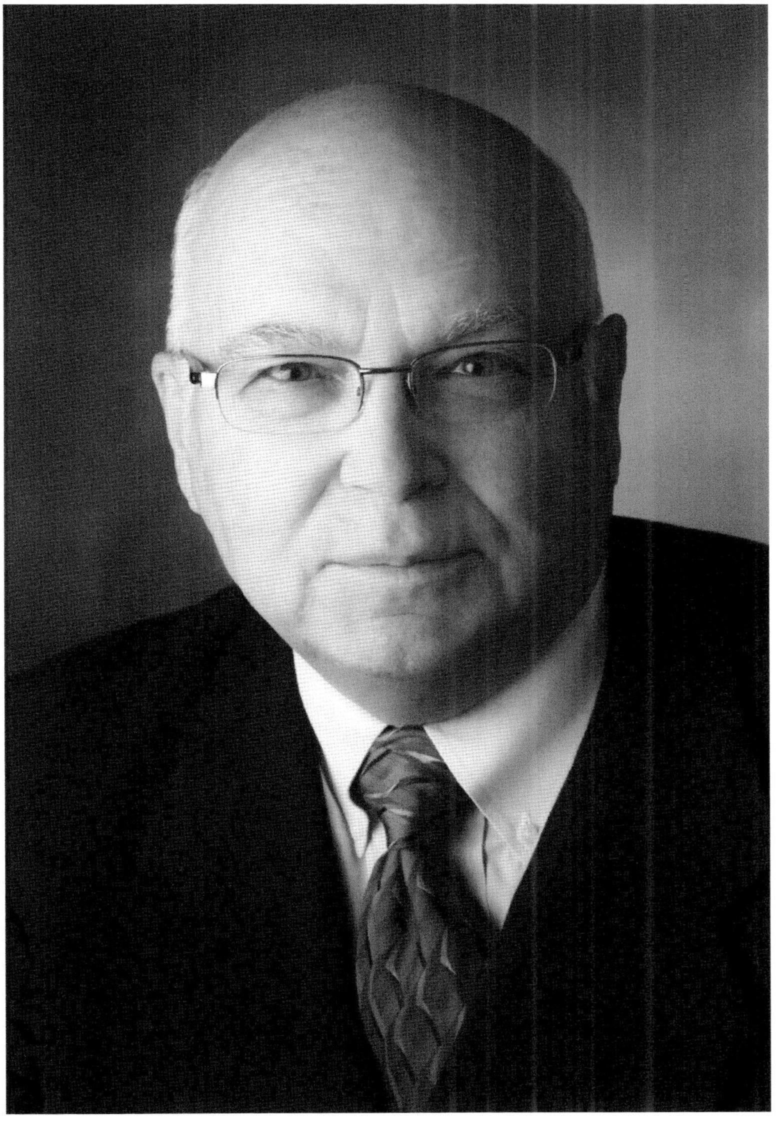

Max Blaufuss
Max Blaufuss is a longtime resident of Pine City and a well-respected businessman. The community came to know him as an administrator at Lakeside Medical Center, a 10-bed hospital and nursing home now connected to Fairview Clinic. Then, he expanded his century-old Lake Superior Laundry plant from Superior, Wisconsin, to Pine City in 2007. It has received rave reviews across the nation due to its efficiency, using low energy and water-recycling systems. The second facility in Pine City helped grow the business and tap into other markets. Blaufuss was named Citizen of the Year in 2011 for his years of dedicated service on numerous projects, including fire hall and library construction and renovation projects. (Courtesy of Max Blaufuss).

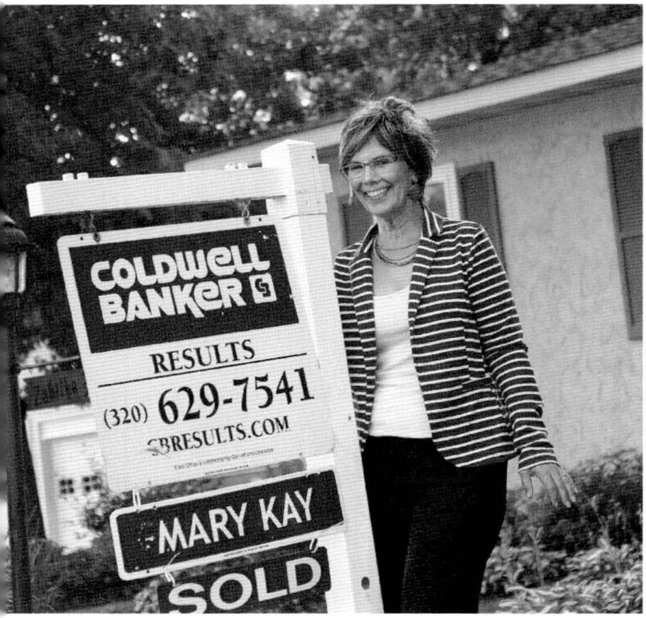

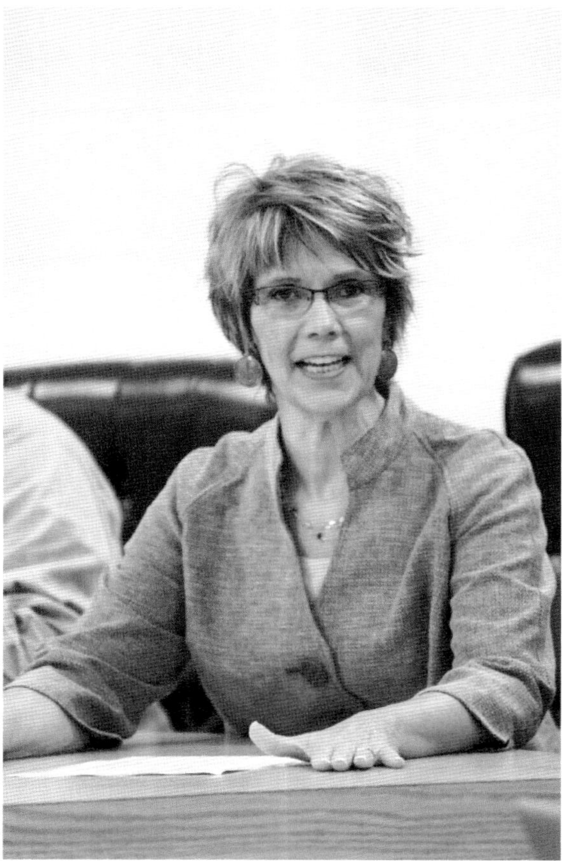

Mary Kay Brautigan

Brautigan sold more homes than anyone in Pine City's history, some over and over again. Originally a Wisconsinite, after her husband, Pat, graduated college in 1971, they ran campgrounds in Door County, Wisconsin, and in Detroit. In 1977, they began managing Pathfinder Village, east of Hinckley. Mary Kay obtained a real estate license to sell campsites. When the couple had their first child, Levi, they resigned from resort management. Mary Kay maintained her license and was hired as a secretary for Century 21 Rush Realty, lasting just three months. Jobless, she was asked to become an agent, landing into the career that ended up becoming her passion. By year three, she was the top producer, a perch she held for 32 years.

Mary Kay Brautigan has been involved in roughly 1,500 sides of real estate property since 1982. She served as president of the Eastern Minnesota Association of Realtors, on the Professional Standards Committee, and on the Board of Directors of Minnesota Association of Realtors from 1998 to 2001. In the 1990s, she added a partner to help with volume, Carole Dahl. In 2002, Brautigan was named Realtor of the Year by the Eastern Minnesota Association of Realtors. She does not think she has a "magic touch." Rather, she says, "I gave everything to my clients, and made them the priority, not me. It's just hard work and being interested in other people's lives." In 1989, she left Century 21 Rush Realty to help Forest Lake's Coldwell Banker Pro IV expand to Pine City. She managed the office until 1999, and then purchased it to help it grow. She renamed it Coldwell Banker Results, a reflection of her expectations.

Brautigan has devoted her time to the Lions Club, the chamber of commerce, Pine Technical College Foundation, Pine Center for the Arts, and more. Besides Levi, Mary Kay and Pat have another son, Adam, and two grandchildren, Madeleine and Quinn. Despite her accomplishments, she is most proud of her children and the tolerance they have had for her inconsistent hours over the years. (Top, photograph by Noah Sikkink; bottom, author's collection.)

CHAPTER EIGHT

Do-gooders and Social Advocacy

There is something about a small town that tends to inscribe people with certain principles: Work, faith, and honesty, among them. There were 24 churches in the Pine City zip code in 2010, more per capita than in either of the Twin Cities. Its people are charitable, and they roll up their sleeves for causes. The people in this chapter are characteristic of the spirit of Pine City, illustrating the notion that Pine Citians give back.

These local legends have taught many people lessons. They urged the residents of Pine City to examine their lives, determine where they are, and what they needed to do to be the kind of person they wanted to be. From a bus driver and florist who photo-documented the community for decades, to a three-generation teacher; from a man who is more than his number on a scale, to a group of friends who have stuck together through the years, something can be learned from each of them. This chapter also tells of an arts champion, a history buff, a philanthropist's contribution that benefited Pine City's library, how a homeless shelter came to life, and how a lay chaplain helped Pine City's young and old.

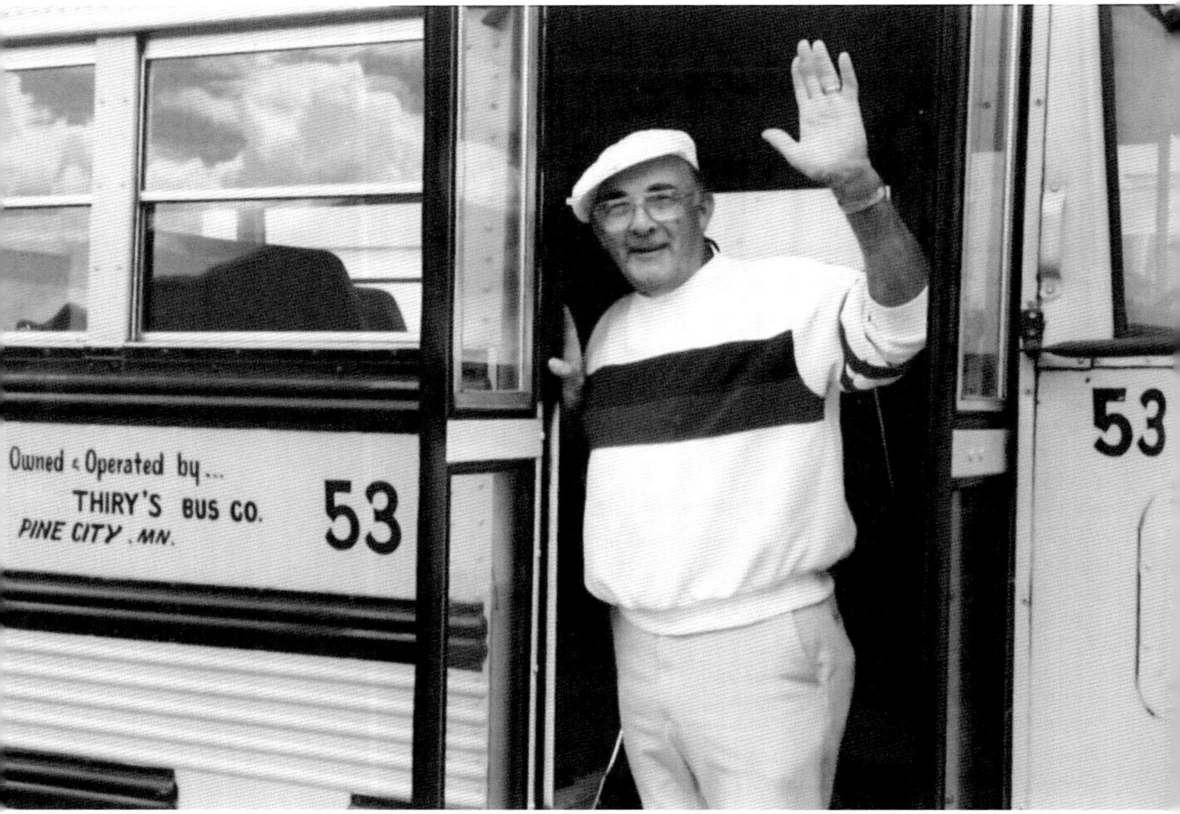

Bob Thiry

In 1929, Bob Thiry started Flower Box Floral & Photography and ran it for 28 years, despite his lenders initially not supporting the business concept. A GI bill helped him get it off the ground. Not only did he make bouquets and arrangements for many of the town's weddings over the course of nearly three decades, he also captured the memorable moments with his camera.

Thiry learned the floral business in New York when he was stationed there in the Navy. He went to several flower shops and offered to volunteer his time, often sweeping the floor and doing miscellaneous jobs while trying to learn the trade. It was in the Big Apple that he met the apple of his eye, Ruth, and the two were married. Thiry went to a famous floral design school, the Tommy Bright School of Floral Design in Chicago.

Cynthia Novy worked for Thiry while she was in high school. He started a school bus route in the late 1950s in the Woodpecker Ridge Neighborhood of Pine City because the children there were not served by the school district's public bus service. He would pick Novy up on the bus and drop her off at the flower shop so she could open it and watch the store until his morning bus route was through. Families had to pay to use Thiry's bus at first, but eventually, the school district contracted with him. Novy interned with Thiry and went on to buy the Flower Box in 1977, but Thiry kept coming in to help out or just to visit. Novy has had the business ever since. (Courtesy of Cynthia Novy.)

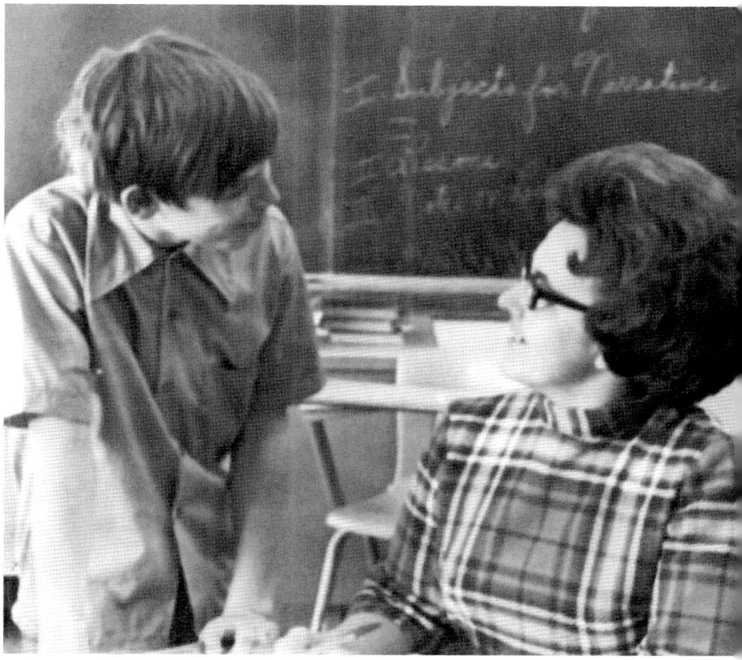

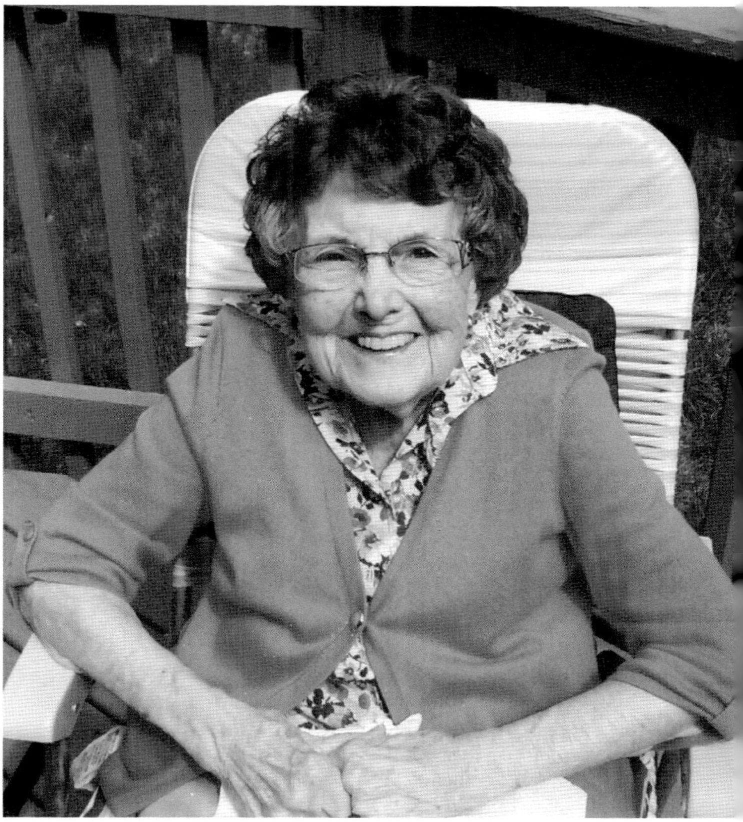

Marian Lones

Marian Anderson Lones began teaching in Pine City in 1947 and retired in 1991, finishing a 30-year career. She missed a few years to raise children, because maternity leave was not an option in those days. Lones taught multiple generations of families. For example, she taught Henry and Janice Korf, as well as all three of their daughters, all three of their sons-in-law, and one of their grandchildren. She was offered the job from Superintendent Victor Ziebarth for $2,200 a year. Medford schools offered her $100 more, but she chose Pine City because she thought it would be an easier commute to St. Paul, where she grew up.

Lones taught English in the seventh, eighth, and ninth grades in her first year at Pine City. That was before the classes consolidated in 1949–1950 and when there were still country schools. Over the years, she appreciated the tight-knit teacher community at Pine City High School. She married Bill Lones, who was born in the house on Third Avenue Southwest that she lives in today. Her father-in-law was Marion Lones, a city councilor when the downtown courthouse and city hall were built. Marian never met Marion.

Lones said, "Kids have to know their limits. I used to lay down the law in the first two days and I earned their respect." She was named Teacher of the Year in 1973 and was a Teacher of Excellence at the state level as well. The top photograph shows Lones and eighth-grader Steve Duzan. (Both, courtesy of Marian Lones.)

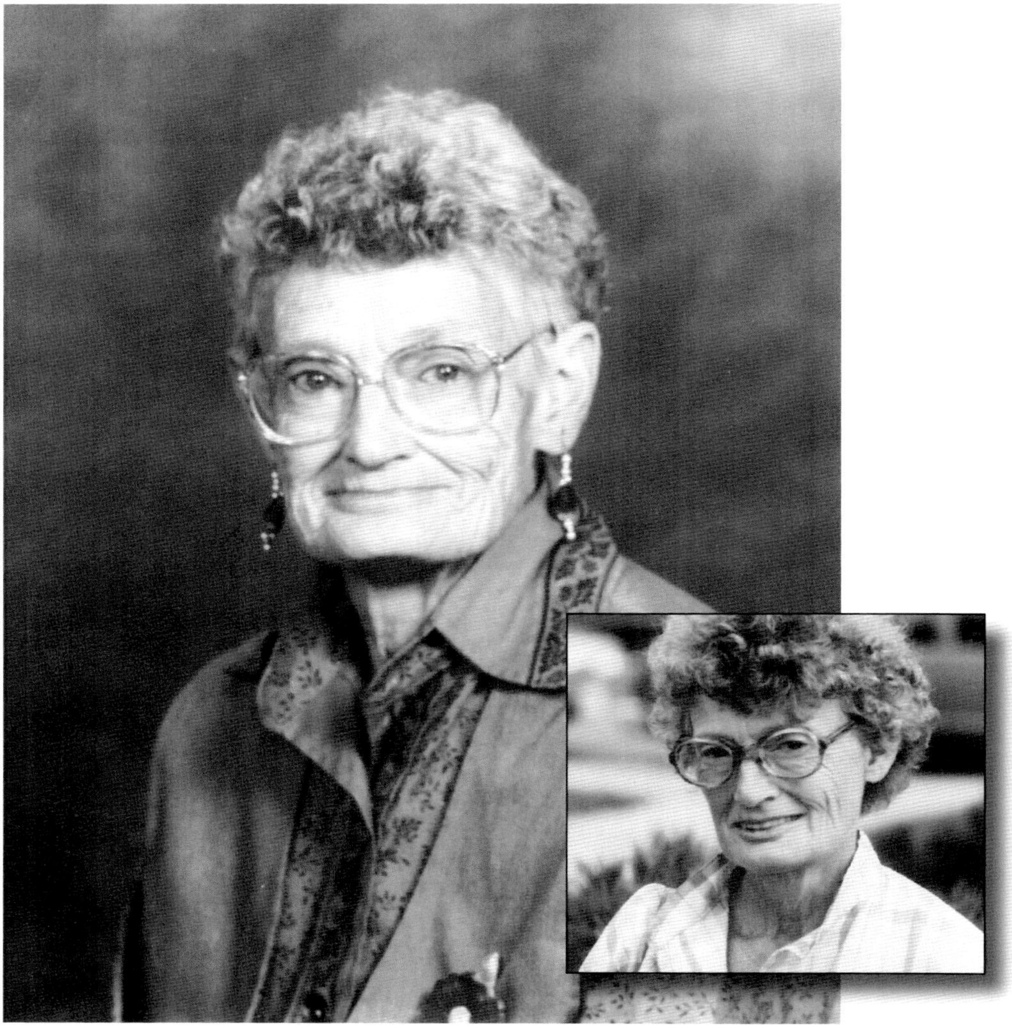

Betty Karas

Betty Jane Karas was born to Albert and Marie Boyle Robinson on September 28, 1925, on a farm in rural Pine City Township. She grew up on the farm and attended a nearby elementary school, later graduating from Pine City High School. She went on to enroll at the University of Cincinnati. While living in Ohio, she was employed by a pottery company. When Betty returned to Minnesota, she married Leslie Karas. They made their home on a dairy farm in rural Pine City, where they raised their seven children.

At one time, Betty worked at Plastech Corporation in Rush City and later as a lab technician at the Land O' Lakes milk-drying plant in Pine City. Throughout her life, she was a professional artist, and she taught art for 23 years to Pine City fourth, fifth, and sixth graders. Karas was a longtime 4-H leader and served in many capacities at the First Presbyterian Church in Pine City and for the wider Presbyterian church. She was active in garden clubs, painting groups, and the Pine City Heritage Players. She had an artistic eye that allowed her to see art in everyday objects, and she passed on that sense of discovery to her children, her students, and everyone she knew. In 1995, Betty Karas was honored as Citizen of the Year. She died at her daughter's Sunrise Township farm in Chisago County, at the age of 79, on August 27, 2005. (Both, courtesy of Robin Raudabaugh.)

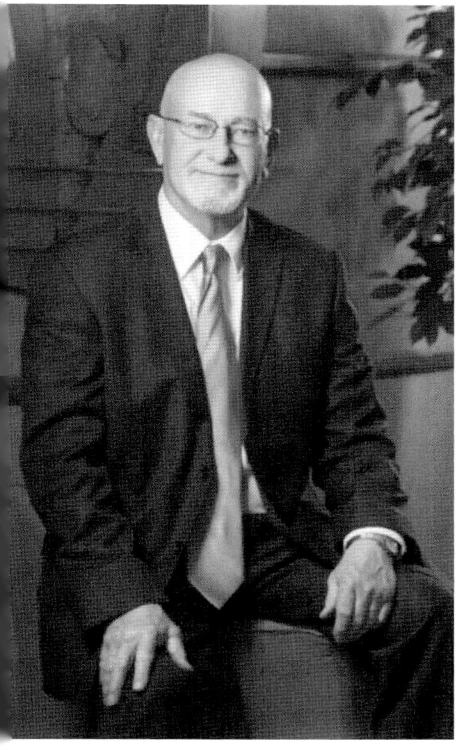

Robert Musgrove

Musgrove came to Pine City in July 1998, at the age of 48, from Sweetwater, Texas. Pine Technical College needed a president after Eugene Biever retired on June 30, 1998. Dr. Musgrove's qualifications were impressive, and he received the post. It was just two years after the school had been established as a state technical college, part of the Minnesota State Colleges and Universities system.

Musgrove received his bachelor of arts degree in English, graduating cum laude from the University of Texas in Austin. He received his master of arts in English and master of education in the state of Virginia. He earned his doctorate in educational administration in 1992 from the University of Texas. While at Pine Technical College, Musgrove helped it through a period of growth and increasing prestige. Under his leadership, the college grew to serve over 1,200 students and to offer programs and degrees in a variety of career fields previously not offered, including unique technology programs. In 2013, *Community College Week* named Pine Technical College one of the nation's Top 50 Community and Technical Colleges.

Musgrove, an Army veteran, is married to T.J., a Pine City realtor, and he is the father of two grown children. In 2007, he was named Citizen of the Year, and in 2011, the Pine City Lions honored him with a Community Leadership Award. (Courtesy of Del Gross.)

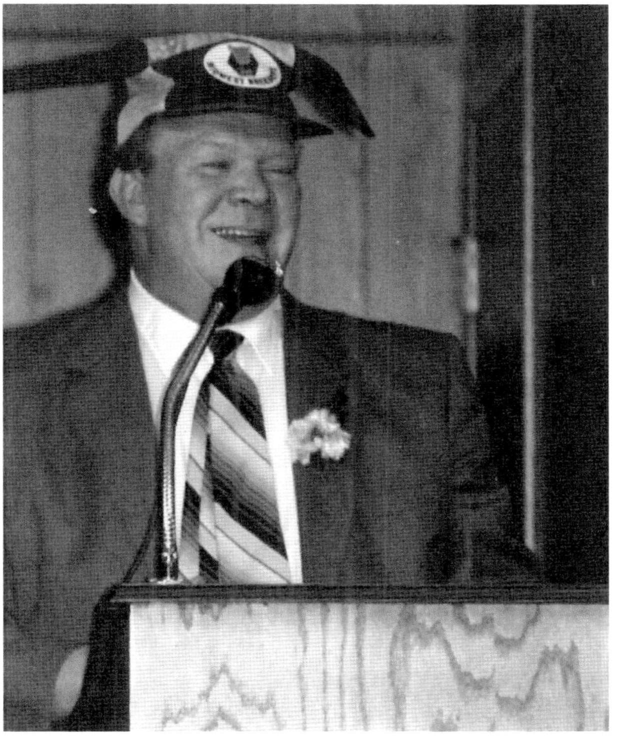

Gene Anderson

Eugene "Gene" Albert Anderson was born in Pokegama Township on November 5, 1933, the son of Carl E. and Elizabeth Cummings Anderson. He attended rural elementary school and Pine City High School, graduating in 1951. He and his wife had a son in 1962.

Besides Bob Haedt, Pine City had another Santa in Gene, who also dressed as a clown. A 1985 Christmas letter addressed to Santa Claus, Route 1, in Pine City was no mystery to the local postal employees. Anderson played Santa from 1966 to 1985, when he wanted to spend Christmas with his own family. He was named Citizen of the Year in 1991. He died on December 13, 1999, at Burnett General Hospital, following a fire at his home. (Courtesy of Tom Larson.)

Johanna Cox

Johanna Katherine Kubinski Cox was born on February 25, 1922, to Kasimierz and Anna Dziakowicz Kubinski in Northeast Minneapolis, where she lived until adulthood. In September 1947, she married Kenneth W. Cox of Pine City at St. Hedwig's Parish in Minneapolis, and then made her home in Pine City, where she lived the rest of her life.

While she and Kenneth were raising nine children, Johanna became known in her church and community for her active volunteer life. Her involvement earned many awards and acknowledgements, including the 1992 Pine City Citizen of the Year. Among her activities were the following: volunteer EMT with the Pine City ambulance service, scouts and 4-H leader, hospice volunteer, actress with the Heritage Players, 55 Alive instructor, Meals on Wheels delivery, Clown and Senior Singer, as well as numerous volunteer positions with her church and St. Mary's School. She was a driving force in getting the new senior center built in Pine City, and she served several terms as the president of the senior group. Cox also was an active member of both the VFW and American Legion Auxiliaries. Her voice was frequently heard on WCMP promoting various causes. In 1972, she began working at Cambridge State Hospital, where she successfully completed training as a psych tech. Cox retired in 1986.

She enjoyed traveling, first with Kenneth, then on her own, to Oregon, Ohio, and Texas to visit family. She traveled to Europe, and in 2002, attended her granddaughter's wedding in Hawaii. Her hobbies were arts and crafts, traveling, gardening, fishing, singing, and flirting. More than any of her own achievements, she was most proud of her wonderful family and friends. She believed strongly in God, her family, and her country. Johanna Cox loved life, lived it to the fullest, and would willingly do an encore. She passed away at her home on Friday, May 28, 2010, at the age of 88. (Both, courtesy of Jessica Carlson.)

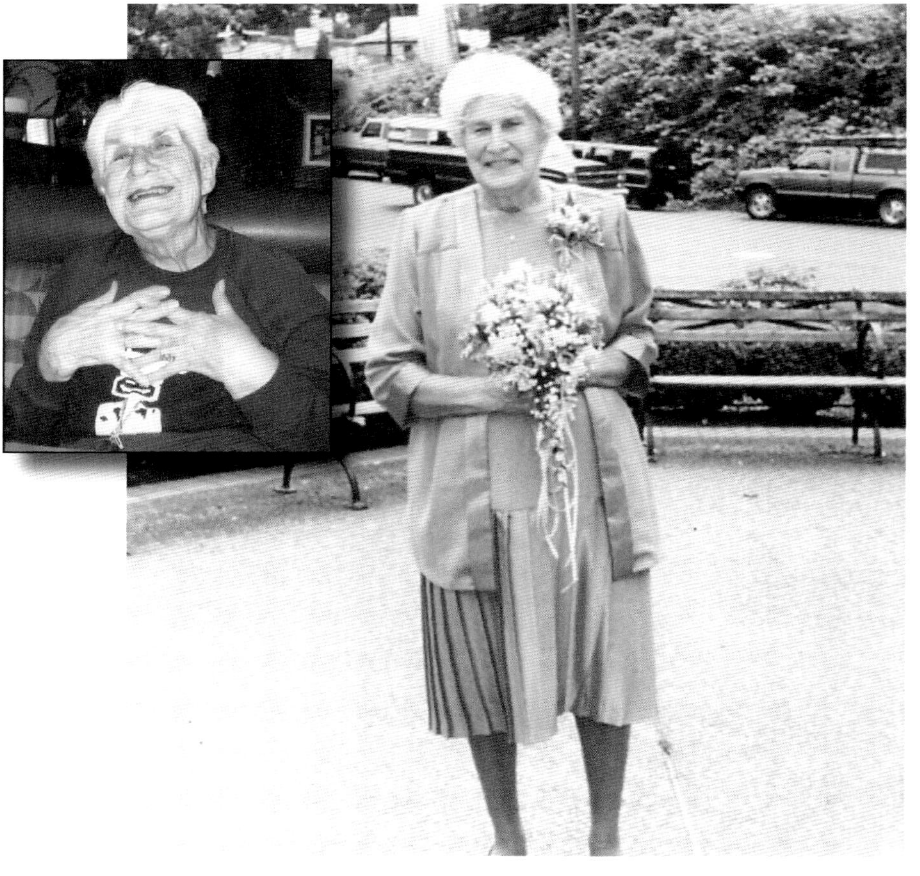

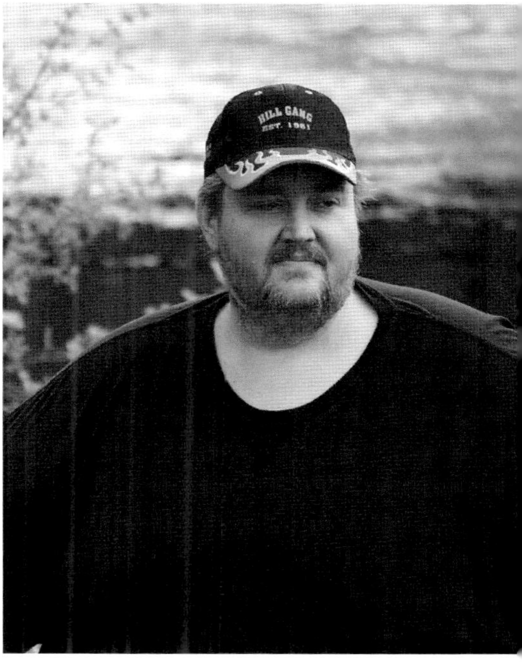

Marty Rike

Marty Rike always lived in Pine City, always was overweight, and was sometimes made fun of in school. But, he never imagined being made a national spectacle of due to his size, over 500 pounds.

In 2007, Marty underwent treatment to break up blood clots in his legs. His doctor suggested water therapy so he accepted an invitation to go tubing. He and fellow tubers set out on the St. Croix River—without regard to the shallow water depth. A sharp rock punctured Marty's tube and he began to drag. He tried to get to shore but the water became deeper. Marty slipped, hurting his ankle, knees and shoulder. That began a difficult, 12-hour rescue involving nearly 50 personnel, and aircraft, from the bi-state area. Pine City Fire tied canoes together and floated Marty to a landing.

After the ordeal, there was a cruel editorial in an area newspaper, followed by a nasty joke by Jay Leno on *The Tonight Show.* Then, a KQRS (92.5 FM) radio show dug into Marty. Pine Citians showed their support for Marty countering the attacks. KQRS responded by inviting Marty to the station for an on-air apology. (Photograph by Noah Sikkink.)

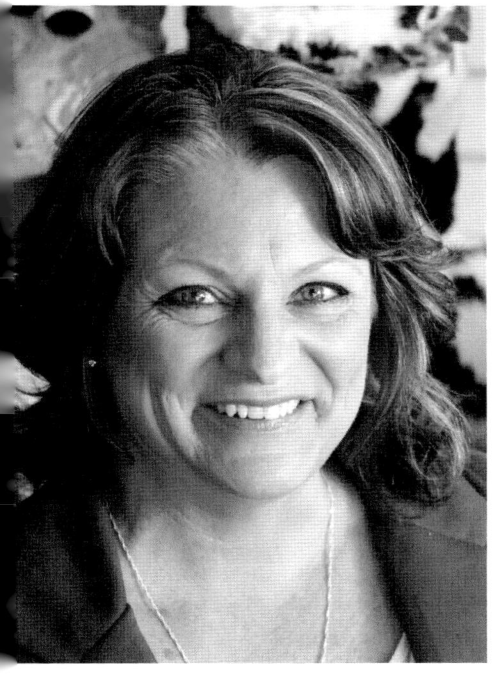

Kris Seuntjens

Many people should take credit for the creation of Pine Center for the Arts, but Kristin "Kris" (Magnusen) Seuntjens wins a big share of the praise.

Growing up with an artist dad, Kris began playing violin at the age of nine. Trained in education, Kris worked at WDSE-TV (PBS, Duluth) and also taught at John Duss Music Conservatory. Her family's Blue Hippo Productions came about in 1988, and subsequently *Rhythm Sticks*, an educational and animated show using a mix of puppets, claymation, and live action. She was also a contributor for the best-seller "Chicken Soup for the Kid's Soul."

While looking for a place to film *Rhythm Sticks,* various Pine City buildings were considered, including a former Methodist church and courthouse. She and her friends became inspired to create an arts center in town to support music, dance, theater and literature. In November 2008, the first arts center event was held: "Ball in the House" performed to a sellout crowd.

With the longstanding tradition of community theater, concerts, and events, Kris feels Pine Center for the Arts helps the city be branded as an arts destination. (Photograph by Noah Sikkink.)

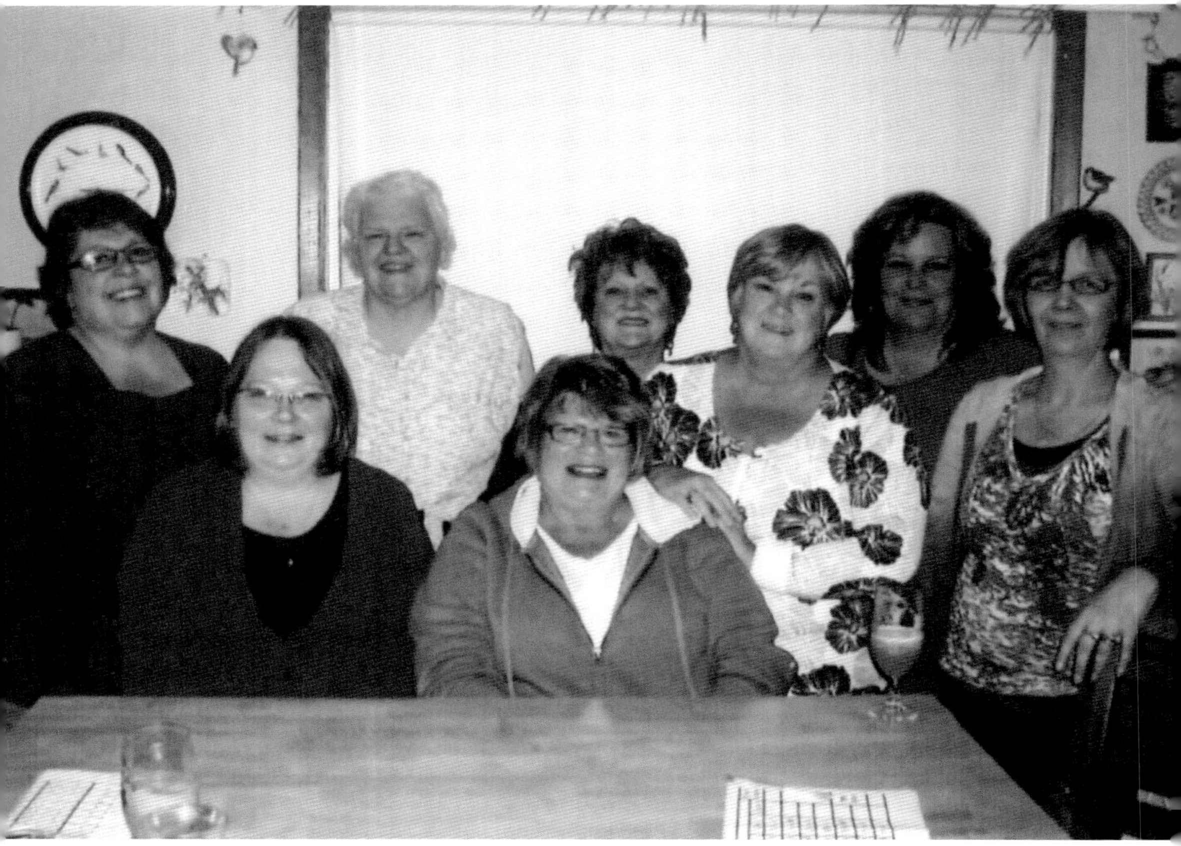

500 Club

In 1984, eight women from Pine City began playing 500 together once a month, taking turns at one another's homes. These women—Chris Horn, Linda Haug, Peg Irlbeck, Denise Novak, Peggy Wasson, Sue Smetana, LeAnn Bergstrom, and Deb Fore—were the founding members of the card club that still meets monthly to this day.

Early on, Wendy Johnson replaced Sue Smetana, and Karen Teich replaced LeAnn Bergstrom, but the rest of the group is intact. Over the years, Lila Irlbeck, Mary Anderson, Shirley Martfeld, Judy Zastera, and Franny Southwick have filled in from time to time so that the required eight players were present. All of these women have meant more to each other than just a little monthly entertainment; they have been there for one another through thick and thin, in sickness and health, from when they were raising toddlers of their own to helping raise their grandchildren. Shown here in 2011 in the home of Chris Horn are, from left to right, (back row) Wendy Johnson, Chris Horn, Linda Haug, Peg Irlbeck, Tammy Kraft, and Denise Novak; (front row) Peggy Wasson and Karen Teich. (Courtesy of Karen Teich.)

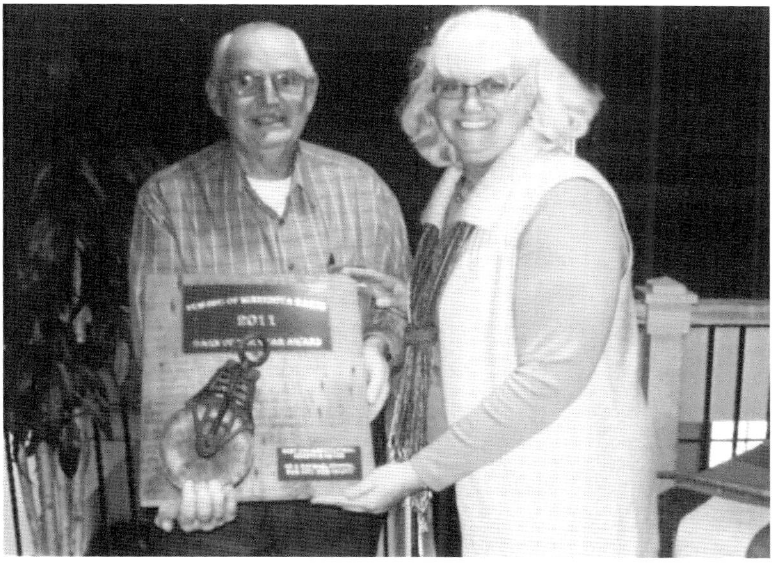

Ed Stoffel

Over the generations, the Stoffel family has saved just about everything that had any kind of bearing on their history. So much so that they were able to open their own museum. With over 80 years of memorabilia, Ed Stoffel, the youngest of 11 children, and his wife, Rachel, have opened the restored barn on their family farm to the public as the Stoffel Family Memorabilia Museum. The collection includes old photographs, antique farm equipment, and the clothes worn by Ed's parents at their 1917 wedding.

Ed has had a longstanding involvement with the Pine County Historical Society, and he has an avid interest in preserving history. The above photograph shows Ed Stoffel and Marlene Pixley (museum curator) receiving the 2011 Barn of the Year award from Friends of Minnesota Barns on behalf of the Stoffel Family Memorabilia Museum. Below, the surviving Stoffel siblings pose in 1995. They are, from left to right, (seated) Ernest, Ed, and George Stoffel; (standing) Elizabeth "Betty" Wurm, Marcella Dion, Dorothy Pixley, Theresa Kowacovich, Rosemary Schultz, Eileen Brenberg, and Dolores Eich. (Both, courtesy of Ed Stoffel.)

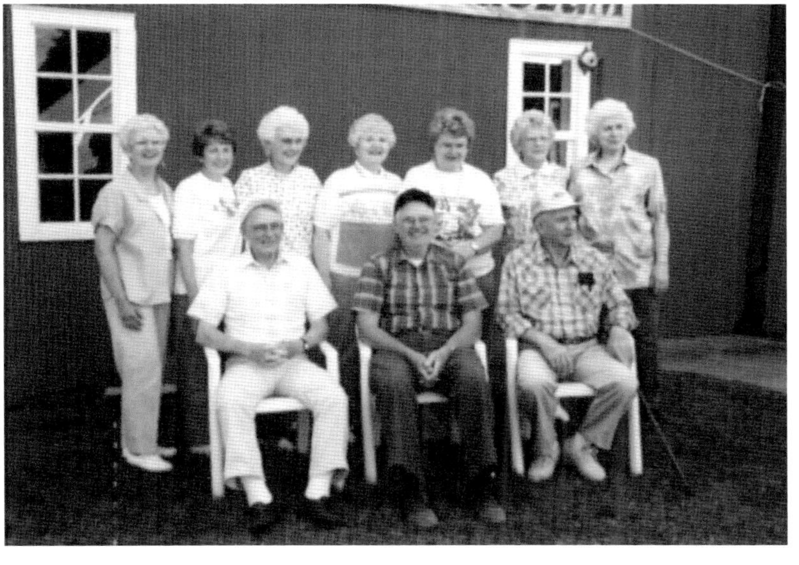

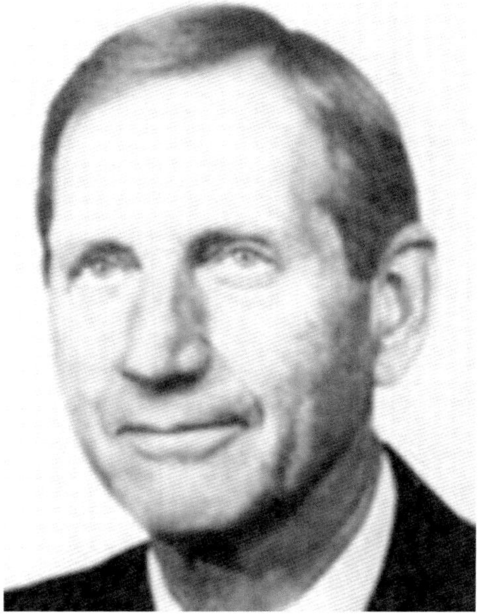

Benjamin C. Boo

Benjamin Boo was Pine City mayor from 1927 to 1930. He was born in Pine City and a graduate of Pine City High School, before serving in the Minnesota National Guard. As of October 14, 1958, he had served in active duty as administration officer at the Duluth Armory for approximately five years. His rank was lieutenant colonel. There, he became the purchasing agent for St. Louis County. He moved back to Pine City, where he was a lawyer, banker, and a lumber dealer. He married Henrietta M. Boo, and they had three boys and three girls. His sons were Benjamin Boo, Dr. James Boo, and Peter Boo.

Ben Jr., born in 1925, was the 33rd mayor of Duluth (1967–1975) and a member of the Minnesota House of Representatives from 1984 to 1993. During his time as mayor, Ben Jr. was involved with advancing tourism in Duluth, including the creation of Spirit Mountain. After leaving office, he became executive director in the Western Lake Superior Sanitary District (WLSSD), a position he held until 1979. He was elected to an open seat in the legislature in a special election in 1983, then reelected in 1984, 1986, 1988, and 1990. At the time, the district included portions of St. Louis County.

Benjamin C. Boo's daughters were Mary Boo, Barbara Boo Jenkins, and Henrietta Lydia Boo, who was born on May 28, 1934. When Henrietta was just 12, her father died. She attended Pine City High School and the University of Minnesota, where she received a dental hygiene degree in 1956. She married Hosea Peter Hudson of North Carolina while working at the University of Minnesota's dental school. Henrietta achieved public fame through a gift of life on September 18, 1990, when Methodist Hospital surgeons did what had never been done before in the nation, simultaneously transplanting to five persons organs from one donor, Pete Oltman III, who died at age 21. Henrietta became the longest-living single-lung transplant patient in Indiana, and one of the longest living in the world. She passed away on May 17, 2001. She is credited with assisting the Pine City Library renovation and expansion in 2011. The Boo family said it would donate $200,000 if the community could match it, which it did. (Author's collection.)

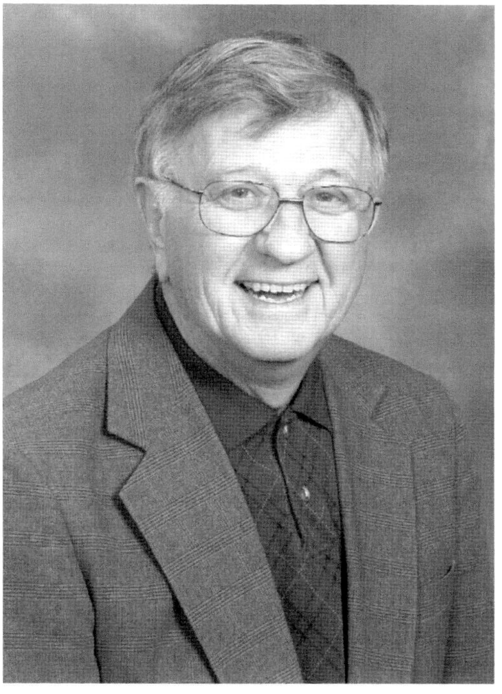

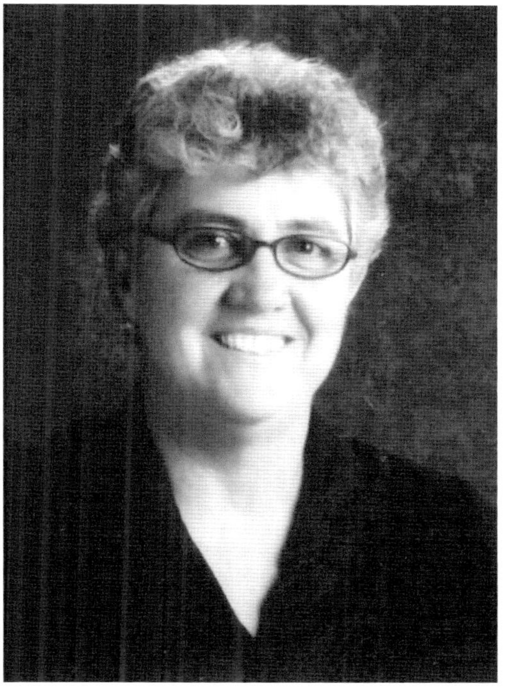

Deacon Gene Biever and Mary K. Sloan

Having worked at Pine City schools since 1977, Mary Kay Sloan noticed that some students slept in their cars in the school's parking lot. Deacon Gene Biever was president of the college in town and noticed homelessness as well. Their heightened sensitivity to people's needs made them realize that something had to be done. Sloan and Biever understood that most were local residents who want to stay in their hometown, but with shelter lacking, they had to leave Pine City in order to escape a homeless life. Sloan and Biever solicited the help of many in the community, championing the cause. A new shelter was opened, the only one between Duluth and the Twin Cities.

Today, local homeless residents have options. Many across the state have had the same vision, but lacked the human capital to meet the need. These two knew how to garner resources. Besides donating thousands of hours to the shelter, they wrote grants and letters and found help for everything to get it off the ground. They organized people to renovate the building, obtain donations of furniture, and perform other tasks. On a typical week, Sloan and Biever spent between 25 and 30 hours at the shelter, answering phones and doing what was needed to keep it operational.

It is because of Mary Kay Sloan and Gene Biever that Pine City—and Minnesota, for that matter—is now more responsive to the issue of homelessness. Sloan was elected to the city council of Pine City in January 2011, having previously served as chair of the planning commission. In 2007, she received the city's first Citizen Planner Award. She was honored for her level of involvement, overall positive effect on the community, length of commitment, and leadership. As a planning commissioner, she was instrumental in educating the general public about planning issues such as density, setbacks, and trail route planning, but she also was instrumental in helping build awareness about homelessness. Biever was Pine City's Citizen of the Year in 1994. (Left, courtesy of Gene Biever; right, courtesy of Mary K. Sloan.)

Bob Foster

Perhaps the front-page article of the *Pine City Pioneer* of May 22, 1997, said it best: "Where there's a need, you'll find Bob Foster." Foster was involved with the local American Legion Post, served with the Veterans of Foreign Wars (VFW) for 27 years, and was the chaplain for both groups. He made many visits to area nursing homes and served as the volunteer minister for 23 years at the Lakeside Nursing Home in Pine City, where he stayed up nights holding the hands of the dying and praying with the sick. He held services there every Sunday—holidays, too—and officiated at almost 300 funerals for town residents.

Foster was a Pine City native, born there on June 16, 1926, one of eight boys and two girls. He and five of his brothers served in the military, five in the Army and one in the Navy. He was an Army aviation engineer from 1943 to 1946, spending much of that time in the South Pacific at places like Okinawa and Iwo Jima. When Foster returned home to Pine City after the war, he married Helen Points of Cambridge, and the two set up residence in Duluth before returning to Pine City, where he was employed by the Coca-Cola Bottling, becoming the plant's sales manager. He then became a Pine City village deputy and, in 1971, was appointed a Pine County sheriff's deputy.

Foster had an affinity toward the town's youth. He organized hygiene-product giveaways; hundreds of former students owe their well-groomed faces, teeth, and hair to him and his wife, Helen. The two made health kits for every fourth grader in Pine City from 1985 to 1992. He was also involved in the "Voices of Democracy" youth essay program and a youth safety patrol. His post was awarded the American Legion's Outstanding Post for Children and Youth in 1989–1990. Foster was awarded the Ray Kreitall Memorial Chaplain Award in 1973–1974, 1979–1980, 1988, and 1990. In 1983, he was named Volunteer of the Year by the Minnesota Association of Health Care Facilities; and, in 1993, he was the 10th District Post Service Officer of the Year. He passed away on July 19, 2002, at the age of 76. (Courtesy of Helen Foster.)

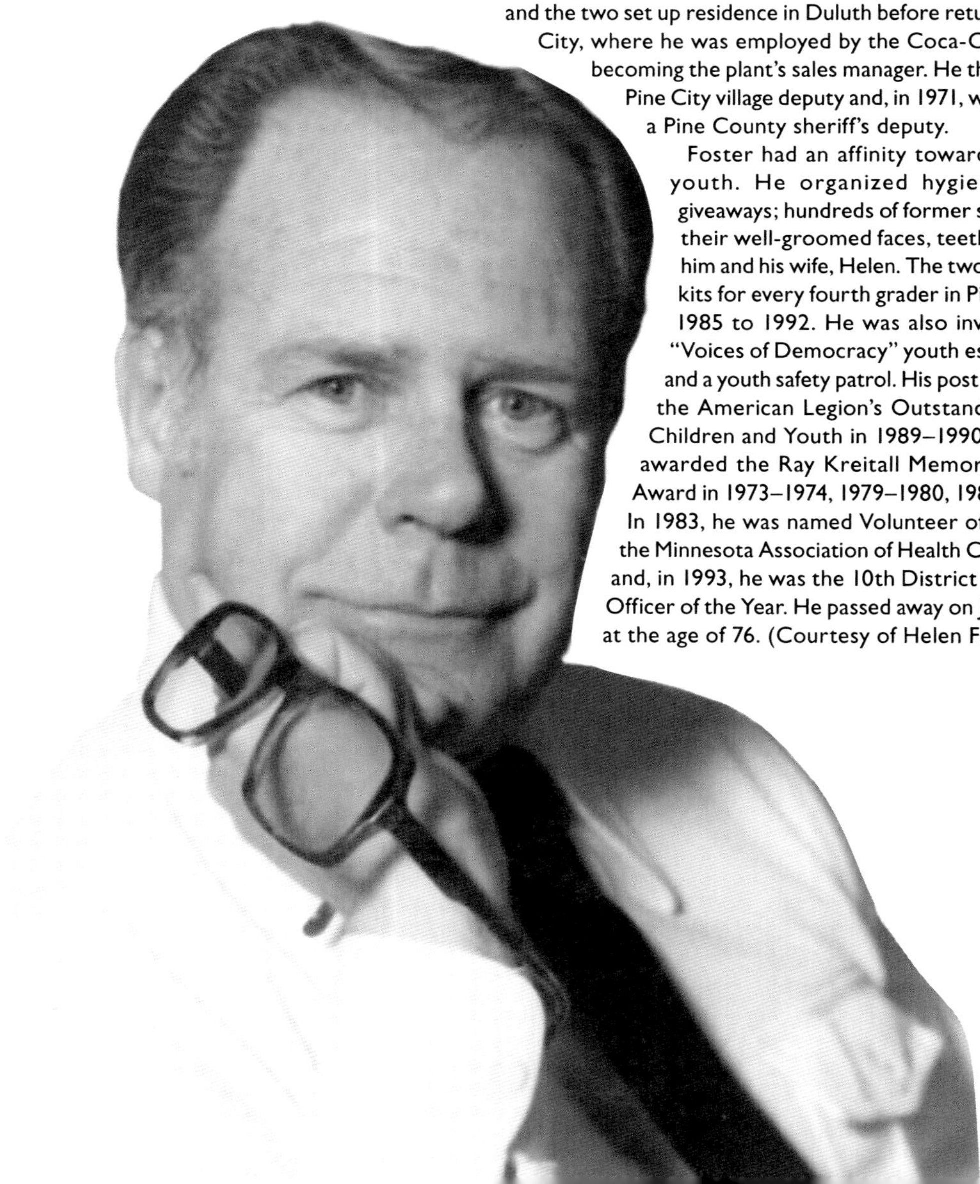

CHAPTER NINE

Their Remembrance Lives On

There are many whose legacy lives on long after they are gone, like Olivia M. Erickson, who was born in March 1883 and died in April 1973. Known as "Redtop," she lived in Redtop, Minnesota, and the unincorporated place near Isle is said to have been named after her.

And then there was Helen J. Myers, a native of Pine City, who founded and was a director for the Russell Bede School, a place of learning for children with various forms of learning disabilities located in San Mateo, California. Myers, a graduate from Notre Dame High School in Belmont, California, began an after-school tutoring program in her home in 1981. She was inspired by her father, Russell Bede, who had a learning disability. In 1983, she renamed the school after him.

Sometimes, disease takes one's life, other times it is sudden tragedy. Let us not forget them, the people in these chapters, and others who come to mind.

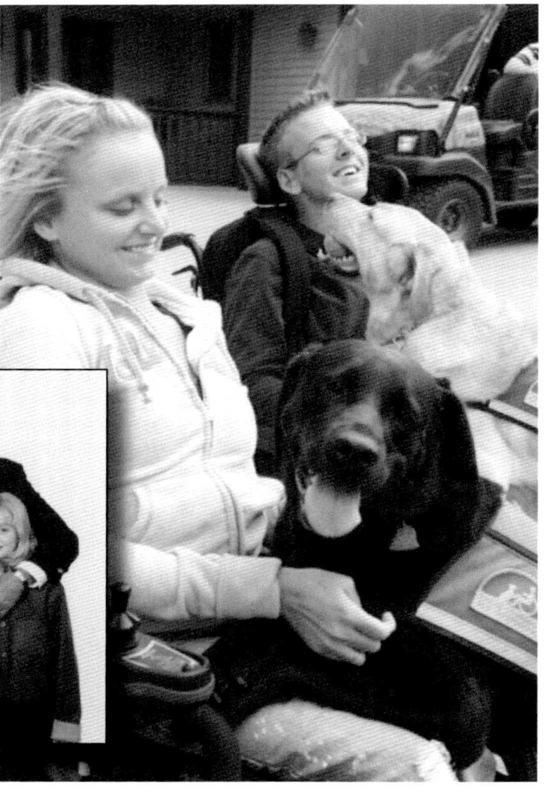

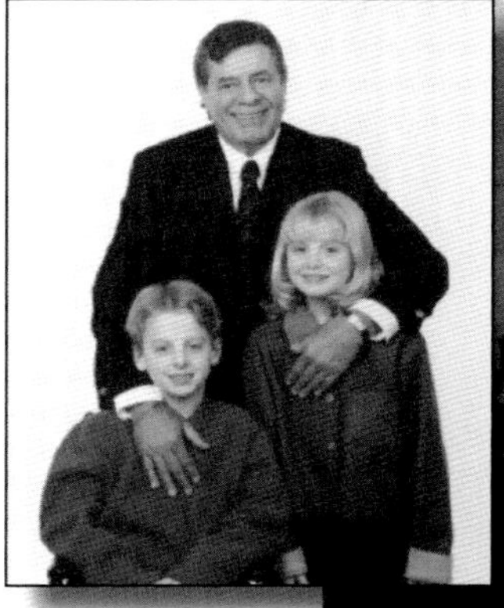

Aubrey and Nick Olson

In 1998–1999, siblings Aubrey Olson and Nicholas Olson were national ambassadors for the Muscular Dystrophy Association. Despite having the disease Friedreich's ataxia (FA), they didn't let it slow them down. Aubrey was able to participate in graduation ceremonies in May at the University of Minnesota and play soccer with a wheelchair team in St. Louis. She was close to completing a degree in child psychology, with a goal of attending law school. When she attended class, she was accompanied by a service dog, Kethry, a black Labrador retriever known for snoring during lectures. Aubrey played power soccer in tournaments across the country, swam, and skied using adaptive skiing equipment. In her spare time, she was a volunteer for a homeless shelter in Minneapolis. Aubrey died at the age of 23, just two months after Nicholas passed away at the age of 21. Nicholas was a mischievous brother, homecoming king, and contributor to research about FA. He crammed more impressive achievements, good deeds, and mischievous fun into his short life than many people manage across multiple decades.

The disease forced Nicholas to use a back brace, then a walker, then a wheelchair, by fourth grade. He appreciated when he received an electric wheelchair. As he grew, the challenges intensified. At age 14, he was hit by a car, suffering broken bones and a brain injury. At the same time, the FA was attacking his vision, hearing, and speech. Yet, he continued to travel with his family, including to Europe; make his friends smile and tease his sisters; attend Pine City High School, where in 2007 he was elected homecoming king; and earn Eagle Scout honors by building a handicapped-accessible ramp at a pavilion at Pine City's Robinson Park. As locomotion and speech became more difficult, he spent more time watching CNN, especially for any news about Pres. Barack Obama, whom he admired.

As MDA National Goodwill Ambassadors, Aubrey and Nick traveled across America for two years, representing MDA and the families it serves. They appeared on the Jerry Lewis Telethon. The entire family became active MDA volunteers after Aubrey and Nick were diagnosed with FA in 1995. (Both, courtesy of the Muscular Dystrophy Association.)

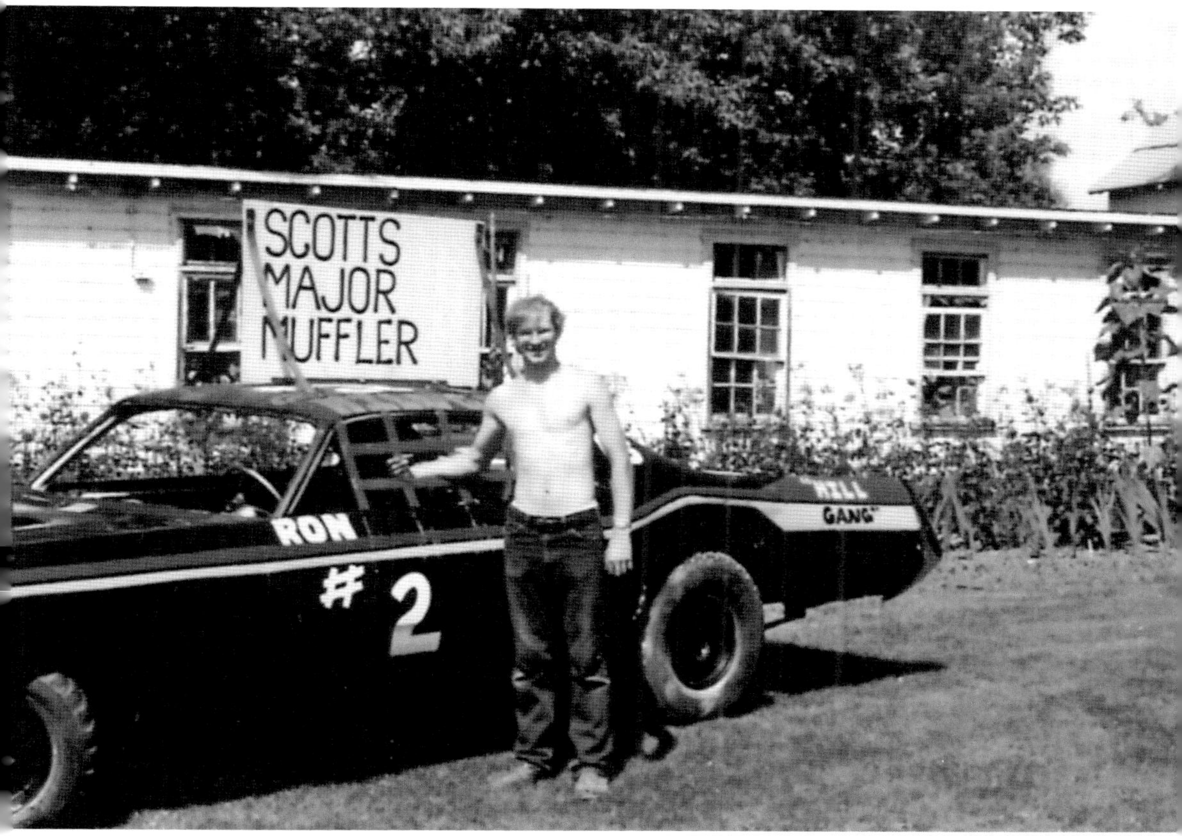

Ronald Cox

Ronald Cox, known as Ronnie to most, was born a twin, with Bobby Cox, on February 12, 1958. He attended elementary school at St. Mary's Catholic School and graduated from Pine City High School in 1976. While still in school, he started participating in demolition derbies. His garage had shelves lined with 30 years of trophies from running in derbies at county fairs across the state. He often came in first place. Ronnie's trademark car was a black, yellow, and orange "Hill Gang" car with the number 2 painted on it. But, as of 2006, he was not able to run any longer. Ronnie suffered from sarcoidosis, an inflammatory lung disease. So, in 2011, at his hometown demolition derby at the Pine County Fair, friends of Ronnie's threw a benefit called "Wreckin' for Ronnie" in front of 5,000 spectators. The funds raised went to medical expenses. The day showcased about 15 cars, all painted the way Ronnie used to paint his in one of the derby heats. A raffle was held, with the prize being a demolition derby car painted in Ronnie's colors.

Cox passed away at the age of 54, just prior to the Pine County Fair, on July 31, 2012. His No. 2 was retired. He has been credited for helping to make the demolition derby in Pine City one of the best around.

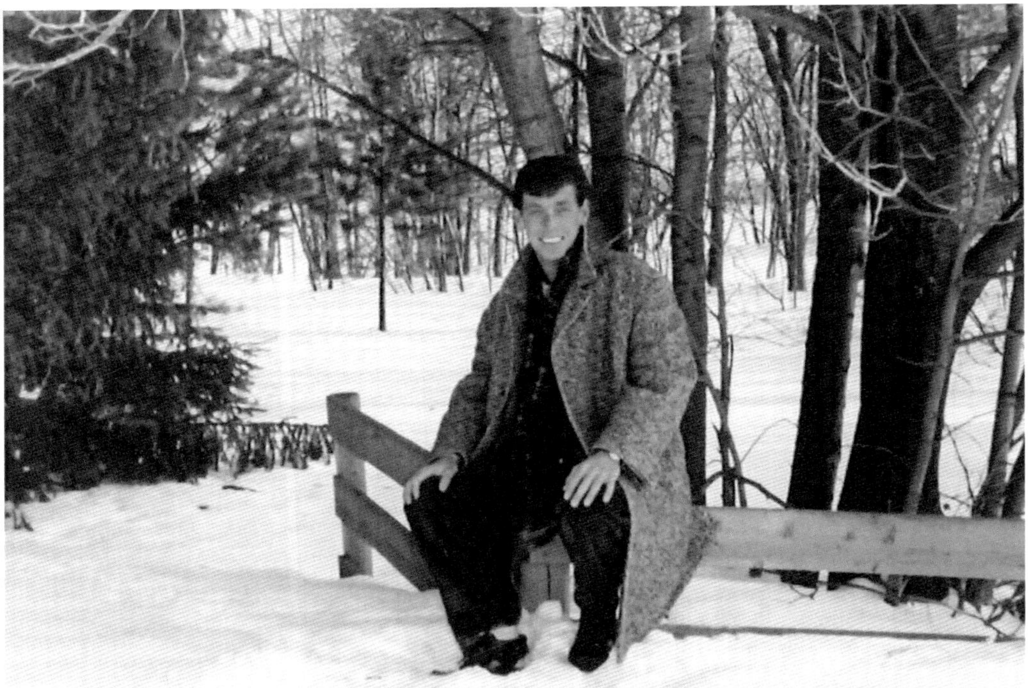

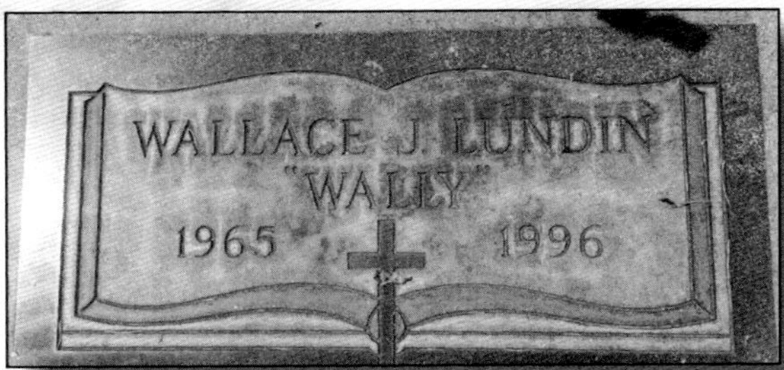

Wally Lundin

Wallace J. Lundin was born on August 1, 1965. Like many rural gay youth, he fled his hometown for the big city, in his case, Minneapolis, after he graduated in 1983. That fall, he landed a job at American Express and started college. He attended the Minnesota School of Business and graduated from National College. After working at American Express for 12 years, in April 1996, he was found dead from asphyxiation in his northeast Minneapolis duplex. Always punctual, coworkers became concerned when he didn't show up for work on Monday morning. The case lay cold for nearly a dozen years. In 2007, DNA evidence linked Rommal Bennett to the murder.

Lundin enjoyed being with friends and was always on the go, traveling to Miami every winter and often talking about moving south because of his displeasure with Minnesota winters. Lundin was one of several gay men murdered in the 1990s whose deaths went unsolved. As a result, Dallas Drake of Minneapolis founded the Center for Homicide Research, the first place in the nation to study gay homicide. Drake has become a relied-upon consultant to homicide investigators. (Top, courtesy of the Lundin family; bottom, author's collection.)

Aaron Anderson

Aaron Mitchell Anderson was born on June 23, 1987. He had light brown hair and brown eyes and a small white birthmark on the lower right side of his abdomen. He was last seen at approximately 4:30 p.m. on April 7, 1989, playing in the yard of his family's Pine City residence bordering the Snake River. His mother left him unattended for a couple of minutes, and he vanished. He has not been seen since, despite extensive search efforts. While authorities believe Aaron may have fallen in the water and drowned, his family believes he may have been abducted. The case remains open and unsolved.

In 1993, Aaron's picture appeared in the music video for the Minnesota-based band Soul Asylum's song "Runaway Train." After his picture was shown, his full name appeared in large capital letters on the screen, along with the words "missing since April 7, 1989." Anyone with information concerning this case should contact the Pine County Sheriff's Office at 320-629-3930. This is a rendering of what Aaron might look like in 2013, at the age of 26. (Both, courtesy of National Center for Missing & Exploited Children.)

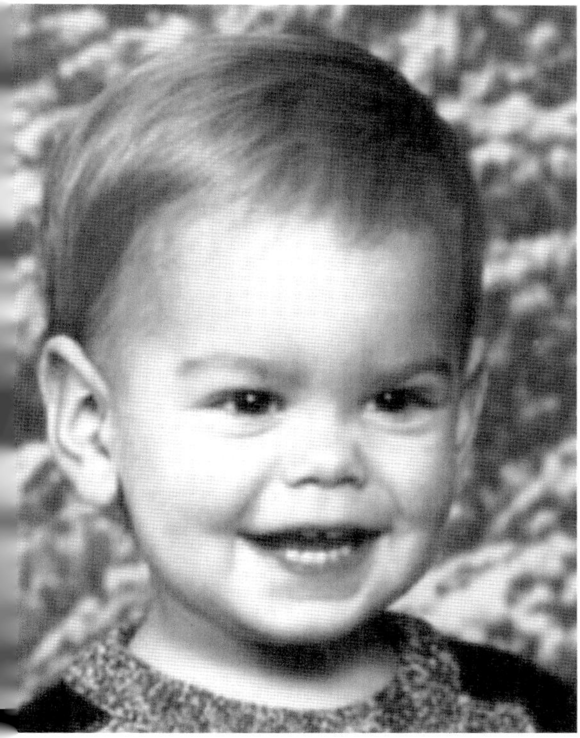

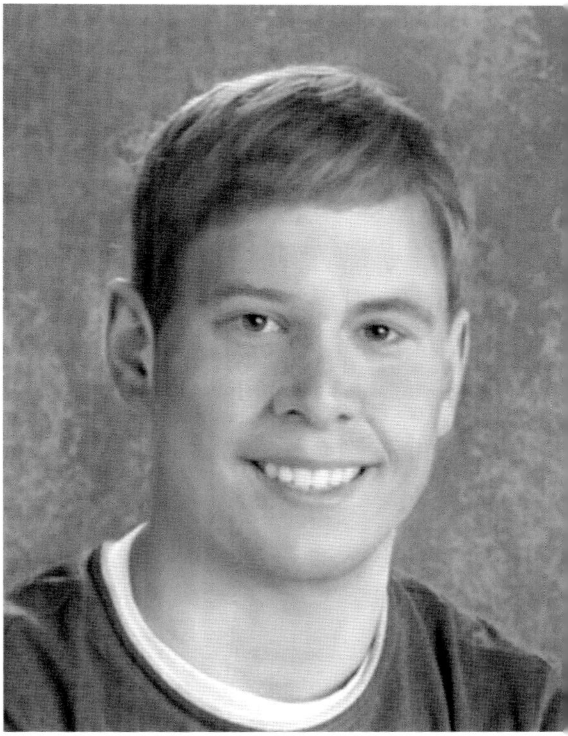

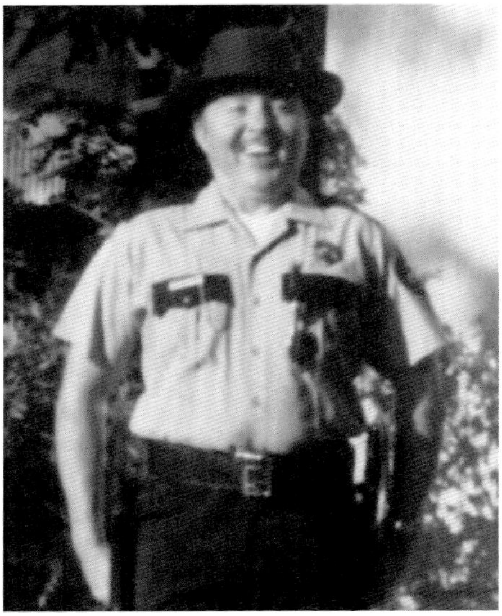

Michael Morrow

After putting in 11 years of service with the Pine County Sheriff's Department, Michael Morrow's life was taken in the line of duty. He was beaten to death with his own flashlight at the age of 53. The date was August 24, 2001, and it was 2:27 a.m. when Deputy Morrow radioed in a traffic stop, saying he was stopping a Chevrolet Citation on County Road 14 north of Pine City. Another deputy was sent to investigate when dispatch was unable to make contact with Morrow after 15 minutes of attempting to do so. Morrow was found with severe head wounds, lying unconscious behind his squad car with the lights still flashing. Broken glass was everywhere, Morrow's flashlight was missing, and his baton was found lying in front of the vehicle with blood on it. After being transported to Rush City Hospital, he was pronounced dead at 5:05 a.m. due to a skull fracture. The suspect's vehicle was found four miles from the scene at 7:00 a.m. with Morrow's flashlight in it and the left window broken out. The suspect, Scott Lange, was 25 at the time. His release date was set for February 20, 2006.

Morrow left behind his wife, Beatrice, two children, Elizabeth and Michael Jr., as well as five grandchildren. His funeral, which brought officers from around the state, was held on Wednesday, August 28, 2001, at the Pine City High School gym. Morrow's badge, No. 425, was retired. (Both, courtesy of Beatrice Morrow.)

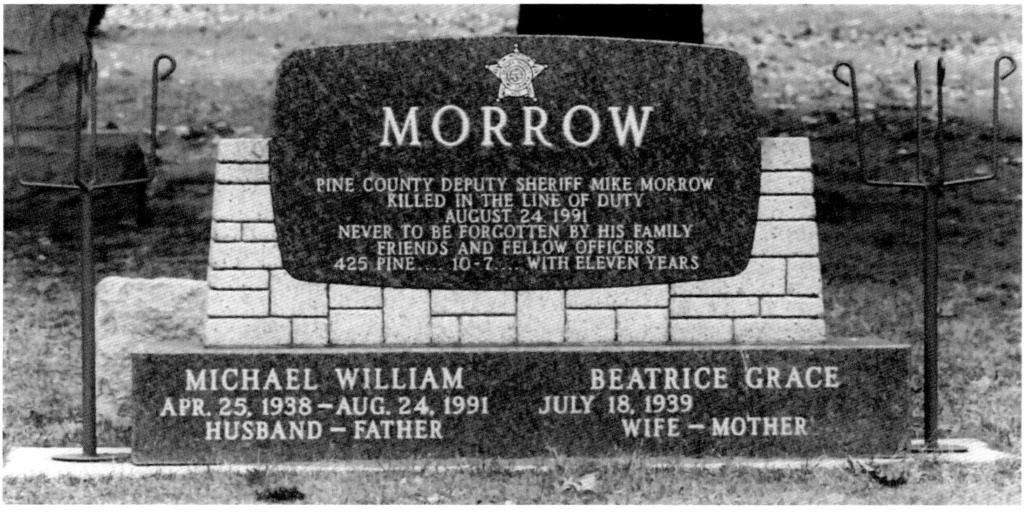

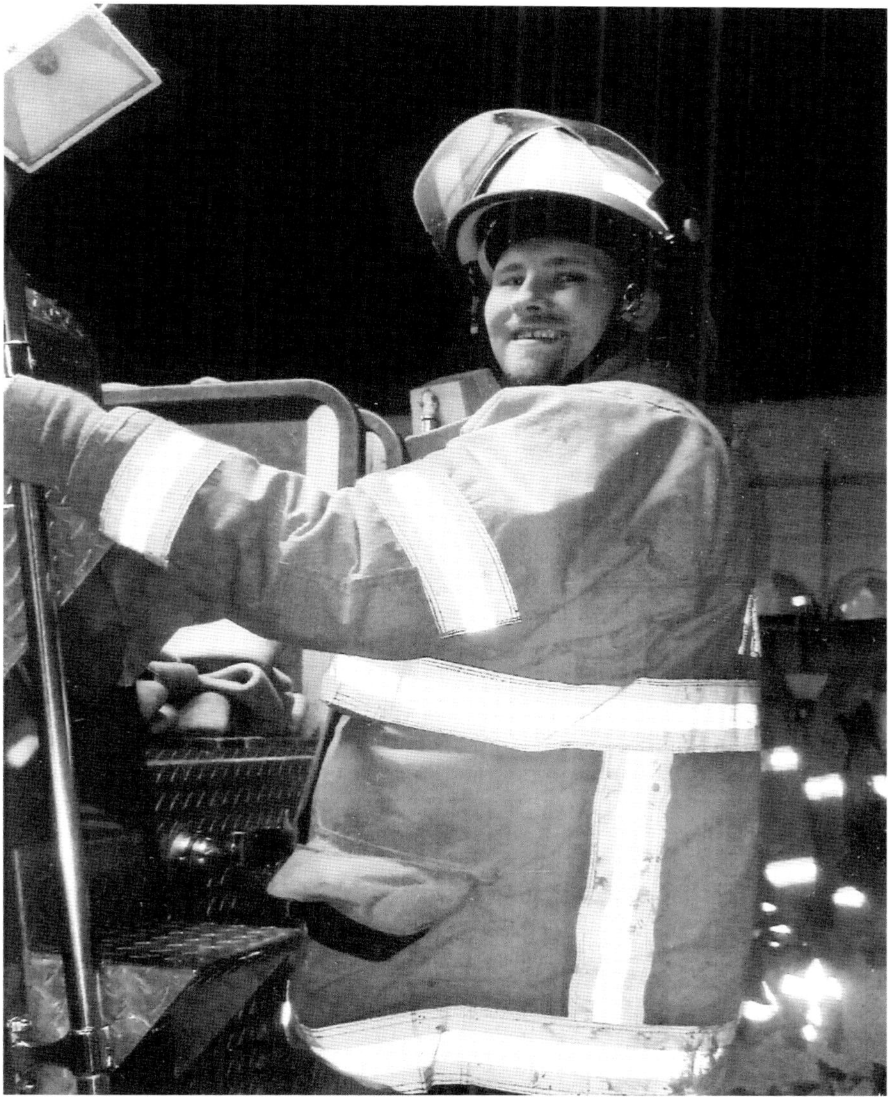

Jeremy Jylka

Jeremy L. Jylka joined the Pine City Fire Department on May 1, 2007. The firefighter died in the line of duty on Tuesday, April 29, 2008, while responding to a grass fire. He was a passenger in a grass rig when he experienced a medical condition and became unresponsive. Another firefighter began CPR, and Jylka was transported by ambulance to Kanabec Hospital in Mora, Minnesota, where he succumbed to his injuries. He was pronounced dead shortly after admittance at the age of 34.

Jylka left behind his wife, Kelley, and his four-year-old daughter, Anica. A full-honors funeral was planned. The wake was held on Sunday, May 4, 2008, at Our Redeemer Lutheran Church in Pine City, with Gov. Tim Pawlenty in attendance. The funeral was held on Monday, May 5, 2008. The Minnesota Fallen Firefighters Memorial Association (MFFMA) color guard assisted, and the service included the fireman's prayer, bagpipes, a procession of trucks, and other traditions.

Born in Two Harbors, Minnesota, Jylka graduated from Staples High School in 1993 and served two years in the US Navy. He worked for Product Fabricators in Pine City. (Courtesy of Kelly Jylka).

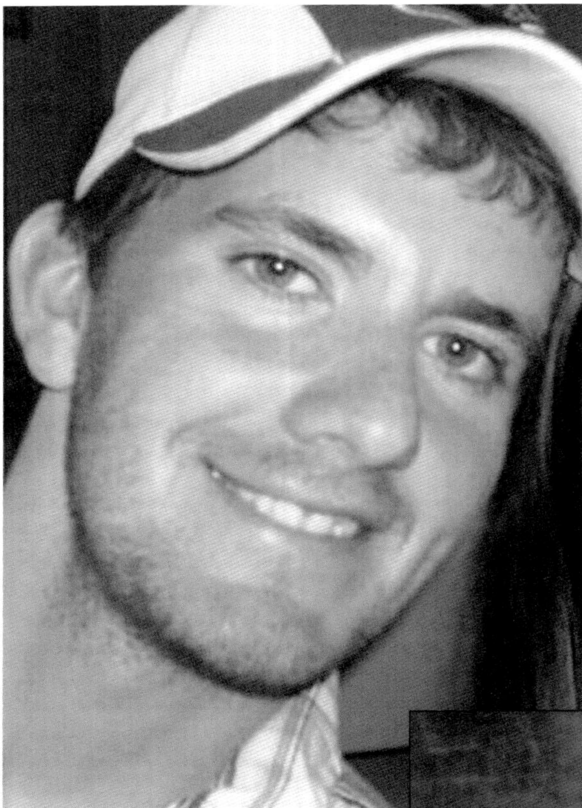

Beau Berglund

Beau Richard Berglund was born on July 25, 1984, in nearby Mora. He had two older siblings, Jade and Holly. Beau attended Pine City Elementary School and Pine City High School. Though he was diagnosed with brain cancer by age 15, that did not stop him from doing the things his brother and dad did, such as fish, hunt, and be outdoors. He especially loved hockey, and he played for Pine City.

Beau died at the age of 25, on August 7, 2009, at Abbott-Northwestern Hospital in Minneapolis. His funeral was held at the Pine City Civic Center (formerly Korbel Arena) on August 12, 2009. The venue was packed with Beau's friends, family, and former teammates. Beau's Dragon hockey number, 32, was retired, and his jersey still adorns the wall there. Beginning in 2010, an annual hockey tournament has been held in his honor. (Both, courtesy of Jade Berglund).

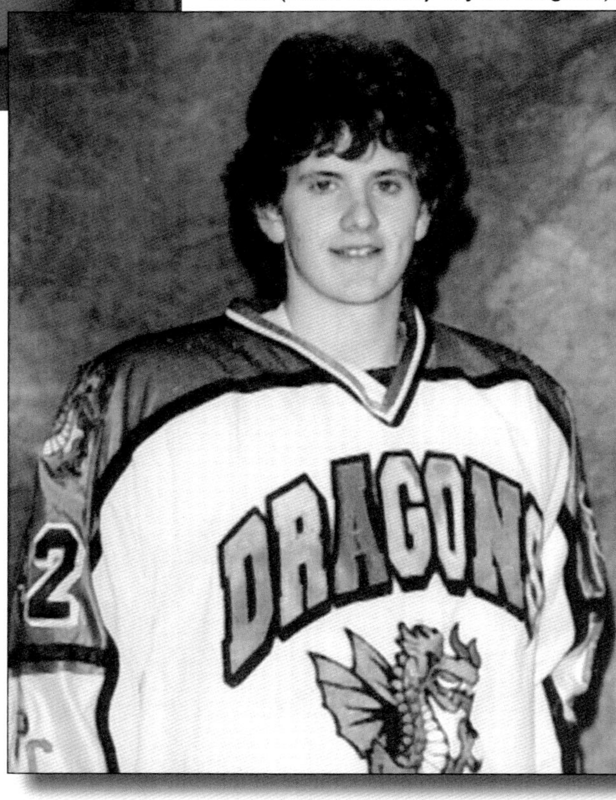

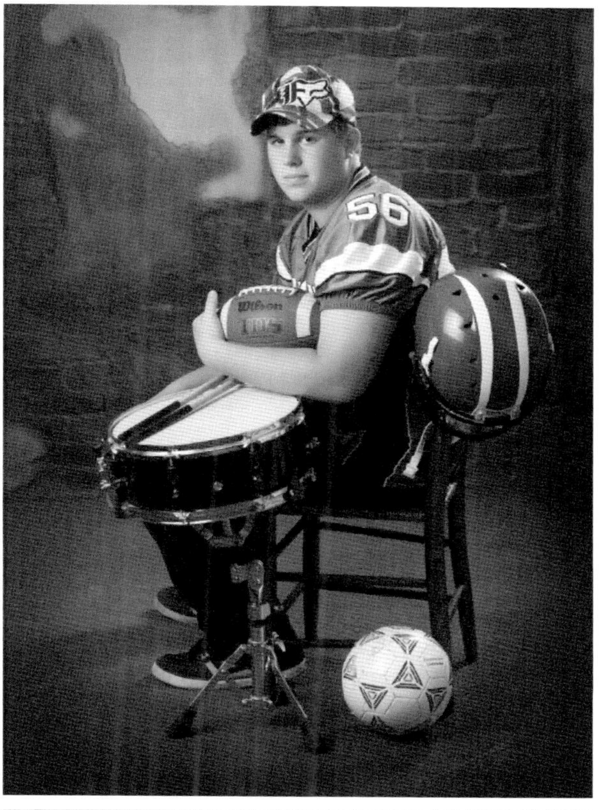

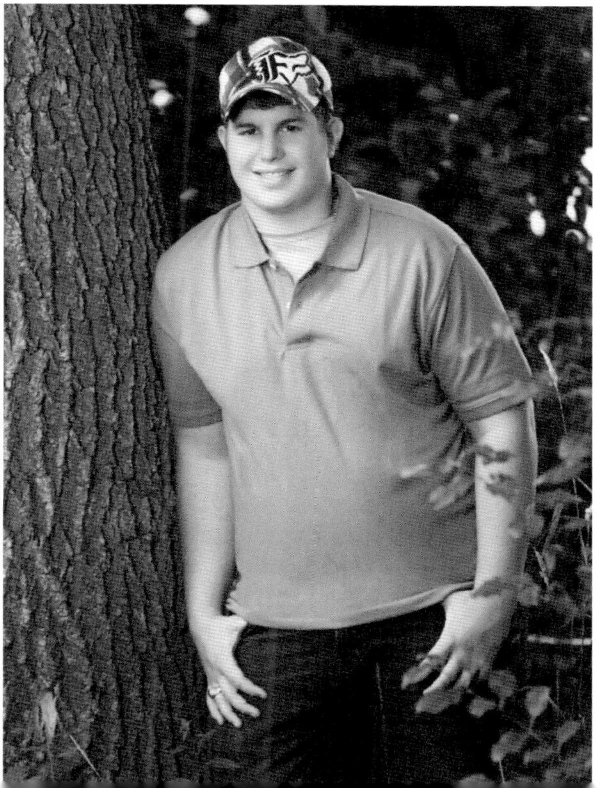

Derek Rootkie

If the number 56 is seen around town, it is due to this guy: Derek Rootkie. He was a senior at Pine City High School when he was diagnosed with acute myeloid leukemia (AML) shortly after his 18th birthday. The community rallied behind Derek, who had played football since the fourth grade and for the varsity Dragons, wearing No. 56. Derek played a number of other sports and the drums. He had plans to go to the University of Minnesota–Duluth for mechanical engineering. In high school, he balanced sports, schoolwork, and two jobs, at the Pizza Pub and at the Old Oak Inn motel.

Fatigue began to set in for Derek, and his doctors told him that leukemia had set in a large portion of his cells. He began chemotherapy treatments. The town came together and held blood drives, as well as a bone marrow drive, and held numerous fundraisers. He was able to walk with his class at Pine City High School at graduation ceremonies. But he passed away on September 8, 2012. Since then, No. 56 has been seen around town in a variety of ways, from displays on vehicles, to store windows and lawn signs. At the final regular-season football game in 2012, the Dragons won 22-17 over Two Harbors. It was a game played in honor of families affected by cancer. Randy Shaver, a KARE-11 news anchor, told Derek's story on a "Tackle Cancer" segment of *Prep Sports Extra*. (Both, courtesy of the Rootkie family).

ABOUT LOCAL ORGANIZATIONS

There are three organizations that are invaluable in conducting historical or genealogical research about the Greater Pine City area. They are:

Pine City Area History Association
315 Main Street S., Suite 110
Pine City, MN 55063
www.facebook.com/PineCityHistory

Pine County Historical Society
c/o Pine County History Museum
PO Box 123
6333 Andersen Alle
Askov, MN 55704
Phone: 320.216.7636
www.pinecountyhistorymuseum.org

Pine County Genealogy Society
P.O. Box 115
Sandstone, MN 55072
www.pinecogen.org

INDEX

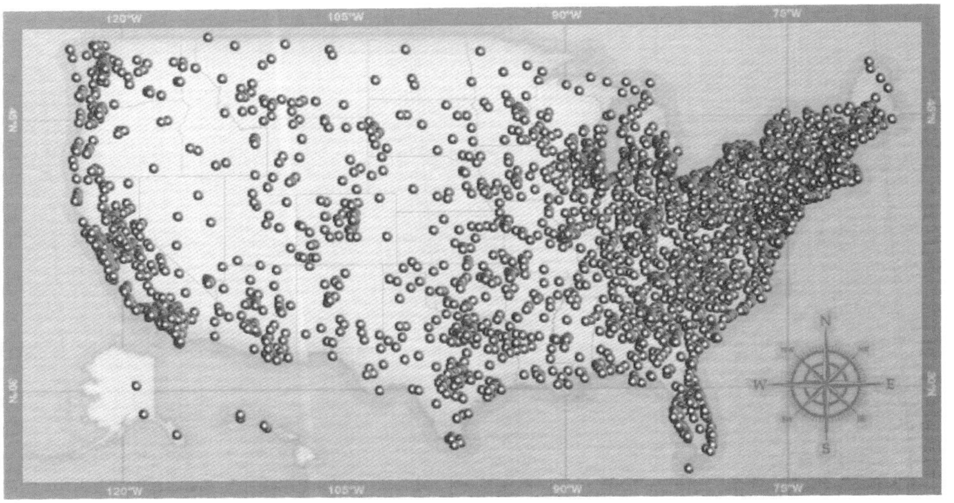
120°W
105°W
90°W
75°W
N
W
E
S